MY MOTHER'S REQUIEM

A Daughter's Memoir

TRISH MacENULTY

PRISM LIGHT
PRESS

"If you want to understand any woman you must first ask about her mother and then listen carefully. . . . The more a daughter knows about the details of her mother's life – without flinching or whining – the stronger the daughter."
Anita Diamant
Prologue, *The Red Tent*

"A lovely mind, had she, and she was always one of my very favorite instructors and humans. My remaining school friends always speak of how much we admired her brilliance - and her complete willingness to be a smartass. Like after the first round of papers we delivered to her for Classical & Romantic Music History, she stood before the class and intoned (in her sort-of Julia Child voice), 'Now, your second paper is due in a few weeks, and I want to exhort you all to write better papers this time, and please: cut. through. the bullshit!'"
Robert Moore
Roz's former student, (who dedicated one of his pieces to her)

Introduction

In the summer of 2004, I moved my 86-year-old mother from Edenton, North Carolina, where she was a well-known and much-loved musician into an assisted living facility near my house in Charlotte. I had no idea what the next few years of my life would be like, but I guessed they might be difficult. They were more than difficult. They were gut-wrenching, sometimes grief-filled years – and yet also more rewarding and soul-stretching than I could possibly have imagined. Sometimes in the throes of despair, I would write essays about what I was going through when I could find the energy. Then I began to think that sharing my experiences of dealing with an elderly parent might be helpful to others who were just embarking on this adventure – as reading about the experiences of others had been helpful to me.

So I started out to write a book about taking care of my mother. However, I found that I could not write about my elderly mother without writing about my younger mother. I couldn't write about my sacrifices without writing about hers. And I couldn't write about being a daughter without writing about being a mother. Then there were all the others who played such important roles in this journey: my brothers, my husband, my daughter, my friends both living and dead, even my dog. Mostly, I realized I couldn't write about the present without writing about the past.

This is my spider web of a story. I have kept the real names of my brothers, my daughter, my mother and myself and many of my friends – with their permission. I have changed the names of my husband (at the time) and his family out of respect for their privacy. I am sure they do not share my perspective of all of the events that I describe. This story is my truth. Theirs may be something entirely different. I have also changed the names of the various places where my mother was housed over these years. Some of them were fine. Some were awful. I learned a lot about the way we treat our elderly and our care givers.

One day while driving in my car, I heard an interview with Terry O'Neill, president of the National Organization for Women, on the NPR show "Here and Now." O'Neill said, "Being a mother is the one factor that correlates strongly with living in poverty in old age." I was shocked. Women are punished for being mothers? She added that we don't have policies in this country that support caregivers, noting that caregiving is largely unpaid and largely done by women.

For my mother, social security represented her only income in her old age, other than what my brothers and I contributed. That, I discovered, is not uncommon. According to the Social Security Administration, about 90 percent of all elderly women live solely on social security. In addition, women live longer than men and their social security payments are less; and few elderly women have private pensions. Another scary statistic: by 2030, one in four American women will be over the age of 65.

And what does this mean for the women who are doing the caregiving? According to a study by the Commonwealth Fund, 25 percent of women who care for a sick or disabled family member rate their own health as fair or poor, and more than half of women caregivers have one or more chronic health conditions. I can attest that while taking care of my mother, I often neglected my health for lack of time, energy and money. The study also states, "Nearly one-third of all caregivers (31%) report a decrease in their family's savings because of caregiving responsibilities. Overall, two of five women caregivers devote more than 20 hours per week to caring for a sick or disabled family member."

Although my mother has always been a very private person, she understood my desire to tell our story. I have tried to paint a broader picture of her than the emotionally fragile old woman she became in her later years. She was so much more. In addition to possessing a wide-ranging intelligence, she was kind, generous, fun, and extraordinarily talented.

The centerpiece of this story is my mother's Requiem, a composition which she wrote as a memorial for two young men who died in separate accidents. This book is also my requiem for friends I have lost, for my mother, and for the long chapter of my life that ended somewhere in the midst of all these events.

ONE PRELUDE

Remember thy servant, O Lord.
Her hands are quiet now,
She moved in quiet rooms.
Her silence now has found her,
Fragile and translucent as a shell polished by the sea.

Rosalind MacEnulty
An American Requiem

ONE

SEPTEMBER 2009

My cell phone starts singing "Love Me Do" at seven in the morning. I've been awake for an hour, lying in bed, thinking, wondering what to do about my crumbling house and my crumbled marriage – abandoned like an old broken sofa by the side of the road. The sound of the phone so early brings on a rush of adrenaline. What now? It's my daughter, Celina, in a quandary about a paper that's due in an hour. I'm almost grateful to be given a problem that I can handle so easily. I get up and shoot her some suggestions by email. Celina is in college now and rarely needs my help anymore, but her moment of desperation brings me back to all those times when she was younger and she forgot her homework or lost her keys or had some other mishap and I always ran to the rescue.

A couple of hours later, my friend Darryl calls. He's agreed to go play Scrabble with my mother on Tuesday and Thursday evenings since I have late classes to teach. He wants to know if I've seen my mother this morning. I haven't.

"Well, she wasn't doing well at all last night," he says. "She was very slow and only able to come up with three-letter words. Then when it was time to go, I asked her if she wanted me to take her upstairs. She said no and then she said yes. So I started to walk with her to the elevator. She was wheeling herself, and she turned and went in the other direction. I tried to correct her, but she insisted I was wrong and when I tried to push her wheelchair to the elevator, she began to fight me."

Oh God, I'm thinking, picturing my tiny mother, her mouth set in grim determination, her silver head lowered like a bull, and her hands with their purple bruises clutching the wheels of her wheelchair. And poor hapless Darryl, ever the gentleman, trying to convince her to go the right way.

"I finally let her go in the other direction and then after she couldn't find the elevator, I pushed her the right way but by then she was very upset." And this too, I can imagine: the resigned despair in her eyes, the fluttering hands, the hang-dog look and the inarticulate stammering.

"Yes," I say. "Every time she goes to the hospital she comes back a step lower. I've no idea what to do."

And it's true. I've no idea what to do. They surely won't keep her at The Sanctuary indefinitely if she's that diminished. They do have a memory care unit – a locked door at the end of the hallway. I've never been inside, but I've heard sounds: people calling out, laughing sometimes, or crying.

It reminds me of a story by Ursula K. Le Guin that I often assign to my students called "The Ones Who Walk Away from Omelas." Le Guin describes a happy, almost perfect society – except for the neglected child kept chained in a basement. This is the price that has to be paid in order for the society to be as delightful and orderly as it is. Everybody studiously ignores the horrid basement and the unspeakable cruelty in which they are all complicit. Though I know the memory care unit is not a bad place nor run by bad people, still, I have ignored it with the same suppressed horror as the people in Le Guin's story ignore the child in the basement.

But why am I even thinking about the memory care unit? We can't afford that. She'd most likely have to go to one of the nursing homes where the lumps of flesh are gathered in their wheelchairs, dozing and drooling and occasionally looking up to ask where they are and if you will take them home.

Then a new thought gives me pause: maybe it's the new prescription the doctor in the hospital gave her. So I call her family doctor and ask him to "d.c." – discontinue – that medication. Maybe I can buy her a few more months. If she can just make it till February 21 when I plan to take her back to the church in Jacksonville, Florida to hear her music one more time. Her Requiem.

TWO

I sit in one of the pews of the Church of the Good Shepherd, an Episcopal church in Jacksonville, Florida, where I grew up. Blue velvet kneelers are propped up in front of each wooden pew. So many times I knelt here as a child, not praying but somehow enjoying the meaningless ritual – stand up, sit down, kneel, sit down, kneel, sit, stand. Religion was cloaked in secrets and mysteries. When you know the ritual, you're in. I liked being a member of that secretive club.

But I am no longer a child. I am 26 years old. I have been a heroin addict and a recent resident of the Florida Correctional Institution for women. I have even more recently graduated from college with high honors. I have a teaching job at a community college and am thinking about going to graduate school. It feels right to return to the fold this Sunday evening to be present at a performance of my mother's Requiem – her masterwork. I am not here out of love for sacred choral music. I am here out of gratitude to the woman who stood by me and waited while I explored the realms of degradation and despair and then who helped me get back on my feet.

I gaze around at the stained glass pictures. It's evening now so the light does not shine through them, and their brilliant colors are muted and dull. Small square and triangular stones make

14

up the floor of the aisles. These floors always fascinated me with their odd hieroglyphs. I inhale the stone smell, old with a fusty sort of holiness. It has been a long time since I've been to my mother's church.

I stopped going regularly when I was about twelve. Before that I had to go because my mother was the organist and the choir director, and I couldn't stay at home alone. Besides, I liked being in that Gothic castle with its secret passageways, dungeons, and sequestered rooms full of pipes for the organ. The choir was my extended family. My godmother was a soprano in the choir. My godfather a baritone. The rest of them were like assorted aunts and uncles. I even adopted the church secretary as my grandmother.

Then I became a teenager, and figured I didn't need all that family anymore and damn sure didn't need to have some stupid God preached at me every Sunday. Of course, as Episcopalians we weren't exactly fire and brimstone, but the liturgy entailed telling God how worthless we are and how thankful we are that his Son died for our sins. And none of it made any sense to me. I was too young to have committed any sins anyway.

But in the ensuing years life has done me the favor of kicking me around a bit, and though I still don't get the dying for my sins bit, I have now committed some grievous sins of my own, and I have come to believe that something larger than me exists, something ineffable. I'm not sure, however, that it lurks in this big stone building with its stained glass depictions of ecstatic saints and doubting disciples. Or maybe it is here. Maybe it's everywhere, like they say.

My brother John (or 'Jo' as we call him in the family), wearing tails and looking magisterial, comes down the aisle, bearing the conductor's baton. An orchestra awaits him. My mother is seated at the console of the big organ with its four keyboards and its row of foot pedals. The choir is robed and ready. The concert begins.

My mother has always composed. At Yale she studied with the famous composer Paul Hindemith; he told the dean that she was his most promising student. In her professional life, she wrote original arrangements for her various choirs to sing, she'd written a couple of commissioned musicals, and she'd even re-scored the music for *The Lost Colony*, an outdoor drama in Manteo, North Carolina.

Marriage to my father, however, had kept her early ambitions in check. My brothers said that he threw her compositions in the fire when she was younger. She told me that the most crushing thing he ever did to her spirit happened one time when he came into the music room of our house and found her working on a composition. Overhearing the work, he sneered and said, "That's facile, isn't it?" He did much worse things, but his snide comment about her work stung the most.

Tonight is her vindication. She's written a piece from her heart, a requiem for two young men. The men (both in their early 20s) died in separate accidents within a couple of weeks of each other. They were sons of close friends of hers. As a woman with sons of her own, as a friend, as a human being, she was deeply affected by this sudden, inexplicable loss of promise. "Why do people die so young?" she wondered. "Why am I still alive?" Not being a particularly religious person, she couldn't fall back on that old stand-by: God's Will.

I'm sitting in the crowded church, listening to this strange sometimes atonal piece. It doesn't sound like traditional church music; the voices haunt. The saints in their stain glassed prisons hold their breaths and listen. Do the dead gather to hear the music written in their honor? The list on the program includes more than just the two who inspired it. There are about thirty names of various church members who have died within the past year. I know a few of them.

And am I thinking about the dead I have known? Two of my cohorts from the bad old days died from drug overdoses. Other acquaintances died in drunk driving accidents, and others might as well be dead, locked away for years. No, I am not acknowledging them or any of the others. I am only looking forward. I have stepped out of my dark past, but I haven't really found my place in the world, and I have no idea that resurrecting this piece of music will become my mission more than a quarter of a century later.

THREE

I place my lips around the regulator, take a breath and fall back off the side of the boat into the greenish-blue water. My hair floats across my face as I turn belly down and swim toward the bottom. The water is murky, churned up sand making a thick filter. I look for my dive buddy, Joel, and spot his fins waving languidly. He's swimming toward the reef. A thin layer of water seeps into my wet suit and begins to warm me.

The current pushes and shoves. The surface is choppy, and my stomach didn't like the ride out. I've always been prone to motion sickness, so scuba has been a challenging hobby, but in the past as soon as I've gotten below the surface my stomach has relaxed and I've been able to enjoy the serene beauty of the coral reefs or the wrecks. Not today. The egg biscuit I had for breakfast taps on the door of my esophagus. I remember my dive instructor advising, "Don't puke in your regulator."

I can no longer hear the purr of the boat engine. The only sound is the steady stream of bubbles pouring out of my regulator. I check my air tank and see it's about three-quarters full. I'm not enjoying the dive. My stomach won't unknot. I feel tired and can't see much of anything. We're above the reef; a few random angel fish slide by. I swim alongside Joel and our eyes meet through the masks. He makes the okay sign, and I make it back.

I'm not really okay, but since this is such a crummy day, I can look forward to a short dive.

A strong arm pulls me back on the boat. My feet with the fins on them are unwieldy. I feel like a clumsy dinosaur until I slip my buoyancy compensator and the tank off my back.

"How are you doing?" Joel asks, pulling off his mask.

"I'm still sea sick," I answer. "I don't understand why."

"Well, it's kinda rough out there."

"Not that rough."

I lean back and don't say anything else. I'm too sick to talk. The other divers are all back on board, and I can hear the boat engine roar as it's pushed full throttle. Once the boat starts speeding over the waves, the tossing will lessen and I'll get a little relief. Joel sits beside me and pats my arm. Joel is an editor at the newspaper where I work. My boyfriend, Hank, is out of town working, a fairly common event, and Joel is one of the people I pal around with when he's gone.

Joel and I put our gear into the back of his car and make our exit from the dive park at Marathon Key. My stomach has finally begun to settle down and I'm hungry. We're driving along U.S. 1 with the wind blowing through the windows and the sun jack-hammering through the clouds. We stop at a little Cuban road-side joint for Cuban coffee and subs.

"Feeling better?" Joel asks. I nod.

"It's funny," I tell him. "The other day at aerobics class I got so tired. I couldn't even finish the class. And then today . . . well, I've never stayed sea sick once I got in the water."

I gaze at palmetto bushes on the other side of the road. A yellow cat slinks under the table. It looks like a scrawny version of my own cat, Monster, who found and adopted me the day after a bad abortion six years earlier.

"Oh."

"What is it?" Joel asks.

"I know why I'm sick," I tell him, setting down my *media noche* on the round mosaic table. "I'm pregnant."

■

As I sail down the escalator at the San Francisco Airport in my long black coat, I look into Hank's eyes and I am reminded of smoky topaz. I slide into those eyes and find myself ensconced in a warm dark place. When Hank looks at me, he sees a woman carrying a burden. He sees cells multiplying, growing fat, thickening against him like a wall.

Hank kisses me when I reach the bottom, not a passionate kiss, but a soft dry kiss. He is shy about kissing in public places, even here in this airport, but he kisses me, and the glow I feel keeps the chill away, the chill I have felt coming like a long delayed winter. He takes my suitcase from the carousel in baggage claim and tosses it into the trunk of a rental car.

I close my eyes when we get in the car. I had no idea that I would be so tired, that pregnancy would be like a drug, that it would fall on me like the San Francisco fog into which we are driving.

"There's damage from the earthquake everywhere," Hank says. "We'll have to stay at a hotel here by the airport. All downtown is closed."

"Mmmm," I answer and nod against the cool windowpane. Then I rouse myself and say, "Not the best time to take a vacation to San Francisco, I guess."

"It won't matter," he says. "We'll go up north and see the mountains, maybe drive into Nevada."

Hank grew up in California, but we live in Florida. Our yard is a rainforest and our swimming pool is an emerald pond. When it is not emerald, but chlorine-doused blue, we drink Cointreau and loll in the water in the moonlight. He travels for ESPN. I work for a newspaper. We planned this trip to California months ago—long before the earthquake happened, before the pregnancy. I told him the news on the phone. I knew he would not be happy about it.

◼

In San Francisco we eat prawns, we buy sour dough bread and Ghirardelli chocolates, we laugh at the seals in the bay because they remind us of our dog, and we drive down windy little streets and visit Chinatown. We appear to be blissfully in love, but we both know that it may be the last time in our lives we ever feel like this.

We leave San Francisco and drive north through small California towns. We steal an apple from an orchard and share it, the sweet juice dripping down our chins. We eat seafood in Eureka and stay in the oldest hotel in town. We drive to Mount Shasta and hike through virgin snow. We stop wherever we see rocks and streams. He collects water in a canteen he has had since he was a boy scout. I sit by the stream, my long black coat fanned on the rock, and drink the cool water from his canteen. The air around me is a fresh new skin. Every single moment seems to be amplified, like the slow motion of the cinema; every moment deepens and widens and holds more than just time.

As I am standing by a grape arbor above Jack London's house, a rainbow stretches across the sky like the trail of a running goddess. I can see the beauty, but I cannot feel it. Hank has grown silent, and I am like someone inside an upturned glass. People will wonder why I am so sad. He's just a man, they'll say, and not a very good one if this is how he treats you. But I am still the fatherless girl, the girl who stuck needles in her arms and straws up her nose and drank her way to oblivion until I found the one person who could drive away the demons.

After we visit Jack London's house where we see two startled deer and the charred ruins of Wolfhouse, we head west into the desert. The unspoken fear that has dogged him ever since he learned I was pregnant has caught up to us and clings to his back. He realizes that I am not going to change my mind. I am going to have this child.

We catapult into gaudy, glitzy Reno. I am perpetually hungry. At three in the morning we eat in the hotel surrounded by gamblers edgy to get back to their games. We glower at each other with raccoon eyes. His ragged fear has turned into rage. My passivity has evolved into stony stoicism. The handshake is over, we retreat to our corners.

We go to Virginia City – dirt and dust and a cold wind blowing by brown shops selling turquoise jewelry. We pace along the sidewalks, saying nothing. Then I see a dusty cemetery with toppled tombstones. In the cemetery I stare at tiny little graves, and I can't help thinking about the last time, my legs up in stirrups, the tube inside me, the sucking sound, the sudden inerasable pain. The hemorrhaging afterwards.

We get back in the car, and his pain spills out of him like oil.

Why, he wants to know, over and over again, why must you do this? Why, I ask, why can you not accept this?

"I want you out of the house," he says.

"Fine," I answer.

And before I know it we are barreling down a desert highway, the Sierras looming up beside us. I look at the dusky mountains and the hills that look soft and rounded as if patted with two soft hands. I see the thrusts of earth, the long lines of sediment sticking out at an angle showing the pattern of a fault line. This scenery is the result of old upheavals. That's how it is. You can start off with everything looking one way, and then something happens, and the landscape is changed forever.

I remember that I fell in love with him because he was so different from every other man I'd ever met. He didn't care about my past. He gave me freedom to come and go. He never said anything he didn't mean. He had a gentle side that he kept hidden behind his humor. Now I am wishing he was more like other people—that we were more like other couples who get married and have children and are happy about it.

Finally, we pull over and stand outside the car watching the sun shoot purple streamers of light as it sets over the desert. The sand reflects the sky like a still lake. The beauty makes me think there must be a God, so I say ask for a miracle, but nothing happens.

The sky blackens. Hank does not look at me.

We get in the car and head to L.A. where he leaves me in a hotel room with a plane ticket home. When the door shuts behind him, I stare at nothing for a long time. Then I go into the white tiled bathroom, take off my clothes, turn on the water in the bathtub and sink down.

I think about my mother – she wasn't perfect, but I never knew anyone who tried harder to be a good mother. Alone, she raised three children, supporting us with her musical talent. Her mother, Skipper, raised four children by herself – during the depression. Skipper was one of the first women to be a licensed riverboat pilot. She worked as a cartographer during World War II. My mother's paternal grandmother supported her son after her husband ran off to be an actor. She worked as a reporter and a probation officer for the courts where her son later served as one of the most powerful judges in Connecticut.

I realize I come from a long line of strong women at least as far back as the Puritans in the 1600s, who left everything they had known and boarded ships to come to America. They and their daughters would lose husbands and children to wars and diseases. Some of their granddaughters would go to college. One of them would become a famous poet. They worked. They persevered.

I don't want to be like them, I'm thinking, as the warm water rises around me. I don't want to be strong. But I might as well wish for brown eyes instead of blue. The earth may be breaking apart under my feet, but the resolve of generations before me and of the new one inside me is leading me to solid ground.

FOUR

Hank calls. He's changed his mind. He sends money and presents for the child he hasn't met. His mother writes me a letter. He sends a check to help with my expenses. I agree to meet with him.

Two years earlier I had moved with my three-month-old daughter to Tallahassee and re-enlisted in graduate school to get a Ph.D. because I figured if I was going to be a single mom, being a college professor was better than working 12-hour days as a freelance journalist. I qualified for food stamps and Medicaid, I taught classes for very little pay, and my mother sent money.

On Derby day, Hank, who has gotten a pilot's license, flies a small rented Cessna to the airport in Ocala, Florida, halfway between Tallahassee and Fort Lauderdale. I drive down with my two-year-old child in the backseat and meet him at the airport. I'm not sure how to respond to him. I'm not even sure how I feel about him anymore, but he's here, and he has a legal right to be a part of his child's life. I'm willing to give him a chance.

Hank gets in the front seat, spins around and takes one look at the child.

"Who are you?" he says.

She stares at him with brown saucer eyes that match his own; at that moment they fall in love with each other, and our fates are sealed. Hank sells his house and moves up to Tallahassee with us.

One day when we pull up to the babysitter's apartment, Celina gets out of the car, looks at Hank and says, "Hank, love you." Then she slams the door and runs inside to play. He's the first person she says that to.

A year after our reunion, we get married at a little wedding chapel in Lake Tahoe and come home with a couple of coffee mugs that say "The Party's at Harvey's." These are our wedding mementoes.

■

My mom had retired from her myriad jobs in Jacksonville and then moved to Edenton, NC, and we'd make occasional forays up there to visit. The drive from Tallahassee to Edenton took an eternity. My mother also came to visit us in Tallahassee at least once that I can remember. I know this because I have a picture from when we went to the opera.

In the picture I have of her from that visit, she is standing by the fountain in front of the auditorium at Florida State University, wearing a dark green velvet dress and holding the hand of four-year-old Celina, who has one leg out in an arabesque and is balancing on the wall of the fountain. My mother is heavier in this picture than she had ever been before – solid, seemingly immoveable.

My mother became old in fits and starts. Every time I saw her, I noticed some surprising new mile marker. On this visit I discovered she could no longer keep up with me when we walked anywhere. I found I needed to walk very, very slowly. Her heart, she explained . . .she had congestive heart failure. I was nonplussed. She never had anything wrong with her heart before – except a murmur she'd had since birth. The past 20 or so years she'd been an inveterate walker. That was her exercise, a way for us to spend time together, to talk and laugh. And now all of a sudden (or so it seemed to me) we were cr-aw-ling. We'd become characters in a movie, moving in slow motion, each step exaggerated and excruciating as the world seemed to stop spinning in space. Of course, I hadn't planned for this when I got her and Celina in the car to go to the opera. I carved out just enough time for us to speed over to campus, find a parking space and sprint to the opera hall. Ha!

During this visit, I kept thinking there was some way to "fix" my mother. At the time I had come across a set of five exercises called the Tibetan rites. A man who had supposedly discovered them in Tibet said these exercises would have old bodies dancing like teenagers.

"Here, Mom, just do this," I said. So with my agile 37-year-old body, I demonstrated the rites in the living room of our little ranch house. Spinning was the first one. I got my mom to slowly spin three times. (You're supposed to build up to 21.)

After the third spin, she was out of breath, and a bright red blood spot suddenly bloomed in her left eye. Shit, I thought, I've killed her. She's had an embolism or something. My mother survived whatever it was. Of course, she was a big disappointment to me, having gone and grown old like that. Where was my playful friend?

This is the last picture I have of my mother without a walker.

The Buddhists teach impermanence – an idea that still confounds me. In my mind my mother is permanently laughing and vigorous, physically strong and intellectually at the top of the mountain. But today (many years later) as I sit on my front porch on a chilly autumn morning, yellow poplar leaves carpeting the ground, I am aware of my own mortality slowly ticking away. My doctor has informed me that my bones have already begun the process of deconstructing themselves. One day my daughter will look at me in shock and dismay as I can no longer keep up with her. And I – the I of this moment – will just be a ghost in her mind.

FIVE

Hank doesn't want to leave Tallahassee. We've been fairly happy here in the land of the canopy road. I have my friends, Hank has his work, and Celina goes to a small private hippie school where the children never have homework or tests and yet still learn as much as kids in the state-sponsored gulags.

Now Hank is being offered a job in Charlotte, North Carolina. Oh, please, I silently intone, please, accept the job. I've lived in Florida all my life, and the opportunities for me to make a living in this college town with its cup running over with Ph.D.s are just about nil. The one full time teaching job I thought I might get went to one of my friends instead.

So when Hank says he has the possibility of a real job with benefits and a salary and not as much as travel, I'm ready to start packing. For one thing, Charlotte is only five hours away from my 81-year-old mother, and I want to see her more than just the couple of times a year we now manage. He's leaning in that direction but first we have to take an exploratory trip to North Carolina.

Hank, Celina, and I are in Hank's truck with Jaxson, our black Labrador retriever. Jaxson is a sweet, dumb moose of a dog with one invaluable ability. He knows how to become invisible. This is an essential skill for a dog to have if you are going to be sneaking him into hotel rooms and other places where large beasts aren't welcome. That first night we check into a cheap motel room on Independence Boulevard, which we will later learn is the ugliest street in Charlotte. A security guard stands at the top of the parking lot, watching as Hank and I lurk around, putting our things in the motel room, waiting for an opportunity to sneak the dog in while Celina stays in the Blazer with the beast. With his full beard and bulging belly, Hank has an uncanny resemblance to Fidel Castro. We must surely look like we are grifters with a dead body to dispose.

The suspicious security guard wanders down past Hank's old Blazer while Hank and I watch from the motel room doorway. He peers into the window of the truck and sees an adorable eight-year-old girl who smiles angelically at him and waves while the 90-pound dog lies at her feet on the floorboards as silent as stone. We laugh about this for months to come. Our little con artist. We couldn't be prouder.

Although Hank isn't happy about the move or the idea of getting up and ironing clothes to wear to work every day, he takes the job. I get a full time teaching gig at a nearby college. The move is a tough one, but necessary. For one thing, I've got a souvenir from my days as an addict – a sometimes debilitating case of hepatitis C. Eventually I need to do something about it, and that something will surely require health insurance. So we find a pretty two-story house with a porch and a creek in the backyard, and we settle into our new lives in suburbia as if we're normal people.

Neither Hank nor I really have the hang of this marriage business. I don't know what his excuse is. He comes from a nuclear family unit, headed by two upstanding Orange County California Republicans. But I have only had the example of my mother and my two older brothers, all of whom did time living with my railing, egotistic, alcoholic father, who (luckily for me) left when I was three. I should perhaps mention the stepfather experiment that didn't work out so well either. Shortly after my mother married this man, he developed a taste for vodka, lots and lots of vodka, and for my teenage babysitter. She didn't repeat the experiment after he skulked out of our lives.

When Hank berates me for not making enough money, I shrug my shoulders and go on doing what I love to do: writing and being involved in various unprofitable artistic ventures. He doesn't like to socialize, and I could hang out with people all day. He's a staunch Republican (though not the church kind), and I am definitely not (though I am fond of certain offbeat churches). But we're affectionate with each other and faithful. He's not a big drinker, and I gave up the last of my legion of bad habits soon after he came into my life. He keeps me sane. When the demons start to close in, he makes me laugh and they disappear.

Our favorite holiday is Halloween. Our first Halloween in Charlotte, Hank and Celina carve a pumpkin. Hank draws the face and then shows Celina how to cut it.

"That's good, babe," he says even when she lops off the jack o'lantern's tooth.

Hank uses his electronic ingenuity to create two glowing eyes that peer from the bushes of our house. He and Celina make ghosts out of old sheets to hang from the trees, and I allow spider webs to accumulate on the porch. We know how to do this much.

■

My mother and I talk on the phone nearly every night. We have always been close, even when I was at my most awful. When I was a teenager, I started doing drugs like a lot of kids in my generation. The difference between me and most other kids is that I was an overachiever. I had to do more and harder drugs than anyone else – cocaine, heroin, Dilaudid, morphine. I fell in love with drugs and built a fortress around myself with them. Throughout those years my mother somehow never gave up on me. She bailed me out of jail. She sent me to drug programs. She told me over and over again, "This is not you. I know who you are." Finally, after my stint in prison, the love affair with dope lost its luster. Then I met Hank on a video shoot in Miami (I was the production assistant, he was the "genius" engineer), and he swept away any vestiges of the old druggie that lingered inside me.

■

Now that we live in North Carolina, I am able to see my mother more often.

My mother was always smarter than anyone else I knew. The damage to that blade of intellect occurred off-stage. The years are blurry. In 1997 she had to have an operation on her back. Something went wrong. She had to have another surgery, and the second surgeon said that the first one had not completed his work. Her spine was actually wobbling. The end result for my mother: two surgeries and a life sentence to painkillers and a walker.

During this time my brother Jo went to Edenton and lived with her. He took care of her as she had done for him when he had lymphoma back in 1991: when he flatlined she happened to be at his side; she ran out and summoned the doctors and nurses who brought him back from his peaceful interlude on the other side. It wasn't the first time she'd saved the life of one of her children.

People have asked why we didn't sue the surgeon who, in addition to leaving her spine wobbling, nicked a nerve, causing her to be in pain for the rest of her life and confined in a cage-like walker. But apparently in North Carolina, a doctor has to intentionally screw you up before you can actually sue for damages.

"If there's a fire, you don't have to prove arson to make an insurance claim," my mother said after yet another attorney turned down her case. "Why can't there just be insurance for medical accidents?"

At this point I don't understand how drastically things have changed since the operation. I only know that she doesn't travel well anymore. Ever since the surgery, Mom has lived on little pink pills. Ever since the surgery, her life has been difficult and often lonely. Her pain eats away at me. But at least I am closer now.

SIX

THE 1960S, JACKSONVILLE, FLORIDA

When my mother lifted her hands, music happened. Those hands summoned the voices of singers, waved on orchestras with a thin white baton, and elicited the dulcet tones of a Bach fugue from a harpsichord, the Wagnerian state trumpets from her four-keyboard pipe organ, and the intricate harmonic gymnastics of Rachmaninoff from her Steinway grand piano. When I picture her from those days, she is always pitching forward, with an armful of music, plowing through life relentlessly from one rehearsal or performance to another.

Wednesday night was always choir rehearsal night. Always. Although over the years she sometimes had bouts of asthma or migraines, she was never sick on Wednesday nights or Sunday mornings, when she sat at the helm of the enormous pipe organ and directed the choir with one hand, her other hand and her feet steadily pouring out music. She generally dozed off during Sunday sermons. Music was her religion.

When she practiced her piano at home, her eyes would close as she swayed with the music; I would watch mystified as she drifted away from me. She told me that sometimes when she played, she would feel as though she were floating outside her body. It scared her a little.

I was my mother's sidekick. My father had gone off to mess up the lives of other women, and my two older brothers had graduated from high school and left home by the time I entered first grade.

Mom wasn't a great cook; we preferred restaurants. At the Derby House, I turned the salt and pepper shakers and the napkin dispenser into an ongoing story about a princess and a prince and a castle. I didn't like to stay home with babysitters, so she brought me to rehearsals. She got no child support until I was seven when my dad, the son of a wealthy industrialist, had finally gotten some of his inheritance. Even then she had to take him to court and he was hard pressed to part with that $75 a month.

The very best part of my childhood was growing up in the theater. Jacksonville had two community theaters and one dinner theater. My mother worked at all three of them as the musical director. In community theater, the actors and singers were not paid, but the musicians were, and theater work was a significant piece of my mother's livelihood.

The Little Theatre was my favorite place to be in the world. During the first weeks of rehearsals, I would make a nest in a loft piled high with black curtains, silks and materials for costumes and sets. For a child there was no more perfect place to daydream or to eavesdrop on unwitting adults.

Once rehearsals moved downstairs to the stage, I'd sit in the middle of the house, an audience of one. Night after night, I watched the shows – *South Pacific; Kiss Me, Kate; Mame;* and my favorite – *Gypsy!* Being a stripper seemed like a fine profession to me. I watched in awe as the actresses came out in their skimpy stripper costumes and bumped and grinded their way across the stage.

My mother had a closet full of black dresses for the orchestra pit. She was often the conductor and the pianist. She wore Estee

Lauder perfume or Jean Nate bath splash. Each evening she carefully applied her "face" – foundation, rouge, eye shadow, mascara and the essential red lipstick – before heading out for the night, with me in tow. She had an aura of elegance and power that enveloped me.

Once or twice a week, she'd get her hair done in a beauty salon until the styles finally moved away from that shellacked helmet look. A hairdresser once made her wait too long, and she stormed out of the beauty shop with her hair wet and stringy. When she shopped, she always told the clerk to "charge it." She had impeccable credit.

Wherever we were, people fawned over my mother.

"Oh, Roz, that was simply wonderful," I heard over and over again after performances and church services. She was gracious when the compliments came, but didn't seem to care much about praise. She was always moving on to the next thing.

Adults would often lean over and ask me, "Are you going to be a musician like your mother?" My mother and I might exchange a quick glance before I adamantly shook my head "no." We both knew the absurdity of the notion. I had no intention of patterning myself after her. In my eyes, she had already perfected the role. Besides, I simply wasn't musically inclined. My mother says I did have perfect pitch as a child. I could identify notes on the piano and knew a third from a fifth, but I knew even then that you had to love something with all your being to play music the way she did, and I much preferred to be outside, stomping in mud puddles and staring into the leafy branches of trees rather than sitting inside at a piano for hours at a time the way she did – and always had.

We did give music a shot. I had piano lessons, guitar lessons, violin lessons, flute lessons and even voice lessons. Though my mother arranged for these various lessons, she didn't seem particularly dismayed that they didn't take.

We discovered I had a natural talent for the theater. When I went on stage, something clicked. But what talent was there wasn't enough to overcome the slide into depression and self-destruction that I took during my teens. One rejection and I was through with theater.

The only thing, the only lifeline, was this. Putting words down on paper. So while my mother played the piano, and later while my daughter sang in the children's choir or took piano lessons, I settled down somewhere to wait with a book or with a pen and a notebook, and my mind left the building.

SEVEN

AUTUMN, 2000

It only takes me a year to lose my teaching job. Not that I really lost it. I was hired as an instructor, a full time untenured position, to teach creative writing and composition classes. I applied for the tenure-track creative writing position, which was unfilled at the time. After a series of interviews, they gave it to a guy who did not have the creative publications or awards that I had. They tell me I can still keep the instructor position and teach four composition classes a term while the new guy teaches the creative writing classes I just taught. Fuck that, I think.

It's not exactly like what had happened to my mother when she graduated from Yale. There was a teaching job open at the University of Miami in Ohio, and the dean of the school of music at Yale recommended my mother for the position. She applied and received a letter back saying, "Your qualifications are certainly impressive, but you can understand that we want a man."

My mother never did work full time at a university. She taught at a public high school for a few years to try to help my step-father get through law school. That didn't work out so well, and she was glad to dump the job as soon as she could.

So I will be like my mother in that regard, I guess. I'll do a little this and a little that and create some sort of living out of it. Hank is not happy about my plan.

It turns out that this is a good year for me not to have a full time gig, anyway, for this is the year that I am going to finally get my mother to stop nagging me. I am going to see if I can get my hepatitis C cured.

Sometime in the 1970s I contracted hepatitis C – most likely in a shooting gallery on the Lower East Side of Manhattan. By the 1980s I had cleaned up my life, and I thought I was pretty much rid of my past. But about 1990 I realized I had an adverse reaction to even the smallest amounts of alcohol. It was easy enough to quit drinking, but a few years later I became desperately fatigued on a regular basis. The disease which had lain dormant for a couple of decades had begun kicking up its heels.

So now that I am on Hank's insurance, I contact a leading specialist in the treatment of hepatitis C, and we schedule a liver biopsy. The biopsy hurts like hell, but when the nurse asks me if I want something for the pain, I tell her, "No, 'something for the pain' is what got me into this mess in the first place."

After the biopsy, the doctor tells me I will have to give myself shots of interferon three times a week for six months. He says there are side effects to the treatment, including and especially depression. The alternative is that I will likely develop liver cancer.

I do my first shot at the doctor's office so that they can make sure I am doing it correctly. I pinch the skin on my thigh and jab the needle in.

"You'll probably experience some flu-like symptoms," the doctor's assistant tells me.

I take Celina to her choir rehearsal that night – the first one of the season – and join the other parents for the annual meeting in the fellowship hall. Suddenly, as we're sitting there, listening to the kids perform their new songs, I begin to shake uncontrollably.

Oh, this doesn't look good, I think. How can I get Celina out of here and go home? I slip out of the meeting through a back door and stand outside, shivering in the August heat. I begin to sing James Brown's "I Feel Good" to convince myself I am okay. Finally, the interminable meeting ends and Celina comes out and finds me.

"Are you okay?" she asks.

"I feel good," I tell her as my trembling hands attempt to open up the car door.

On the way home, I continue to sing "I feel good" as loudly as I can. I am crying and shaking with my terrified child in the passenger seat. When we get home, I sink into a hot tub of water filled with lavender bath powder while Hank, who never really believed I was sick until tonight, takes care of our daughter.

I am so delirious I'm not sure what year it is. That night I relive my years as a junkie. I am baptized in the waters of the past, immersed, drowning, former comrades and forgotten crimes resurface to leer at my beaten body. When dawn finally arrives, I have new respect for the phrase "dark night of the soul."

After that I give myself the shots at night so that I will sleep through the side effects. I never get the crazy chills again, but I need to sleep extra on the day after the shots.

At least during the treatment, my fatigue is predictable. I know which will be good days and which will be "bed" days. More importantly, the six-month treatment provides time to forgive myself. Perhaps the side effects of the medication—fatigue, short-term memory loss, skin rash and hair loss—create some sort of unconscious penance for the irresponsible way I once treated my faithful body.

■

In October of 2000 my friend Kitty from Tallahassee visits us because she needs to see the doctors at Duke University for some experimental stem cell treatment. Kitty, who is in her early 30s, has stage four breast cancer. In Tallahassee, it was a tradition for Kitty to wear a witch costume and give out candy on Halloween while we took Celina trick or treating. She's the only one of my friends accepted by Hank, the only one he feels comfortable enough around to actually let stay in our house overnight.

While Kitty stays with us in Charlotte, she and I spend our days, sitting on the couch and watching the leaves fall outside the tall windows that look out onto the woods behind the house. Kitty says we're wearing lead suits. But this time with her is one of the most peaceful interludes of my entire life.

Kitty, whose curly dark hair is only now growing back from the last round of chemo, dresses up as chemo-witch for Halloween. Celina, who is also dressed as a witch, could not be happier. We come home from trick or treating, make caramel apples and share the spoils. Jaxson snatches a candy bar and eats it wrapper and all. When Kitty goes back to Tallahassee, she strides onto the plane, wearing a mask that she has decorated with cat whiskers to protect herself from germs.

I probably should do the same thing, but I don't have her panache. The hepatitis C drugs mess with my immune system. For Thanksgiving we go out to California to be with Hank's family and I catch a cold on the way out. I am pretty sure I am going to die in the land of the shopping mall as I lie comatose in the guest room. I don't die. But I do get numerous sinus infections, my fingernails grow ridges, and every time I take a shower, handfuls of my hair pile up over the drain. I get a cut on my finger that won't heal for months. But I never, ever get depressed. I just keep counting off the shots.

Three months after I start treatment, I take a blood test. The technician screws up, causing blood to bubble out of my vein like a fountain when she takes out the needle. Celina looks on horrified. That's probably the day she decides she will never take drugs. I survive the blood lab people, and a few days later I get the results in the mail.

That Christmas we go to see my mom in Edenton. One of Mom's friends has gone away for the holidays and we're staying at her gorgeous house on the Albemarle Sound. Christmas day I give my mother the piece of paper with the results in a decorated envelope. When she reads "test results for Hepatitis C – negative," she starts to cry. I have three more months of shots to inject just to be sure.

EIGHT

"You come from a long line of strong women," I tell Celina. Celina is twelve now, and getting a taste of life's disappointments. I often tell her the story of my grandmother, Skipper, who, during the Great Depression, comforted the distraught sheriff who had come to evict her and her four children from the home she herself had designed overlooking the Long Island Sound.

The other story I don't tell her but which I often remember when I think about the women in our family is that of my mother and the terrible night when I woke to the sound of her screams: "Fire! Fire!"

I was seven years old and encased in dreamless slumber when her panicked screams finally chiseled their way through my consciousness. My feet hit the floor and I dashed out of my bedroom in my flowered nightgown. When I ran into the living room, I found no flames – only a giant with his arm around my mother's neck as he dragged her toward the kitchen door. My mother craned her head around and saw me. Then she screamed out, "run."

It was March and the night was cool and black as I burst out of the house and ran across the weedy lawn, oblivious to the sand spurs. I ran to our neighbor's house and began to pound on the jalousied window door. My best friend, Katie, lived in this house. Katie's mother opened the door. I saw her dad in the background, buckling his belt. They pulled me in, and I told them what I saw.

I stood in their bedroom as Nella called the police.

"What if he isn't a bad guy?" I said.

"Oh, he's a bad guy, honey," Nella told me. I don't remember what her husband did while all this was going on, but soon we heard sirens slicing the night. And the next thing I remember I was sitting on my mother's lap with her warm, comforting arms wrapped around me while an enormous policeman asked me what the man looked like. But I had no idea. I did not know if he was black or white, young or old. The only things I noticed in those few moments were my mother's face and the open front door.

Later, when I was older I learned what really happened: the front door had not been opened by mother's attacker. He had kicked in the back door. As my mother heard the pounding of his foot on the flimsy door and the cracking of the wood, she dialed the operator and screamed fire and our address, believing that she would get a faster response that way. She had opened the front door not to escape from the man but so her child could escape. The man had come in and dragged her through the kitchen out the splintered back door to the backyard where he shoved her to the ground, held a knife to her throat and raped her. After the police arrived, my mother seemed like a fortress as she held me.

We moved away from that house and away from the dark woods where I had played war with the neighborhood kids and into a second story apartment with a solid door. My mother also let me have a dog, a very protective chow-chow. She would not be caught off guard again.

The only time I saw my mother cry during my childhood was on the day we took my brother David to the train station. At 17, he'd joined the U.S. Navy, where he would travel the world playing the trombone in the Navy Band. My other brother, Jo, was at the Eastman School of Music on a full scholarship.

My mother cried when her youngest son left, but otherwise, she kept a tight rein on her emotions. Once when she was the chorus teacher at a disadvantaged high school, she was confronted by some young thugs during a period of racial unrest.

"Why aren't you afraid of us? All the other teachers are scared," one of them asked her.

"All you can do is hurt me," she answered. "And I'm not afraid of being hurt."

They left her alone.

My brothers remember a frailer person than I do – a woman so defeated by her disastrous marriage that she would lie on the couch for days. But she did get up. She got up to give piano lessons in the converted garage where the two Steinways (hers and my father's) nestled next to each other. She could always work. When my brothers were teenagers, she drove them on cold mornings to their early band rehearsals, she took them on their paper routes, and she somehow kept the family afloat while her husband drank and consorted with other women.

Once while taking my brothers to the beach (before I was born), she stopped at a red light and looked over at the car next to her. My father was in the car – with another woman and her children – heading to the beach.

"He never went to the beach with *us*," she would say when she told me this story. She didn't seem angry so much as incredulous.

45

My brothers were fourteen and fifteen when my father left. We grew up in different families. I was not awakened by the early morning brawls. I did not see the devastation that my father wrought on my mother's psyche. Instead, I grew up with a woman who loved to laugh, who entertained at countless parties with her piano and her wit, who rolled down hills with me as a child, who bowed to no one – a woman who was fearless and generally happy.

Then she got old.

NINE

Hank, Celina and I are piled into the Blazer. God, how we miss Tallahassee where we had a 45-minute jaunt down to the coast for some play at a spit of land called Mashes Sands, followed by a meal of stuffed shrimp or blackened grouper at Angelo's Seafood Restaurant.

Hank and I are chasing some semblance of happiness, which somehow eludes us in Charlotte. He doesn't care for life in suburbia. I think it's just fine. There are woods behind our house and a little creek, and a neighborhood full of girls. Celina and the gang rove from house to house in a pack, cleaning out refrigerators and scattering girl stuff in the bedrooms. But I do miss the water, so we're heading towards the ocean with a stopover in Edenton to see my mom.

Edenton, North Carolina, managed to escape the developer's ravenous maw that ate up most of the American South during the 20th Century. Situated on the Albemarle Sound, the town is a warren of streets lined with antebellum mansions and historic houses that sport Georgian columns or Victorian curlicues. Each house has its own style, some with cupolas on top and a few with the original glass window panes from a century or so ago. You won't find a Walmart in these city limits.

My mother moved to Edenton a year or so before Celina was born. She took a job as the music director of an Episcopal church that had been established in 1736. She was 70 years old. She discovered Edenton because in the summer she was musical director of *The Lost Colony* on the Outer Banks. When it was time to "retire," she gave up her church job and theater gigs in Jacksonville and moved to the smaller church and the smaller town.

She kept her job at *The Lost Colony*, where during the summer she sometimes lived in a big apartment complex called The Grove, populated by young actors and singers. I knew better than to call her late at night after the show because she usually wouldn't be home. She was busy being the life of the cast parties.

During the rest of the year, she lived in a 250-year-old pink house with wide sloping floorboards. The living room was bright with pretty white interior shutters on the windows. The ancient white book shelves and the big black Steinway were also there. My mother held choir rehearsals in the living room, and there always seemed to be people coming in and out.

One summer when we still lived in Florida, we came up for a visit and went to see *The Lost Colony*. As we sat on the bleachers, I looked up. There was my mother standing on the hill, conducting the choir below with a blue flashlight beam.

"Look, Celina," I said. "There's Grandma Roz."

Celina was awestruck. My daughter was seeing her grandmother as if for the first time, making music happen with a wave of her hands.

But after the botched operation, my mother quit *The Lost Colony*. She couldn't make it up the hill in the walker.

Now she lived in Edenton year-round. We'd breeze in and she'd make time to go out for a meal or two, and then we'd breeze out, and she'd go back to her busy life of rehearsals and performances. Even after the back surgery, she still maintained a full schedule. Or so I thought.

■

We tromp up the stairs of the old pink house and enter. Mom greets us with a bright smile. She's sitting in her chair, her walker in front of her. Celina hugs her and Hank says, "How are you, Roz?"

"I'm fine. How are you?" My mom and Hank get along fairly well.

My mother keeps a candy dish full of York peppermint patties on the table for choir members. Celina and I scarf down a couple. Then Hank and I leave Celina and my mother to entertain each other while we check in to the Travelodge. I know that Celina will be playing the new piano pieces she's learned or practicing a new choir song with my mother accompanying her. Or maybe they'll paint pictures together. Those two never have a problem finding something to do.

As usual, we take Mom out to dinner. She wears one of her colorful dresses with a necklace of red Chinese beads. At the table over crab cakes and shrimp, Mom and Hank wind up discussing computer synthesizers and how musical vibrations work.

"The speed of the vibrations determines the pitch," she is explaining to us. "The size of the vibrational waves determines the volume. That's how you can make the same sound loud or soft. And then there are variations that determine the quality of a note."

Hank takes the conversation up an esoteric notch or two over my head, but I'm happy that these two smart people can find something to talk about, and especially thrilled that they deftly manage not to talk about politics. In that arena, they don't have anything in common. My mother, though not the most politically active person in the world, did get out and support the Socialist Party candidate back in the 1940s. She has fairly strong opinions about the idiocy of George W. Bush. Hank will not reach that conclusion for several more years.

When the check comes, Mom tries to pay, but Hank insists on getting the bill.

That night while Celina stays with Grandma Roz, Hank and I study the North Carolina map in our room at the Travelodge.

"Let's go down to New Bern and then to Charleston and back up to Charlotte this way," Hank says. Our original plan was to come back through Edenton, but I agree this gives us a chance to see more of the state.

The next morning we arrive at my mother's to pick up Celina and say good-bye to my mother. My mother is in her chair and we're gathering up Celina and her stuff.

"Mom, we've had a change of plans," I tell her. "We're not going to be coming back through Edenton on our way home."

I know she's going to be disappointed, but I am completely unprepared for what happens next. My mother, tiny and frailer than I have ever seen her, sinks back into the cushions of her chair. Her face crumples and the good-time girl begins to weep.

TEN

CHRISTMAS 2002

Hank and I have been practicing for tragedy for a few years. We'd had to put Jaxson down in early 2001. Well, I did. As I pulled out of the garage with the sick old dog in the backseat, Hank and Celina stood in the doorway, Celina wailing and Hank barely able to breathe. Then at the end of 2001, my friend and Celina's godmother, Kitty, died of breast cancer. She was only 33 years old.

With elderly parents we are always expecting the "news." While we wait for the inevitable, like farmers watching the skies for ice storms, disaster comes from a completely unexpected direction. In the summer of 2002, Hank's sister Beth, a golf pro at an exclusive resort, is diagnosed with ovarian cancer. She is six months younger than I am.

■

We've been going to California for Thanksgiving or Christmas for the past ten years. We often take off for the mountains there to give Celina a chance to play in the snow. We stop in rustic little restaurants for hot chocolate. Occasionally, Hank and I even leave Celina with the grandparents and go out on our own, something we almost never do at home. We are always more in love with each other in California. We go to the different beaches. We take Celina and the dog to the park where Hank played as a boy.

This Christmas is different. This Christmas we linger nearby. The shopping is less frenzied, the dinners more subdued. This Christmas as we sit in the family room, Beth comes through the doorway, gaunt, hollowed, stoop-shouldered. Tears fall at their leisure from lashless eyelids as she recounts these long six months since July: the trips to the emergency room, the good nurses who bathed her as if she were a baby, the scar from sternum to pubis, the row of chairs in the chemo room. She takes off her wig and swigs from a beer, this soldier who looks at us from the middle of the trench, and the words pour like coins from a torn pocket. We are the dream of home she's falling toward, the place where she plans to be born again.

Usually Southern California is dry in the winter, but this Christmas it won't stop raining. My mother-in-law Jean tries to gather the strength to be the mother she has always been, cooking and cleaning, even though she's in her 70s now. But she's shell-shocked from these past six months. Still she manages to make dinner every night, and she and I indulge in our annual conversation marathon at the dining table. Hank Senior has put up a tree and as usual it's given birth to several litters of presents.

We have the dog with us. We always do. The dogs have blurred in my mother-in-law's mind. Satan, Jaxson, and now Merlyn. Each one black, each one male, each one a lab. Merlyn is the sneakiest of the three. Something glinting on the coffee table is an invitation for a quick snatch and dash – and there goes one of your favorite pair of earrings. Merlyn was born trouble – maybe that's why he has become my dog instead of Hank's.

■

I remember the first time I met Jean and Hank Senior, the day I stumbled out of the back seat of the rental car, barefoot and clutching a two-year-old Celina. Celina had been crying after the five hour flight so I sat in the back seat and held her and sang songs with her while Hank drove and Jaxson rode in the front. I'll never forget the look of surprise on Celina's face as two elderly people swooped out of the house and fell upon her in adoration. For the first time in Celina's life, I simply let her go as Jean took her from me and fussed over her and Hank Senior stood by, chuckling in admiration.

And that's how it was every time. For those one or two weeks of the year I was able to relinquish my role. I could let go of my maternal vigilance and relax. It was wonderful.

"My God," Jean confided to me. "If I'd known he had you in his life all those years, I wouldn't have been so worried about him." But for the six years that Hank and I were together before Celina was born they hadn't met me. Hank Senior didn't say much about the past. He just sat in his recliner with the sports channel on and let Celina muss his hair and pretended that she had "stinky feet" which always sent her into paroxysms of laughter.

◼

Now ten years later Celina, with her pants rolled up, steps outside into the inches-deep water and lets it graze her bony white ankles.

"It's a flood," she says, looking at the grassy lake in her grandfather's tidy lawn. The drops continue to spike the water and ripple. The cat prowls to the window, watching this cold California rain. Almost Christmas, Celina almost grown, the child within struggles to manage the lanky bones, the beauty that has captured her wild-hearted spirit. Gingerly she comes back inside searching for fuzzy slippers for her chilled little feet, laughing and pushing back her long hair, a mermaid walking into the living room on new legs.

Beth teaches Celina and me how to play Texas Hold 'Em. Celina's a natural at the game. I guess her acting talent helps her bluff. I'm always the first one out of chips. We play for hours. The year before I'd almost gotten back on a plane and gone home when Beth started quoting Ann Coulter, but this year Beth and I put our politics aside. Cancer will do that.

At night we sit together in the family room: Hank's parents, brother, sister, nephew, and Celina and I. Merlyn scours the floor for dropped crumbs. We watch movies or play Clue. We eat chocolate-covered cherries and Christmas cookies. A fire burns in the fireplace. While Celina and her cousin are occupied in another room, Beth tells Hank that she thinks she'll be lucky if she lives another five years. Turns out she's off by one. She'll be around for six more years.

TWO INTERLUDE

Why do we weep?
The moon beckoned and your bright and shining soul said
"Yes!"
Leaping free.
We wept.
We still weep on our sad planet,
While your untarnished soul reaches radiance,
The expanding universe will not hold you;
Time will not stretch to touch you.
Why do we weep?

Rosalind MacEnulty
An American Requiem

ONE

In 2003, I worry constantly about money. I make my living from a series of freelance writing jobs and teaching the odd composition course as an adjunct at a nearby university. I've had one novel published by an independent publisher in Britain, but Hollywood, for some unfathomable reason, has not yet come calling. I don't have health insurance. Hank pays the mortgage on the house and some of the household bills, but when it comes to my car payments and Celina's private school and Celina's clothes and any material goods I desire, I need to come up with the bucks.

One Tuesday in mid-September, I'm working on a newsletter for a volunteer organization in Florida when Hank walks in my office and says: "There's a category five hurricane heading straight for your mother."

I wheel around in my chair and stare at him. His eyes widen as if to say, you better do something.

"Shit," I say.

I call up my mother and tell her I'm coming over to Edenton to get her. She does not protest. Within an hour I am on the highway, hoping I don't get stuck in the storm.

When Hurricane Dora gathered up her skirts and flounced toward Jacksonville back in September of 1964, my mother could barely contain her excitement. She bought cans of food, Sterno, and an oil lamp. She taped up windows the way Skipper, the old salt, had taught her. We lived two blocks from the river so we were bound to see some action. That first afternoon when Dora was merely flirting with the city on the river, we went outside with an umbrella to walk Tojo, my old red chow. I laughed hysterically as the wind blew our umbrella inside out. My mother pretended she was Mary Poppins.

My mother loved storms, especially big, terrifying storms. And she taught me to love them. That night when Dora was no longer just toying with us, the wind moaned long and loud outside our windows. The whole world shivered. The rain bucketed our town while I slept happily in my bed. In the morning we went outside to meet the river which had gotten friendly overnight and decided to visit houses a block away from its banks. We waded down to the new shoreline and saw people in canoes or rowboats where once there had only been cars. Tree limbs had been amputated and cast all about the place.

There was no school and no work, just summer camp in the dining room, cooking pork and beans over a Sterno can and reading stories by candlelight until our power was restored and the subdued river returned to its home.

But my mother is old now, and I have heard too many tales from survivors of Hurricane Andrew to take the storm heading toward Edenton lightly. I must make the five-hour trek to get my mother out of its path.

The rain is falling lightly when I arrive. Sandy, my mother's landlord and upstairs neighbor, gushes in relief when she sees me. I quickly pack a suitcase for my mother and grab the package of Poise pads from her small bathroom. My mother has never mentioned her incontinence.

Because of the walker, Mother can no longer get out of her apartment through the backdoor. The back steps are too rickety. She still has a car, an old blue Buick, that she no longer drives. She keeps thinking she'll get hand controls, but that seems like a bad idea. Instead Diane, her part-time caretaker, uses it to go to the store for her a couple of times a week or to take her to doctor's appointments.

I load my mother's things into my station wagon and pull to the front of the driveway. Mother clomps out onto the porch on her walker. She turns the walker sideways when she gets to the steps. With one hand she holds onto the walker and with the other she grasps the rails and slowly, very slowly, lowers one foot at a time and that way manages to get down the steps. I help her get into the car, fold up the walker, and shove it in the back. Then we're off with Hurricane Isabel fast on our heels.

◼

Prior to my mother's impromptu stay with us, I had established a nice little routine for my life – carpool Celina and three other girls to school every other morning, take Merlyn for a walk in the park, come home and work on my computer all day, then go get Celina and the other girls, drive to choir, piano lessons or dance lessons, come home, make some pasta and cheese and broccoli or spinach for Celina (every night!) and then help her with her practicing or homework, or carpool to choir practice and back, and then it's (Thank you, Jesus!) time for bed.

While I'm on my timetable, Hank usually works in his corner office upstairs with his television on. He found he couldn't hack ironing clothes every morning and so he quit his corporate television job and now works at home, designing video equipment for a company based in California. Sometimes he sleeps all day and works all night.

Hank's a great cook, and fairly regularly we'll make "family taco dinner." He fries up the shells for us – soft for me, medium for Celina and hard for him – while I chop vegetables and Celina grates cheese. He heats refried beans for us, and cooks meat for himself. His guacamole tastes like California with cumin, cilantro, salt, onion and a bit of chopped tomato. Sometimes Celina and I will wake up in the morning and find him in the kitchen, egg shells and flour covering the counters.

"Cakes and eggs, babe?" he'll ask Celina, knowing that nothing would make her happier. I heat up the maple syrup.

On Tuesday nights we all watch the military/courtroom-drama television show, JAG, and on weekends we get a movie. JAG happens to be one of those right-wing propaganda shows that once actually featured (I kid you not) Iran-Contra henchman Ollie North as a good guy(!), but I love the female character, Mac, because she's a recovering alcoholic and because she always chooses the wrong guy. Sometimes as I'm pulling out of the driveway on another mission to drive Celina to some rehearsal or another, I paraphrase the opening of the show: "With the same daring and tenacity her own mother used getting her to ballet class, she fights evil and overcomes all traffic jams to get her daughter to choir practice on time." Celina laughs every time.

This is our weird, humdrum little life. It works for us. In fact, we like it.

And now Mother is here like a rhino in the living room.

◼

Hank has to go to California for work, which is a relief for me as I can focus more on my mother and less on balancing the interests competing for my attention. She can't get upstairs so I've made a bed for her in the living room – a box spring and mattress half on the couch and half on the large plastic boxes that Hank uses to ship video cameras back and forth to California. I also place an old speaker by the toilet in the bathroom as a prop so she can push herself off the toilet seat, which is too low for her.

Her presence irritates me like an annoying buzz that only I can hear. We have a local supermarket that emits a high-range squeal audible only to teenagers to keep them from loitering. When my mother is around, I feel like a 13-year-old standing outside that store.

It's morning. I've taken Celina to school and now I'm back home, unloading the dishwasher. I've got a deadline to meet, and Mom sits at the table, wanting to be friendly, to talk. I haven't slept well because my mother has to have the television on all night and she is hard of hearing.

"What kind of tree is that?" my mother asks, looking out the window.

"I don't know," I reply irritably.

"There are so many different kinds of trees," she says pointlessly.

This is something I really don't feel like conversing about. In fact, I don't want to converse at all. I want to keep the bubble of my own thoughts around me. This is one of the beauties of my life as it is – mornings when Hank is usually sleeping, Celina is off at school and I am virtually alone with the delicious silence of my house.

"I have work to do," I tell my mother. "Is there anything you need before I go upstairs?"

"No," she says. "Is something wrong?"

She must wonder why the daughter who has always loved her and enjoyed her company is suddenly taciturn and sullen. I can't give her a proper answer. The truth is I don't want her here. My life is full with work, husband and child. I realize I am being thoughtless, ungrateful and selfish. What I don't realize quite yet is that I am going to need to make room in my life for her – and it's coming sooner than I think.

So later after I've gotten some work done, I make an effort to be a better daughter. I play Scrabble with her, and I take her out to lunch (though it's not easy to take her anywhere). I bring her with me to Celina's choir rehearsals. And that old bond between mother and child starts to knit itself back together.

Then two weeks after the daring rescue of my mother, Sandy says it's safe for Mom to come back to Edenton. Hank, who has returned from his trip, and Celina are both happy to see her go. As a child, Celina was protective of my mother, but she's a teenager now, and this old, needy woman who constantly calls out my name isn't looking like a sweet deal. Celina has owned me lock, stock, and barrel for all of her thirteen years. The idea of having to share me with someone else is intolerable.

When I drive my mom back to Edenton, we find a war zone with blue tarps over damaged roofs and work crews still trying to get trees out of the roads. My mother's house is undamaged, and the old brick church where she works is fine. Mom is glad

to be back, but I have the feeling it's time for me to start antici-
pating the next stage of her life. I know that she is almost un-
bearably lonely here. And yet it is her life. Her music. Her job.
Her friends. Still it's not enough.

After my mother leaves, Hank tells me that his sister Beth's
cancer has returned after a brief remission.

"It's looking grim," he says.

"God, your poor parents," I answer.

"The next few years are going to be bad," he says. He crosses
his arms over his chest and gazes at me as if we are the Tsar and
Tsarina facing the red hordes. We're in for a hard ride.

TWO

As I begin to realize just how hard things have gotten for my mother, I try to visit her as often as I can – usually with Celina but sometimes by myself or with the dog. Ever since her own grandmother (Skipper's mother Gammie) made her look at a piece of dog fur under a microscope, my mother has never been an animal person. But she has always tolerated my need to have at least one animal in my life. So she never complains when I show up with a big, ungainly beast – a beast which tends to sweep valuable objects off the coffee table with a swipe of his happy tail.

And even though she doesn't love him, Merlyn adores her as he does all women. Fortunately, he doesn't try to mount her. But he does like to put his cold nose on any bare body part he can find, and her shriek of surprise is always good for a laugh.

When I visit, we get her friend Marion to come with us on an outing. Mother admires Marion a great deal for having been married five times and having lived in Europe and for being a flagrant atheist in a southern town of church-going Christians who love to pray for people. One of my mother's favorite Edenton moments is when one of the Christians said she was going to pray for someone in poor health and then looked at Marion and said, "And you can just hope." The town understands and loves Marion.

That spring after the hurricane I go to visit my mother. Sleeping at her place is traumatic for me. She has to get up several times in the night to go to the bathroom, and the sound of the walker thunking around on the wood plank floor jars me awake without fail. Sometimes my mother has nightmares and starts moaning loudly in her sleep. This has happened off and on since I was a child and I always attribute it to The Terrible Night. But still it scares the hell out of me.

This particular night I am sleeping soundly for once on the uncomfortable little rollaway bed, when suddenly a loud incessant singing jolts me awake. What the hell? And it doesn't stop. Loud. Louder. Louder still. Finally, I get up and stagger into her room. There she is sound asleep, the TV blaring loud enough for people three blocks away to hear it. She has rolled over on the remote control.

"Mom," I yell. No answer. "Mom!"

I wrest the remote control from under her slumbering body. She wakes and immediately feels guilty for stealing sleep from me.

I grumble back to bed, also feeling guilty. Fortunately, we are good at forgiveness. We need to be or else neither of us would survive the other. Sometimes my mother wonders whether she somehow caused me to become a drug addict in my youth. I honestly can't say. I was allowed to do just about anything I wanted to do my whole life. Perhaps she could have kept a tighter rein. Perhaps she could have provided more guidance. But I decided long ago to take responsibility for my own actions. I made bad choices then; I could make better choices now.

When my mother was young and planning to marry my father, her sister Hazel predicted the marriage would never work. "Who will find the keys?" she asked. Hazel was right. They were not a good match. Not only could neither of them find the keys, they both needed to be the center of attention. This was easy for my mother. All she needed was a piano. She was famous for her improvisational style. You want to hear "Happy Birthday"? She can play it in at least five different styles from boogie woogie to horror movie. One of her friends told me that once he was listening to her play the organ during a church service. Which Bach cantata is that, he wondered. Then he realized it wasn't Bach at all. She had taken a Broadway tune and turned it into faux-Bach, and nobody was the wiser. Another time she composed some music that fooled knowledgeable people into thinking they were listening to some newly discovered piece by Mozart.

Brilliant as she is, my mother has always had a bit of the absent-minded professor in her. There is the story, famous in our family, of the time she left the baby outside while she was practicing. She had completely forgotten about him until a friend showed up and wanted to see the baby.

"The baby?" my mother asked and then realized with horror she'd left him outside in his little swing and now it was raining.

Like all mothers, my mother had a set of maxims that she thought were important to impart to me: if you can't say anything nice, then don't say anything at all (unless it's irresistibly funny); it's as easy to fall in love with a rich man as it is with a poor man (a nice idea in theory); if you want to commit suicide, wait until tomorrow (advice which has, it turns out, saved my life).

My mother was fascinated by the idea of suicide when she was young. Then when she was a teenager, the woman next door hung herself, leaving behind her daughter, who was a close friend of my mother, and a grief-stricken husband.

"You not only kill yourself, you kill everyone who ever loved you," my mother said. Suicide was no longer romantic. Not to say that she didn't later consider it. Once she told me she had merely been waiting for me to turn 18 before taking her life. Then when I turned 18, I was in more trouble than ever and the timing for a self-imposed departure on her part wasn't good.

Still, the threat of suicide was a great controlling device. When I was sixteen and wanted to rent a beach house with a friend for the weekend, she threatened to kill herself to get me to back down. I did, of course, but it was a dreadful mistake on her part. That was one of the few friends I had who wasn't heading to prison or death by overdose.

THREE

As my mother transitions from elderly to "frail elderly," my daughter is getting ready to make the transition from middle school to high school. They are both graduating, in a way. And I've got to figure out what is the best next step for both of them – and how to afford it.

Celina is in the eighth grade and attends a small private school about 30 minutes from our house. There are only 16 kids in her entire grade, and even though they have their cliques, they also like to do things in a pack – go to movies, amusement parks, parties and dances. For the three years she has been there, I have written the school play. Celina was the lead the first year but only because I was out of town and someone else gave her the lead role. After that I made sure that the plays were heavy on "ensembles" and light on leads. But there's no doubt that every time she gets on a stage, Celina is riveting.

For the eighth grade play, I create a pastiche of Shakespeare's plays, and we ask the kids to audition by reading a short mono-logue from Romeo and Juliet. We've gone through all of the kids when it's Celina's turn. She comes in, all legs and elbows and big brown eyes. She doesn't have the sophistication of some of those other world-traveled girls, but when she's done reading the part, my friend Kerry, who is directing the play, and I just look at each other. She's in another league entirely.

High school will be different. She will have to leave this warm cocoon. I'm thinking now might be a good time to switch to public school where her neighborhood friends go. It's been rough coming up with eight grand a year for this school even though they let me pay by the month and they're pretty lenient when those payments are late.

Celina, on the other hand, decides she doesn't want to go to public school. She'd tried it once and said it was like jail. I know that the standard liberal stance is to send your child to public school for the diversity and all that, but maybe those other liberal parents did not have the same experiences I had with the public school system.

I went to elementary school in Jacksonville, Florida where every day felt like an interminable sentence. I was bored beyond redemption. When I was in the fourth grade, my teacher warned us as we were preparing to take a field trip to the zoo not to sit on the public toilets because some "fat colored lady" might have sat on the seat before we did. I was shocked. My mother had taught me that bigotry was unacceptable. Of course, schools weren't even integrated at the time – a fact that hadn't quite registered in my consciousness. By fifth and sixth grades I started getting into trouble – shoplifting, scrawling bad words on my desk. Maybe it's the only way I could stand the tedium. Maybe those childhood traumas were beginning to make themselves evident.

After sixth grade I went to the newly built Episcopal private school for the next three years. By then I was already on the path to ruin, but at least I learned a lot. In the seventh grade I memorized a huge section of Hiawatha just to impress our lovely young English teacher. In eighth grade, a teacher named Mr. M., who only liked a few of the handsome older boys, taught us "The Lovesong of J. Alfred Prufrock" by T. S. Eliot and changed my life forever. I had never known such music or despair could be conveyed by mere words. He also made us read *Great Expectations*, and I've been a slave to stories ever since.

My mother was fairly hands off when it came to my schooling as were most of the parents of the time. I think she found school superfluous to education. When she was in high school, she often refused to go to school on Wednesdays. Instead she took the bus to town and educated herself in museums and libraries or by going to the courthouse to watch trials.

"Five days of school a week seemed a bit excessive to me," my mother often told me.

My mother did come to my elementary school once when I had refused to eat the cafeteria food. To this day I shudder to think of those grits that you could stick a fork into and raise up above your head like a dead jellyfish or those cold foul-smelling little orange fish sticks. It was lunchtime when my mother came to speak to the principal.

"I notice you aren't eating the cafeteria food," my mother said to the principal who had a deli sandwich on her desk. "Why would you expect a child to eat that garbage?"

■

Now Celina's in the eighth grade, and we have to figure out where she'll go to school next year. This is almost like getting ready for college. Everyone signs up for open houses at the "big three" – the three powerhouse private schools where Charlotte's elite send their children. I'm still holding out hope for public school, but some strange instinct draws her to the one school I would never have imagined for her. It's a large private school where the "old money" families send their children.

We take a tour of the campus. The "athletic center" is better than those at most colleges. The classes are small. The teachers, top of the line. The fine arts building is state of the art. I try to keep my inner roughneck in check as we smile at the admissions counselors and the other moms whose every movement reeks of money and privilege and impeccable three-story homes.

Not only does Celina like the place. They like her. I realize that even though we are white, we are the diversity that school seeks. Most of the other students have gone there since kindergarten. Celina is fresh blood. She might as well be from another planet compared to those kids with their perfect hair and their trust funds. A few weeks after we apply she gets an acceptance letter and what is even more startling – a scholarship. Not for the whole thing, but enough so that if I watch my pennies I'll be able to make the payments.

When we lived in Tallahassee, she went to a very small "hands-on" learning school, like Montessori only with a little more structure. It wasn't a particularly expensive place, but I was even poorer then so I split janitorial duties with another mother to get half off the monthly tuition. Mopping those woods floors where my daughter and her friends had been playing, pouring Lysol into toilets, scrubbing sinks and wiping down tables in the evenings in the empty school house – those were the most meaningful jobs I ever did.

■

As eighth grade comes to a close, Celina and I are prowling through the mall, searching for the ear-piercing place. I know it's un-American, but I'm not much of a shopper –especially these days when checks always seem to be in the mail but not in the mailbox. I may buy new clothes for Celina, but for myself, it's usually Goodwill – or some discount place if I'm feeling extravagant. We find the boutique (hair bows, cheap jewelry, and lots of stuff that is pink and plastic) beside the food court: Ear Piercing – Free.

Inside a young woman whips out a cardboard tray with tiny birthstone earrings, and my daughter locks on the fake emeralds. The piercing is free. The earrings cost 35 bucks.

Celina sits on a stool and the young woman uses a ballpoint pen to mark the spot where the hole will go. The girl offers my daughter a mirror, but Celina just wants to get it over with. She's petrified.

"Do you want me to let you know when it's coming or just do it?" the girl asks.

"Just do it," Celina says with a tight smile. A few seconds later, a green stone sticks out of her ear lobe on a gold stem.

■

We had intended to do this a week earlier on her 14th birthday, but those plans were ambushed by a well-meaning science teacher who told her that in spite of her "remarkable" gift for engineering (her rockets went higher than anyone else's) and how much she had impressed him with the self-propelled car she built, she would not be getting the science award at the end of the year. Her right-brained tendencies (terrible organizational skills and an inability to get homework turned in on time) had exacted a heavy price. She would not be eligible.

When I picked up my child from school that day, I had not been expecting this storm of grief. It was her birthday, after all, and I'd just been there a few hours earlier with pizza and cup-cakes. But now she was inconsolable.

"Everyone thinks I'm an idiot," she sobbed. "It's always the same ones who always get the awards. No one knows that I'm smart."

It was not a minor issue. The birthday plans I had mapped out went down the drain, and I spent the rest of the day com-forting my broken-hearted girl.

So a week later, the day before her eighth grade graduation, the day before the dreaded awards ceremony, we are finally strolling out of the mall with a couple of pretzels and a pair of newly adorned ear lobes.

As we drive to the ceremony the next day, Hank can speak of nothing but piercing. My daughter sits in the backseat in her new black dress with spaghetti straps, her strappy black shoes with wedged high heels, a slight sheen of gloss on her lips, her thick golden-brown hair gleaming as it falls past her shoulder blades and he can see nothing but the tiny green dots on her ears.

"What's it going to be next, babe? A tongue stud? How about a nose ring? I know a girl who wore a bone from her dead poodle in her nose. It was quite the conversation piece." Hank's teasing has a sharp edge to it.

Celina has never been a prissy girl. She scorned some of her classmates whose lives revolved around shopping and make up counters. She called them "nail polish girls." She had never shown any interest in earrings. In fact, I was the one had insisted that at fourteen, it was time. She had shrugged noncommittally and said, okay. It was only when it looked like it might not hap-pen in time for graduation that she had finally pleaded, "Can we please go get my ears pierced today?"

We pull up to the country club for the graduation ceremony. Celina looks as if she is going to a hanging.

"Will you please tell her that she looks nice?" I hiss to Hank right before we go in to the reception room.

"What?" He's clueless. "Oh. You look nice, babe."

That helps a little, but the day is doomed from the start. She is leaving a school she loves and sixteen close friends. And worst of all, she will not be getting an award.

She smiles through everything – the family portrait, the tedious speeches, the snapshots with happy friends, the hugs and good-byes. She smiles and smiles and smiles until finally we are in the car on the way home and then she weeps. She weeps like a little girl.

FOUR

Shortly after Celina's graduation, I am driving down a busy street in Charlotte when my station wagon, my quintessential "mom" car, makes an awful grinding sound and then shudders to a halt. It only takes a couple of hours for the tow truck to arrive and take me and the Blue Monster, so named by one of Celina's friends, to the transmission shop where the experts are baffled.

This is not a happy time for me. My collection of short stories came out recently, and while the reviews were generally favorable, several said the stories were "depressing." But mostly I am worried about my mother.

Then comes the call. Sandy, my mother's landlord, tells me that my mother is in the hospital for something unspecified. I call the hospital and speak to Mom.

"Do you need me to come get you?" I ask.

"No, it's too much of a bother," she says. Then she begins to cry.

My car is in the shop, so I find a ride to a car rental place, rent a little white economy car and drive the five hours to Edenton. When I walk in the hospital room, I find my mother lying in the bed looking like a bewildered child. For a moment it is as if we are strangers.

A nurse comes in, smiles and busies herself taking my mother's stats. I stare out the window at the flat silver lake on the other side of the parking lot and wonder what's coming next.

The doctors can't find anything seriously wrong with my mother. She's dehydrated they say so they pump her full of fluids and the next day she's ready to go home. Before she's released I go over to the church and meet with several of her choir members, hoping to find some way that she can stay in Edenton. They knit their brows. They're concerned, but they aren't her family. I can't expect anyone to take her in and care for her.

"Mom, I think you should come home with me. I've found an assisted living place near my house," I tell her.

"No, no. We can't afford it," she says.

So I leave her with a make shift care arrangement and drive home feeling as if I have abandoned her on an ice floe.

When I get home, my car is supposedly fixed. I have my summer arts camp job, and for two weeks I forget about my problems as I revel in poetry and play writing with my brilliant teenage prodigies.

But the car is not fixed, and neither is my mother. Mom is back in the hospital. This time I decide I will not leave without her.

■

Hank and Celina are not thrilled. My mother's plaintive cry "Trish!" rings through our house. She needs help getting to the bathroom. She can't get out of the chair. She forgets which door is the closet and which is the bathroom. She throws our busy lives into slow motion. They don't understand. They can't see who she really is. They can't see past the illusion of the body, sheathed in papery skin. I know that in reality, in my reality, she is an exciting, fun-loving person with a terrific sense of humor. They, however, see someone who cries and is no fun at all. To them she's like the worrywart fish in *The Cat and the Hat.*

One night we decide to watch one of Hank's favorite movies, "Shrek." I think Hank secretly identifies with the large green ogre, a soft-hearted grouch. It is not an unreasonable comparison.

We love watching movies together, and we mistakenly assume my mother will enjoy this family ritual of ours: the popcorn, the pillows piled in front of the TV, the dog nosing his way into the circle. We place Mom in her portable recliner and turn the television up loud enough for her to hear it, and we proceed to enjoy the movie, Hank chuckling at the witty banter between Shrek and Donkey. But we are not even halfway through when my mother grows frantic. She frets and moans and says, "Oh, this is terrible. This is terrible."

Hank and I look at each other. My lips tighten over my teeth. Celina is silent.

"What is it, Mom?" I ask. "What's wrong?"

But she can't tell me what's wrong. She can only moan and flail about. Hank and Celina disperse. I turn off the movie. The night is ruined. (In fact, we never watch that movie again.) My mother doesn't seem to notice. All she knows is that now my attention has turned to her, and there are no distractions.

■

With my helpless mother in the house, I sigh constantly. I have never before understood the emotional significance of the sigh. But now I get it. A sigh is your very spirit crying its quiet distress. A sigh is your futile prayer to whatever gods might over-hear it. You understand you are beyond help. There is no answer. So you sigh.

Then my brother David shows up. David is the hero in any narrative. He's the one who goes into a poverty-ridden school where the children are looking forward to a life of gang violence and prison and teaches them to play chess and takes them to the White House and shows them the world and the children grow up and get scholarships to Ivy League schools, and if perchance they still get in trouble, he goes to court and convinces the judge to give them another chance. He's the one who came to find me when I was holed up with another junkie in the Battery and took me back to the drug program in the 1970s. He's the one who will chase down a purse snatcher for twenty blocks until finally the perpetrator in frustration throws the purse down and keeps going.

I wrap my arms around him in relief.

David and I take a tour of an assisted living place near my house. He agrees that it's a decent enough place. The price is somewhat daunting, but right now Mother has enough savings that we can get her in there and pay for a few months. And at this point we're not able to look much further than that. Perhaps it's a failure of imagination, or that annoying habit I have (as Hank loves to point out) of believing that everything will just work out. "God will take care of it," Hank says in a mincing voice even though I've never said that (out loud).

Even as he's nearing 60, David still bears a strong resemblance to the muscular weight-lifter he was in high school. He has a newscaster's deep voice and he brings a Spockian logic to problems. After we look at the assisted living place, we take Mother to an outdoor cafe near my house. David and I discuss her options: should Mom go into the assisted living facility, should we try a little harder to find someone to stay with her in Edenton?

Mom then puts her hand out and says, "But where will I be sleeping tonight?"

"You'll be at my house, Mom, with us. Just like you have been all week," I tell her. I don't cry. I don't bang my head on the metal table. I don't rip open my blouse and beat my chest. But I want to.

Later these lapses won't bother me so much. Occasionally, I'll snap at my mother when she says something absurd. Other times I'll just answer the question and move on. Everyone who has had a parent lose his or her mind knows the shock of the first time. Every single one of us thought it would never happen to our parents. Sure, old people in the movies or on TV are ditzy as hell, but not our parents. Then it happens right in front of us. And if it happened to those gods of our childhood, we can no longer deny it will happen to us. *Lord, let me die first* becomes our unspoken prayer.

Celina is not happy. To her, my mother is a rival. And sometimes I think my mother feels the same way about her. My mother never took to grandmother-hood the way some people do. Don't get me wrong. My mother thinks Celina is lovely, but she doesn't feel the same way that Hank's parents seem to feel about grandchildren – something to dote on and brag about.

■

My mother is not convinced by our arguments that assisted living is the way to go. She does not want to leave her job, and who can blame her? She wants to go back to her piano, her choir, her pipe organ at the church. She will struggle up the narrow steps every Sunday to the balcony of the church where she will lift her hands and make music happen.

My brother shrugs his shoulders. This is what she wants.

"But it won't work," I tell him.

"We have to let her try," he says.

So I pack mother's toilet seat into the trunk and her walker in the back seat of the rental car that David is using to take her home. Hank and Celina come out onto the porch. They are both way more cheerful than I am. I hug David goodbye and then hold my mother. Nothing about this feels right. I am helpless to do anything about it. She's as happy to be going home as Hank and Celina are to see her go.

■

So my mother leaves and I turn my attention to getting Celina ready for her new school. She is going into the lion's den alone. She will need fashionable clothing, not just the hand-me-downs from the neighborhood teenager who happens to be her size and a couple of years older. It's been a lean summer for me, and Hank with his usual generosity spots her the customary C-note to go shopping for school clothes. Well, I decide, she'll have to figure out a way to impress the kids with something other than her sartorial savoir faire.

"I'm not worried," she says with a weak smile. The kid is scared shitless. Me, too. And this year I have no one to carpool with. No one else at the school lives in the hinterlands where we live. That means that for the next two and a half years I'll be driving a half hour there and back every single morning during rush hour and 20 minutes there and back every afternoon. That's almost two hours a day in a car. And of course I'll be calling on my fiction writing skills fairly regularly as I make up excuses for why we're late almost every day.

FIVE

The third time my mother goes into the hospital that summer is, I decide, the last time. No more consulting with brothers. No more trying to patch together a system of care for her. She is 86 years old. She is crippled. Her mind is faltering. Her independent life is over.

I feel as if my chest has caved in. I walk around carrying a tray of pain as if it were hors d'oeuvres. No one wants any. A friend asks me why I don't just give myself permission to own the pain. "Go ahead and grieve," she says. I put that on my "to do" list. But first I have to go and take her away from her old life for good. On top of it all, another hurricane is heading for the North Carolina coast where she lives.

On Monday August 1, 2004, I'm back at the rental car place because once again the Blue Monster is in the shop. I'm now on a first-name basis with the manager. He gives me a compact, and I drive to Edenton with a purpose. I am getting her and taking her and as many of her things as I can fit in this little car. I am commandeering her life. In Edenton, they will have parties for her. They will celebrate her. They will make a cake in the shape of a piano. They will print a huge story in the local paper about this gifted woman who came to a small historic village and played the organ for their church services, created a community

82

chorus, wrote music for them, and taught them to sing like angels. For her it will be like getting to attend her own funeral. It will be sad, but it will not be depressing. She will be the belle of the ball.

While a light steady rain falls, I pack and load, pack and load. She does what I tell her to do like an obedient little girl. When I've finished cramming everything I can get inside the car, she lowers herself into the front seat. I fold up her walker and jam it in the back seat on top of the boxes of books and kitchen items and music manuscripts. I lean over and help her buckle her seat belt. Then I shut the door and run around to the driver's side. Clouds hunker over the Sound. Hurricane Alex is brewing off the coast, and we are leaving it and Edenton behind. The roads are slick. I back into the busy street, put the car in drive and go. My mother's Edenton life disappears in the mist.

■

Later that day my mother is sitting on the bed of her new "home" – a second-floor room in an assisted-living place called The Oaks. We both suddenly feel sick. I am positive that this is the wrong thing. This has been an awful mistake. My mother smiles stiffly, trying to be brave.

"The carpet is pretty," she says. But we both hate the place and everything about it. And mostly I hate myself. Should I have moved her in with me, I wonder? But how would I ever get any work done? Would Hank and Celina leave me if I did? And where would we put the piano? The management here has promised that we could keep the piano in the parlor. Of course, it's not the best idea, leaving a Steinway grand out where any senile person could spill Ensure all over the keys, but at least Mom can entertain people, which is what she lives for.

The main reason my mother cannot live in our house with us is that we are not always there. And this is the one thing I know she needs: the company of others, not just her moody daughter and her daughter's equally moody family. She needs friends, admirers, and co-conspirators. In a little cabinet in my heart where I keep the things that hurt me most is the memory of her telling me that in her apartment in Edenton sometimes she screamed at the top of her lungs just to see if anyone would hear her, to see if anyone would come. My mother had friends in Edenton, but her best friend, Marion, had just been moved to an assisted living place in Long Island to be near her daughter. And her other friends had lives of their own. And a few (to my continued wonder) seemed to have abandoned her altogether.

So I stifle the anguish roiling in my chest.

"I'll come play Scrabble with you every day," I promise. "I'll take you out places. I won't leave you here all the time."

She clutches me. I am her lifeline as she was once mine. We will do this together.

■

"The *Alice in Wonderland* was mine as a child," I explain to my brothers. "It was a gift from someone."

They concede the book. We are sitting on the floor of the living room of my mother's apartment in Edenton, divvying up our mother's stuff. We don't have many conflicts except a few minor skirmishes over the books.

"Oh, here's the *Boston School of Cooking*," Jo says, gently opening the old relic as if it were the original Dead Sea Scrolls. I wouldn't mind having that, but Jo is the cook.

All three of us want the Kierkegaard. I'm sure David already has a copy. He takes the Bertrand Russell instead since it was his to begin with. I don't know why I think I'm going to have some profound metamorphosis and wake up one morning as an intellectual. Jo gets the Kierkegaard.

I always thought it was a bad idea for Mom not to assign things to each of us, but the division turns out to be fairly easy. We each wind up with the things that mean the most to us or that we need. Jo lays claim to the old table from the days of Lincoln, but he has no room for it so I'll keep it at my house. I have already sequestered the bird of paradise plates and that makes up for anything else that I might desire but which they might desire more. In fact, I don't want much when it comes to Mom's things. Stuff feels rather burdensome to me. David takes the beautiful old crystal wine glasses. Jo and I don't drink so that only seems fair. He takes lamps for his New York apartment. Fortunately, the pictures will go to her new place because there would surely be strong disagreement over who should get the wheelbarrow painting that Andy Griffith gave her. They had met when she was the music director at *The Lost Colony* and his wife to be even sang in a performance of her Requiem. When she admired the picture hanging on his wall, he sent it over to her house the next day.

I take "George and Martha," the porcelain figurines that once belonged to Gammie, Skipper's mother and that my mother somehow played with as a child. It's possible that George and Martha are worth some money, but we'll never know. I would have to be starving before I'd sell them.

We're too engrossed in the dismantling of our mother's Edenton existence to absorb the finality of it. The moment one of us begins to feel it, we close our mouths, lips tight together. Almost everyone at some point, I suppose, realizes they must face a time like this. We know that our parents cannot go on forever doing whatever it is they do. Change must come. We see it happening to the parents of our friends. The inevitable. But when that particular experience comes your way, it is more wrenching than you felt possible. My mother will never again live on her own, I realize, as I empty the kitchen drawers of her old silverware. She will not play the organ every Sunday as she had for most of the past 70 years. She will not put together shows. She will no longer shelter a choir in her living room on Wednesday nights.

"Her first organ playing job was at the age of 14 or maybe 13," I say out loud as I stack piles of music into boxes. But my brothers know this. As I'm packing away her music, I find about ten or so copies of "An American Requiem" in old tattered black folders. Something tells me to keep these scores. Someday maybe we'll get enough money to hire someone to put the Requiem in computer format and submit it to a publisher. I'm pretty sure this is the one thing I need to hang onto.

In spite of what we are doing, the fact that my brothers and I are together is a rare and happy enough event that it keeps us from becoming morose. Besides, we are packing and cleaning machines now. The ants abandoning the ant farm after the queen is gone.

We've advertised a yard sale for the next day, and Sandy has offered to help. We're hoping that the furniture will sell. It's going cheap. A few of Mother's acquaintances drop by on Friday while we're in the midst of packing and deciding what to sell, what to keep, what to give away. I mistakenly think they're visiting with us, but really they're nosing around our mother's belongings early trying to stake their claims. David is irritated with them, but we go ahead and get rid of a few things. One woman wants to buy the little books of Shakespeare plays that are probably a century old. I've lived my whole life, knowing those little books were always available if I needed them (although I'd long ago absconded with her tattered copy of *The Collected Works*). Once, I actually performed a reading of the entirety of Romeo and Juliet for my mother, using one of those little books. And she, saintly woman, sat on the living room couch (this same couch now in need of a new home) and served as my audience. I have no idea if the books are worth anything, but I'm so tired of packing and the truck I've rented hasn't even an inch of space left. So I sadly, regretfully, let them go for a few dollars, knowing I'll never feel good about doing that.

Friday night, we go to the only Italian joint in town. We talk politics and though we are all on the same side, for a moment it gets heated between my two brothers.

I have a feeling their anger has nothing to do with politics and everything to do with why we are here or maybe it's just an eruption from some long ago childhood battle that happened before I was born. The argument subsides, and we move back into that place where we know and understand each other better than anyone else ever can. I idolized my big brothers when I was a child, and I still hold them in high regard though now I can acknowledge their imperfections, too. And they seem to love me as if I were still the long-haired, laughing little girl they tossed back and forth between them as brawny teenage boys.

We have been with each other through a lifetime of mistakes, miracles and accolades. We are each other's biggest fans. When I was in prison, I would call David almost every week for my allotted phone call. He told me later that someone, who was supposedly an expert on fucked-up people such as myself, had told him to cut me off. "Once a junkie, always . . ." this genius told him. And what did my brother know? He had never been a drug addict. But he was always there when I called, willing to talk to me, willing to laugh or be horrified by my observations of prison life, whichever was appropriate.

"You wouldn't believe how many thieves there are in this place," I once told him without a trace of irony, and he burst out laughing. He also made sure I got the Sunday *New York Times* every week, which was one of the things that probably saved me. It gave me a connection to a world that I could aspire to, a world of educated banter and beautiful clothes, far away from the raucous, simple-minded bullying and poorly made prison uniforms that constituted my life at the time.

For some reason I was not in regular communication with my other brother, Jo, during those years. He was dealing with issues of his own – a divorce, illness and too much time spent on a barstool before he found AA. But years later when I'd gotten into an unfortunate relationship, he was the one to drive twelve hours to where I lived and handle the hostilities. Whenever he visited, which had become fairly frequent in recent years, we would meditate together, I would listen to his poems, and he would read my stories.

My brothers and I have always been united by love and admiration for our mother and bitterness toward our father. Our father is living in Jacksonville Beach beset by dementia. We rarely see him.

■

The next morning the vultures arrive. We have one absolutely beautiful vase for which I am asking fifteen dollars. It's probably worth 75. Some white-haired crone tries to bargain me down on the price. But I am tired of haggling, and I refuse. I'll keep the damn thing first. Behind my back she convinces Sandy to let her have it for five dollars. When I realize what has happened, I want to snatch it out of her hands and smash it to little porcelain bits on the sidewalk. That's how I feel at the end of the day of bargaining away my mother's life.

When the apartment is emptied, we scrub and mop every inch of the place, and then we drive away. Jo takes off in his loaded van with Ralph Nader stickers on the bumper. David takes off in Mother's old Buick, loaded with boxes and lamps. And I drive away in the filled-to-the-brim rental truck. Even the cab is filled with her belongings. How I am going to unload that truck by myself I have no idea. When I get back to Charlotte, I dragoon Celina into helping me. Hank will have no part of it.

I spend the next day unloading. Celina and I somehow get Mother's small, but very heavy Clavinova onto a hand truck and through the delivery entrance and then into Mother's new room. I hang up the pictures and try to make it look like "home," but my mother is not home and she knows it. Then we swallow back our tears and play a game of Scrabble.

I'm not placing bets on her lasting much longer. How can she survive without that busy admiring world of hers? The change is cataclysmic.

THREE VARIATIONS ON A THEME

Remember thy servant, O Lord.
He was not ready to leave us;
Nor were we ready to see him go.
The dark scissors of death have separated us.
He accepted danger. Its strong and shining thread
Led him from this tangled maze.
Help us, Lord, in thy great wisdom
To accept his acceptance.

Rosalind MacEnulty
An American Requiem

ONE

Celina and I are in Carolina beach to stay for a night at a rented condo with my niece, Sharen, her husband and son and her mother, Camille, and Camille's husband. Camille is Jo's first wife. I had not spent any significant amount of time with Camille since I'd lived for a year with her and Jo when I was fifteen. Yet I still feel great affection for her.

"Mom's not much of a cook," Celina explains to the group as we sit around the glass table noshing on snacks.

"Except for pancakes," I tell them.

"That's right. She makes great pancakes."

"And you know who I learned how to make pancakes from?" I ask. Then I nod over at Camille. Camille and I share a glance. She seems pleased that her brief stint as my stand-in mother has left a mark.

Camille knows that I've been taking care of my mom for a while. Her mother lived with them up until about a year ago when they finally moved her to a nursing home where she died last May.

Later as we stand on the balcony and watch the Atlantic knit itself upon the shore, Camille says, "It wasn't until my mother died that I realized I had finally relinquished that role – the daughter role. For years I was constantly tethered, afraid to go

93

anywhere without my cell phone, constantly on the alert for the next emergency."

She could easily be describing my life.

FALL 2004

I go to see my mother every day at The Oaks. I take her out often. My social life, which wasn't too active to begin with, dries up completely. If I'm not taking Celina to choir or some school function then I am with my mother, playing Scrabble or just driving her somewhere so she can be out.

But God she complains.

"The food in this place is awful. They put the sandwich on the same plate with the fruit cocktail and the bread gets soaked. It's terrible. The quality of the food is so cheap. It's practically inedible."

The lunch when I first visited the place to check it out was pretty good, but soon after she moves in, some corporation in California buys the place and slashes the budget. Somebody's getting rich, but it's not the people who work here.

"This is the Republican vision for the world," I tell her.

She also complains about her fellow inmates. At the dinner table, one woman can only talk about her dead husband. Another woman, younger than most of the rest, has had a stroke and cries all the time and rails against the family who has "dumped" her in this place. Someone else enlivens the meal-time conversations with accounts of her bowel movements. The worst thing for my mother is when they use double negatives. She's a grammar snob.

Once when I am out of town for a day, Hank and Celina go to visit my mom. Hank later reports that she was down in the parlor vociferously complaining that the other residents wouldn't shut up about their insipid grandchildren while he and

Celina grinned and hoped that all the hearing aids in the vicinity were broken.

My mother likes the staff, but seeing how they are treated by the distant corporate entity infuriates her. They fire people for no apparent reason. They expect part-timers to work full time but don't pay them for the work or give them benefits.

Meanwhile the cost of her room is about 400 dollars a month more than her social security check. I'm wondering how we're going to cover that since my income is so sporadic. On top of everything, Mom's Steinway is supposed to arrive, but the transport date keeps getting postponed.

She's been there about six weeks when I take her out with me to do some errands. As we pull into the parking lot of her new "home", she chokes back a sob that slices me open.

"It's just so depressing," she says. "They're all so old and sick."

I want to scream out in frustration. I want to stab myself in the brain. I have tried so hard to make things right for her, to make her happy. I don't know what else to do.

We walk into the building, she slowly on her walker and me forcing myself to take small slow steps. Inside the main room, a volunteer is playing a game with some of the residents to keep their minds stimulated.

"What language would a Hispanic person speak besides English?"

As we wait for the elevator, I listen to see if anyone has the answer. Silence. Mom is right. She doesn't belong here.

A few nights later my mother says, "I don't think I need assisted living. What about one of those independent living places?"

We are only now learning the different categories of places: independent living, assisted living, nursing homes, memory care units. But just thinking of moving her again exhausts me, makes me long for a padded cell and a valium-drip. Besides, she's made a couple of friends at this place. Her new friends are both smokers and she sits outside with them on the smoking porch like the bad kids who skip class in high school and make snide remarks about all the other kids.

As I'm hoping Mom will settle in, I'm also hoping Celina will adjust to her new school. Every day at 3:30 I pull into the pickup line at the school, my dented 1999 Taurus wagon like an elephant in a line of jaguars. Everyone else drives a Volvo, a Beemer, a Benz, a Jag, a Suburban or an Escalade. I'll see my girl sitting off by herself or with the one other girl who it turns out did come from her old school.

"How did it go?" I ask when she plops down in the seat with her enormous book bag in her lap. She shrugs. A fairly large group of kids from her middle school went to the other private school down the street. She's wishing desperately she had chosen differently. In fact, the other girl is already lobbying her parents. Please, dear child, I'm thinking, don't ask me to try to transfer you. I'm getting used to doing the impossible but that one seems a bit too daunting.

Two days after my mother's plea to move, I emerge from yoga class at the Y – the one thing I insist on doing for myself – and pick up a magazine for Senior Living. I find an ad for an independent living place called The Landings just a ten minute drive from my house. And the price for an apartment is actually four hundred dollars less than my mother's social security check.

The next day Mom and I go to look at the place. Instead of the small room she has in assisted living, she would have a small two-bedroom apartment with a kitchen. Of course, there aren't any med-techs on staff, and if you fall, you're on your own. There's a big difference between independent and assisted living.

At The Landings, they only serve one meal a day and not even that on weekends, but Mom is still able to prepare some meals for herself, and I can bring dinner or take her out on weekends. The clincher is that the living room is just large enough to comfortably fit the piano, which is supposed to arrive on Tuesday.

We write a check that day.

TWO

OCTOBER 2004

I learn very quickly that the management at The Landings is not dissimilar to some of the more cold-hearted fascists who ran the women's correctional institution where I spent 11 months of my wayward youth. The main dame in charge is a tall blond with Doberman-white teeth and high heels that could puncture an old man's jugular if he got in her way.

"We just love our seniors," she says.

■

What happens is this: I need a truck for two reasons. The first reason is that I'm going to Tallahassee to retrieve a bed for my daughter. Celina's godmother, Kitty, who died of breast cancer back in 2001, wanted Celina to have her gorgeous antique four-poster bed. But I have never been able to figure out a way to get the bed up to Charlotte, so it was getting dusty in Kitty's mother's garage. About this time I come up with a plan. I will ride down to Tallahassee with a friend who happens to be going there for a conference. I will rent a truck, pick up the bed, bring the bed to Charlotte, unload the bed, take the truck to the assisted living place, load up my mother's things, take them over to The Landings, unload the truck again and then deposit it at a U-Haul place in Charlotte all for the weekend rate. It's brilliant!

I didn't, however, check my horoscope for the weekend, which probably read: "People hate you, and they're going to let you know it."

The ride to Tallahassee is uneventful. I get dropped off at Kitty's mother's red brick ranch house. I go around back past the garden, where Kitty used to grow fresh mint, to the back door, which is the way I always went to Kitty's mama's house. Kitty had her own house a few blocks away but we spent a lot of time over here. Kitty loved her mother, a feisty Democrat who had a fierce reputation among her former high school English students.

But Cathy, Kitty's mother, is not the one who answers the door. Instead Kitty's sister looks at me through the screen. I stand on the steps, holding my little overnight bag like a hobo looking for a little hospitality.

"What do you want?" she asks.

"Is Cathy here?" I ask.

"She's not available. What do you want?"

"I'm here for the bed."

"Now? You want the bed now?"

"Well, yeah."

"I can't believe this."

After an extremely unpleasant interchange, I get the idea that Kitty's sister is angry because I've left the bed in the garage for three years. It's not that it's taken up all that much space – it's only a headboard and a footboard. But somehow this minor imposition has evolved into a major transgression. Kitty's sister insists that I get Kitty's executor to oversee the transfer of the bed from the garage into the truck, which I still haven't picked up yet.

Fortunately, Cathy comes out and rescues me. We hop into her pick-up truck with Kitty's precious poodle – the irrepressible Mythos – and go run some errands. Cathy has the softest, gentlest southern voice. It's like someone drawing you a warm bath on a chilly day. We go get some lunch and some gas for Cathy's truck, and I think about Kitty and wish she were with us today. How much lighter and less alone in the world I might feel.

Cathy drops me off at the rental place where I pick up a truck; Kitty's executor comes over and with a roll of her eyes, signs a piece of paper and then helps me load the bed. Then I complete the eight-hour drive in the truck with the bed. I get home, unload the bed and drive immediately over to my mother's place to start getting her things out of there. I'm loading up clothes, books, lamps, small pieces of furniture, boxes of music, including the old black Requiem folders, and the Clavinova, which weighs as much as a brick outhouse. I do it by myself and with the help of a maintenance guy when I can find one.

Sunday afternoon I drive over to The Landings with the truck full of goods. I go to the front desk and ask them for the key to my mother's apartment. The piano has already arrived and is in the apartment. I've given the people a deposit, but apparently we haven't signed the lease yet.

"I'm sorry," the woman at the front desk says, "you can't go in there until you sign the lease."

"But . . .but our piano is already in there. And I've paid a deposit."

The woman at the front desk makes a phone call to her boss lady at home. I'm standing in this lobby, sweating from the September heat, beat up from an 8-hour drive in a bouncy truck the day before, muscles aching from packing and loading, toting barges and lifting bales. And they tell me, no, I cannot unload that truck today. I will have to wait until tomorrow. At that moment, I realize I am going to hate these people. And nothing changes my mind.

THREE

As 2004 slides into 2005, I'm still earning a catch-as-catch-can living, and at the same time trying to keep my mother on an even emotional keel. I decide to offer a creative writing class to a few people who've been asking for one, and I bring my mother along to get her out of her apartment and around younger people. She's not used to her social set being limited to the upper decades and so this is a welcome change for her.

The group meets one evening a week. I assign writing exercises, and then we share what we've written. Then we write some more. Mother loves coming to the group. She's working on a musical but mostly in the class she writes memories from her life. The others in the group enjoy hearing them. In the meantime I'm learning new facts about her life, especially her childhood.

She explains that she was not named after the famous actress Rosalind Russell, who was in fact only 11 years old when my mother was born. Rather she was named after one of her mother's friends, Rosalind Brown Simons, an accomplished pianist who had studied in London. Skipper taught my mother piano lessons until she was five years old, at which time her instruction was turned over to Rosalind Brown Simons. When the Great Depression hit, the family could no longer afford piano lessons. But by that time my mother had learned enough that she could practice and learn new pieces on her own.

"The Depression didn't stop me," she said.

While in high school, my mother was offered both an art and a music scholarship to Yale. It wasn't a difficult decision. She chose the music scholarship.

"One of my best memories is when the dean told me that Paul Hindemith said I was the most talented student in the whole school," she said. "I never forgot it."

Hindemith, apparently, liked to play with electric trains.

"All kinds of people – Einstein, for example – would come play with his trains. Since they were all geniuses, it was very elaborate and you had to know what you were doing to keep the train on the tracks. It was an extraordinary place."

Sometimes I resent the fact that my mother left New England or at least didn't take us back there after she divorced my father. My cousins still live there and get together for holidays. I wonder how different my life might have been. And yet, I do love Florida where I grew up. Even now I yearn for it and steadily plot a course out of my landlocked life back to the swamps, rivers and lakes of that endangered place.

■

My mother's depression stalks her like a big game hunter in her apartment at The Landings. The doors to the outside are too heavy for her to lift, and the management is too cheap to get those automatic door openers for handicapped people. She feels trapped inside and she becomes alternately morose and frantic. Sometimes I come over and take her out in the car just to look at something besides the ivory walls. She loves the way the clouds bunch up on the horizon and turn psychedelic at sunset. Other times we'll just go outside and sit on a wooden bench and watch the sun set over the water treatment plant just down the road. Charlotte has lovely skies, and bare black trees where you can occasionally catch the fleeting glimpse of deer. During these times we talk. When you spend a lifetime getting to know someone, you think there is nothing left, but she still has stories.

One day she explained that Skipper, which is what we had always called my grandmother, was not known as Skipper when my mother was a child. She was called "Mrs. Field."

"I thought it was awful never to be called by your first name," my mother mused. "It's like she was anonymous."

Mrs. Field was the consummate "lady" in spite of her girl scouting. Being a lady didn't mean girliness, prissiness, or even snobbishness. It was a certain way of carrying oneself. It meant being kind, courteous and dignified. Skipper's mother, Gammie, on the other hand, took her ladyness to an extreme.

"She would never be caught carrying her own parcels. And she wouldn't be caught playing cards on Sunday, especially since she always managed to slide them under the couch if company came," Mother said with a laugh.

Shortly after ice cream cones came into vogue in 1904, Skipper played a not so ladylike joke on an insufferable relative by explaining that you ate an ice cream cone from the bottom up.

The thing my mother never mentioned until I finally asked about it (and I wouldn't have known to ask if not for my cousin Roy) was that Skipper had had a boyfriend.

"Oh, yes, he was my organ teacher," my mother said. "But she was only doing it to get even."

"How old were you?" I asked.

"Oh, about eleven."

"And she was still married to Lewis?"

"Yes," she said. Lewis, like my own father, was a philanderer, indulging in adulterous affairs without a qualm, and an alcoholic, who once showed up at a fancy social function in Washington without his trousers on.

"One time a little girl asked me if my father was Colonel Field. When I said, yes, she responded, 'Oooooh'," my mother said, laughing. "His reputation was that bad."

"Really? I thought you meant she was impressed."

"No," Mother said. "Everyone knew about him."

My mother remembers overhearing her father on the phone, fixing a trial.

"Don't worry. I know that judge. We'll take care of it," he said.

That was how she learned how the system worked. He was an influential man, a skillful attorney who became a judge at a young age. According to my mother, the world turned a blind eye to his behavior. Or most of the world did. Eventually, after his divorce from Skipper, he was strong-armed into marrying one of his mistresses, the sister of his Mafioso chauffeur. Or so the story goes.

One of her worst memories involves watching a boy drown. It was a summer day, and people had gathered at the river to swim and picnic. The little boy's leg got caught in the lock under the bridge.

"The horrible thing is that there was a carpenter there who said he could break the mechanism, but the firemen wouldn't let him do it," she told me.

"Why not?" I asked.

"I don't know. I suppose they insisted on doing it their way. It seemed to me that the carpenter was the only one who knew what he was talking about, but he left in disgust. The boy drowned, and there was nothing we could do but watch it happen when the tide came in."

As we sit on the wooden bench and the evening dusk rises in a wave of darkness from the horizon, I can see the pain of that memory etched on my mother's face, her hazel eyes looking back at a life vanishing before her eyes.

■

The Comandante of The Landings is a bully, pure and simple. She's reportedly got the owner of the place wrapped around her perfectly manicured finger. She cruises into work in her Cadillac and hurries off to lunch with her slightly smaller but no less blond assistant. They are always hurrying somewhere, blowing by in a hurricane of perfume.

Fortunately we don't have much truck with them.

In her little apartment, Mom is claustrophobic and lonely. To combat both issues, she keeps her door open and plays her piano, hoping to lure in admirers. She's pretty effective at it. People wander by, hear Bach or Debussy, and stick their head in the door, curious. Slowly, but surely, she makes a few friends.

One of them is a woman named Carol, a retired art teacher. My mother's hobby for many years has been watercolors. Some of them are pretty good. Celina still has the painting of a clown walking a chicken on a leash that my mother painted when Celina was just a baby. So Carol and my mother decide to paint together. The Landings has an art studio. We saw it when they took us on a tour of the place. What we hadn't noticed is that no one was actually using it. Like so many of the amenities at The Landings, it is only there for show. The tables aren't placed at a convenient height for painting, and my mom, being handicapped, has great difficulty in there. But no adjustments will be made. Still somehow my mother and Carol manage to paint together.

Carol has a daughter my age, and like me her daughter is constantly stopping by to help her mother with one thing or another. Mom gets confused and calls the daughter "Carol's mother."

"Carol's daughter," I correct her.

"Oh, yes. Of course," she replies, but next time she does it again, mentioning something about "Carol's mother." And that's what we are: mothers to our own mothers. I am constantly wiping my mother's face, washing her hair for her, and exhorting her to get out and do things with friends.

■

Celina is also trying to find a way to fit in at her new school. She's been pestering me to try to get her into the other private school, but it's not doable. We've already gotten a scholarship at this place, and it would be way too late to get one anywhere else. She's despondent, but one day she comes eagerly over to the car when I pull up.

"There's auditions for a play," she says, her eyes bright. I can't help but remember the three-year-old Celina who stood on a five-inch curb and exclaimed, "It's a stage!"

"Do you want me to come with you?" I ask.

"Would you?"

So I find a seat in the back of the auditorium to watch the auditions. The kids are good, but Celina's cold reading is brilliant. She's funny and quick. The woman who will be directing the show is not actually a teacher. She's been hired from a community acting group. After the auditions, she bounces back to where Celina and I are sitting together. Her eyebrows leap to her hairline when she sees me. I'm the only mother there, but she seems friendly and enthusiastic about Celina.

"You've got a real instinct for theater," she says to Celina. Then still smiling, "I'm not going to cast you in this show, but I hope you'll audition for one of the shows I'm doing in the community. You're really good."

Celina and I are confused. If she's so good, why isn't the woman going to put her in the show?

"It's probably because you're a freshman," I tell her as we're driving away. But later we find out that another freshman was put in the show. It's baffling.

Over the next few years Celina will have her share of successes and crushing disappointments. For the disappointments, I usually trot out the old story about being a finalist in a screenwriting competition and being sure that I was going to Hollywood and then not making it and feeling like the air had been sucked from the planet, or the sun had suddenly expired. And then a couple of weeks later my friend Mikey died and I had to take over his classes and be there with my friends to help them as they grieved and suddenly not getting that award and that new life in Hollywood didn't matter so much. I don't think this story helps, but I tell it anyway.

■

Although Celina's audition didn't land her a role in that show, it did garner attention from the school's young theatrical genius – a senior.

"Your audition rocked my socks," he told her in the hallway the next day. And as the director of the student-directed play that year, he took her under his wing. Celina found herself ensconced with the nicest, smartest, most intellectually adventurous group of kids in the school. Hallelujah.

■

But there are still a few bumps in the road.

One day I pull up to the school to pick up Celina. She lands in the passenger seat like a wounded bird.

"What's wrong?" I ask her.

Immediately she begins to sob, heart-wrenching, wheezing, mucus-manufacturing, chest-heaving sobs. The story emerges in fits and starts.

"There were these boys . . .in one of the classrooms . . . and I had to go in there to get a . . .book I'd forgotten."

Blood begins pounding in my head like African drums.

"They saw me and they started laughing. One of them said . . . 'it's that girl . . .Celina . . . she's so weird.' . . . and they kept laughing at me."

"What did you do, honey?"

"I turned and ran!" she screams at me.

So there are a lot of things worse than being laughed at, but at that moment with my child sobbing in my car, I'm wanting to go kick some juvenile ass. Rage seethes through me like red hot lava. I'm pissed off at these unknown boys but even more pissed off with myself for letting her come to this school full of rich assholes. (I know. Many of the parents turn out to be incredibly kind and some of these kids will become her lifelong friends, but none of that is registering in the moment.) I can't do anything except try to stifle a terrible memory that suddenly surfaces.

Our paths only crossed once. She was on a blue bike riding across the newly built wooden bridge that spanned the Willow Branch Creek. She didn't have a "cool" bike with a banana seat like we did. She was not cool. She was blond and pale and plump. She wore the plaid skirt and plain white shirt of the Catholic School. My friend Carmen and I spied her. There were two of us and one of her.

"Fatty Patty," we taunted. She tried to ride past us, but as soon as she crossed the bridge and was on the concrete walkway, we closed in. "Fat bitch," we called her. One of us grabbed her bike and the other pushed her and she fell to the ground. Perhaps she skinned her leg or the palms of her hands as she fell. But there she was on the ground while we stood above her. Tears streamed down her face in helpless impotent rage. She screamed at us to leave her alone as she stood and lifted up her bike. Tears streaked her red face. Even as she rode off on her blue bike, pedaling furiously to escape our insults, I knew she was – at that moment – far superior to us. My throat constricted. I wanted to call out, "I'm sorry. Please . . ." I doubt I could have articulated what was in my heart. But if I could have, it would have been "forgive me" – anything to erase the sudden shame I felt. I was a kid with a heart full of pain and she was my mirror.

I guess I figured that I'd see her again somewhere and I could make it up to her. But I never did see her again. She was probably afraid to come through the park after that – that beautiful city park with its old oaks, its thick carpet of grass and the playground and basketball court just past the azalea bushes.

My karma wasn't exactly instant, but it came. In December Carmen and I and the park boys rode our banana-seat bicycles on a mission. We were headed to the barbershop that belonged to Harold's grandfather, located in what we then called "colored town." This was in the late 1960s, and the good folks who divvied up the tax dollars neglected to fix the roads in this area of town. When the front tire of the bike I was riding hit a pothole, I flew face first over the handlebars, grinding my lips on the gravel road.

Hours of plastic surgery restored my lips but left me looking freakish with oversized lips on my small face and a scar running down my chin.

"You'll grow into the lips and the scar will fade," the plastic surgeon assured us.

It didn't matter what the future held. I became a pariah among the park kids with Carmen as their ring leader. They called me names. They laughed at me. They told me I was ugly. I had not yet read *The Metamorphosis* but I knew how it felt to wake up one day as a cockroach. Unlike the girl on the blue bike, I did not lash out angrily. I suppose I thought they were right. I was hideous to look at and not worthy of their company.

Eventually I found a new friend. She also earned the disapproval of the park kids. She was a "rich kid," they accused. But they kept their taunts in check because already she possessed something, some aura of redneck aristocracy, that alarmed the boys and cowed the girls.

Soon Carmen concocted an excuse for a fight. She claimed I was after a boy that she liked. I had no interest in the boy and I didn't want to fight Carmen though if it came down to it, I thought I could win. Carmen was soft and plump, and though I was small, I was wiry and came equipped with a gut full of rage.

It came down to it. My new friend and I were playing tetherball, the one game I was really good at it because I could smack the hell out of that ball, when Carmen showed up, like a gunslinger in a Western, and issued her challenge. I reluctantly followed her to a grassy spot behind the azalea bushes. The other kids circled around us, all but one of them rooting for Carmen. I felt like a fool standing in the circle. I wasn't mad at Carmen. I didn't hate her. But I was supposed to beat her up or get beaten up.

My new friend stood in the crowd of park kids, arms crossed, green eyes narrowed, waiting to see what I would do. So when Carmen came after me, I balled my fist as if I were getting ready to smack the tetherball, and I hit her. Soon all was a confusion of yells, slaps and punches. Then Carmen began crying, her face turned red, and the tears made a snotty mess of her face. She yelled that I had hurt her.

"I'm sorry," I said.

"You go to hell!" she screamed.

There was nothing I could do. My green-eyed friend and I walked away.

That was a long time ago, and yet I still have pockets of shame and guilt. The girl on the blue bike is one of them.

FOUR

My Uncle Dave died in the summer of 2005. He was the second of the "Field kids" to go. We didn't go to his service. It had been many years since Mother had seen him, but she was saddened by his death. She had often told me the story of how for days he searched the waterways around their town in a rowboat after the hurricane of 1938 to find a friend of his who had disappeared with his boat. The boat was found, but not the friend.

Uncle Dave was wealthy, and I had hoped he might leave some money to help Mom get by, but he didn't. It didn't matter. We would survive. If I had to sacrifice a few luxuries or even a few necessities, it would never equal the sacrifices she made for me.

■

In early September, in a year of hurricanes and floods, Hank and I decide to strip and revarnish our back deck. We've been putting it off for several years while humidity, rain, snow and neglect take their toll. We can wait no longer. The wood is turning green, and I worry it will soon begin to rot out beneath us.

We have the television on constantly that weekend. Hurricane Katrina is battering New Orleans and vicinity, and like most people we are horrified and fascinated at the same time. Coming from Florida, we have a deep respect for hurricanes. We feel the same way about alligators. They're scary and unpredictable and yet they somehow define us—or at least they did. We no longer live in Florida or anywhere near a coast, and we do not envy the people in the path of this storm.

The weather is balmy in Charlotte—perfect for working outdoors. While I stand on the front porch admiring the clear Carolina blue sky, a large cobalt-blue butterfly with black trim etched on its wings comes dancing in front of me. Though I come from a family of rationalists, I tend to believe in signs, omens, messages from the gods. This butterfly making hieroglyphs in the air makes me think of transitions and transformations. Mother's health, physical and emotional, is so erratic, I wonder if the universe is sending me a warning. But when I speak to her later that day, she sounds fine.

Hank gets out the power washer. The work is long and laborious, and the green gunk so ingrained that I have to hold the hard, pulsing power washer just inches away from the wood. I shred much of it. It's good to have something to do besides watch the bungling in New Orleans that's costing people their lives. I am full of outrage, but like most people I don't have much to offer besides a paltry monetary donation.

The hurricane passes and, though it was a bad one, it seems not to be as devastating as has been feared; the country will soon resume business as usual. Our televisions will return to their regularly scheduled programming, or so we think.

My life, at the time, seems to be on an even keel. A week earlier I went to a "radical forgiveness" workshop. The afternoon of the workshop I was piled on the floor with about thirty other people like puppies, everyone touching two or three other people in a human chain. Somehow in that moment I managed to let go of forty-something years of anger toward my father. I did this by letting myself remember how I felt about him when I was a little girl. Because he'd left us when I was so young, I didn't know him well, and yet at one point I had loved him. I had loved him because he was my daddy and I didn't know any better. I had loved him unconditionally. This was something I had not allowed myself to feel for him in all these years—simple, uncomplicated love. It didn't matter that he was a shitty father. It didn't matter whether he deserved it or not. I simply let myself feel what I had once felt for a brief time in my younger life, and it was good—like something black and putrid had been scrubbed from my insides.

■

On Monday the levees break in New Orleans and the poorest people in our land are left to drown before our eyes. My husband and I have the deck stripped and next we have to apply coats of varnish. At night we can't work and so I stayed glued to the TV, a sick feeling in the pit of my stomach. We are all culpable in this travesty.

Eventually I turn away and go to bed. I wake up at 3 a.m. completely alert. Hank, who is often up all night, is nonplussed when he finds me working at my computer.

"What are you doing?" he asks.

"I can't sleep. For some reason I'm wide awake."

And so I work until morning when I take Celina to school and then go to Mom's apartment to tend to her needs. I wash her feet, put ointment and band aids on her toes and put on her compression hose. Then we sit in the warm light from the windows, talking about hurricanes. One family story is that my mother's favorite grandmother, Gammie, was so frightened by an enormous hurricane that hit Connecticut in the summer of 1938 that she died of a heart attack soon afterwards.

Around 11 that morning, the phone rings at my mother's apartment. I answer it. It's my brother Jo.

"I need to tell you what he happened," he says in a gentle voice. "You can decide when and how to tell Momma. You know whether or not she can handle it. Daddy is dead. He died in the hospital this morning at 2:45."

I hang up the phone, and something completely unexpected happens: I burst into tears. "Daddy's dead," I say. I kneel down and place my head in my mother's lap, and I let her comfort me. My father, whom I hardly ever thought about, was gone.

We drop our plans for the day and drive over to a coffee shop. As I sit there with my cup of cappuccino, I feel such grief. My mother also grieves. She grieves for the years she had lost to this man who had demeaned and vilified her, this man who slept with his students and brawled with men whose wives he took a liking to. She grieves for the brilliant young woman she was, whose musical talents overshadowed her husband's, much to her chagrin and his rage.

She starts to tell me one of the stories, but I stop her. I've heard them all – the burned manuscripts, the master's degree she'd earned at Yale but didn't take so as not to be his "equal," the sly insults that came from his charming mouth. I do not want to drink from that bitter cup on this day: Tuesday, September 6, 2005. We go to my house. I head upstairs to work, leaving her on the front porch to enjoy the weather. When I come back out, she's sobbing.

■

A couple of weeks later, my brothers and I meet in Jacksonville for my father's memorial service. He always said that when he died, everything he had would go to me and my brothers. He didn't have a lot when he died except for the Steinway. What else there was of value (a Cadillac and a condo) belonged as much to his wife as to him. We thought it might have been nice to have some of his books (he had an extensive library) or some token to remember we actually had a father. Then after the service, a middle-aged man we have never met before comes up to us and tells us, "Your father told me I was like the son he always wished he had."

We stared at him, dumbfounded.

"Well, I'm glad he got to have that experience with *someone*," I respond, glancing at the widened eyes of my brothers.

"When they moved to the beach condo, he gave me all these books," he tells us. "I didn't know what to do with them so I donated most of them to the library." Because, of course, why would the writer in the family want them?

■

What I learn is that my fate at fifty is to be needed but not necessarily wanted. Is there any cliché my life is not fulfilling, I wonder, dabbing hormone cream on my neck each night to prevent the heat coil inside me from glowing red. I spend my evenings playing Scrabble with my elderly mother so she's not lonely. Mornings and afternoons I drive my teenage daughter to school in a seven-year-old station wagon that makes a horrible squeal, which no mechanic can identify. I stand in the checkout line at the supermarket with an enormous package of incontinence pads, resisting the urge to explain to the cashier that it's not for me. I get a perfunctory kiss and squeeze from my husband before I totter off to bed each night.

This is not how I envisioned my life. Perhaps that's the problem. I didn't have a real vision. I didn't make a plan. I set goals for various accomplishments, but I didn't really have any idea beyond "write and publish a novel."

Lest it seem as if I do nothing but measure my life in coffee spoons, I should add that morning drives to school with Celina are respites of light and laughter. We blend in with the morning traffic, and I explain "lane science" as I shift from one lane to the next. We listen to her music – CDs by Bright Eyes or the *Almost Famous* soundtrack. Early on, I explain what's going on in Conor Oberst's lyrics in the song "Lua" when he says to the girl "[you] just keep goin' to the bathroom, always say you'll be right back."

"She's doing drugs in the bathroom, baby," I tell her.

We have a special street we like to look down as we crawl past it. It's called English Gardens and looks like it leads to some lovely alternate dimension where no one has any worries.

We also talk about whatever she has to do that day. One day she begins to recite the "5 C's" of public speaking. When she gets to "confidence," we spontaneously break into the Sound of Music: "I have confidence in me!" We're laughing like lunatics by the time she gets out of the car to go to school. Then I go over to my mother's and she's a crying wreck.

■

I'm going through my mother's things. She's always wanting help with "all these papers." So many letters. So many people who admired her over the years. I open one of the cards from one of her Lost Colony friends and begin to read . . . *"I've been listening to our performances of '80 & '81: Vivaldi's Gloria and Faure's Requiem. Although the recording quality pretty much sucks, the phrasing & musicality, artistry & passion, still shine through profoundly. I want very much to obtain recordings of us doing Haydn's Mass in Time of War, the Vaughn Williams' Serenade to Music that we sang in the gardens for Princess Anne. If you have copies of these, could you, would you make a copy for me and send it? I miss it all so much.*

"As for me, I'm doing better. Time has been the only thing that's dulled the pain of losing Jose & I can tell it's finally working. My health is still holding up okay. I take 5 doses of AZT every day which gets tiresome, but I figure the alternative is less than acceptable!

"You're a great lady, Roz. You've been a tremendous influence in my life & continue to be one to this day. I love you."

There's no date on the card. The writer is probably one of her many gay friends who died of AIDS. She gets sad when she thinks of them. I don't show her the card, but I can't bring myself to throw it away. I place it in a box of other letters and cards – a reminder of who she is.

She needs reminders because in her present circumstances she feels like a nonentity.

Celina has the same problem. Her second year of high school proves challenging. The seniors who had been her saviors the year before have graduated. She tries to find friends in her own grade, but most of them simply don't know what to make of her. Celina sometimes imitates the girls' reaction to anything that doesn't conform with their idea of the world: "Different . . .is well, *different.*" And different isn't a good thing to be. She does find some friends but they are not among the "double-names" –

the pretty girls who all wear their blond hair parted on the same side. One boy manages to really get under her skin. As they sit outside after school, he brags about all the expensive cars his father owns. And then I pull up in the carpool line in my station wagon with the annoying squeal and the two fist-sized holes in the back bumper where an SUV had rammed me and instead of fixing the car, I used the insurance money to pay for tuition one month.

But Celina manages. The theater continues to be her refuge and her source of friendships. We ultimately realize why this school is worth the money: the drama program is innovative and exciting and driven by the students themselves. It is there that Celina is introduced to experimental theater with its intellectual and artistic challenges. There she finds her métier.

While we are obviously different from the other families there, Celina is generally happy with her two strange parents, both of whom work at home. She considers us more interesting than the lawyers and surgeons and CEOs who parent the other kids. She can let drop that her mother is a writer and her father has an Emmy for his television engineering work on the Olympics. In her political science class, she is far more knowledgeable about the issues and the different stances of the two main parties because she grew up hearing us argue about Clinton, then Bush, same-sex marriage, the Iraq invasion, global warming, or whatever is the cable news outrage *du jour*.

And she still has the Charlotte Children's Choir. I spent my childhood entertaining myself while my mother was in one rehearsal or performance after another. I am spending my daughter's childhood in much the same way. The highlight happens in her tenth grade year when her choir is the featured choir in a concert at Carnegie Hall. As Hank and I sit up in the balcony of that enormous, ornate hall and listen to those angelic voices, I think of my mother, who also once played in Carnegie Hall as the guest pianist in a symphony orchestra. My thoughts are sentimental, I'll admit, but musicians seem to me to walk with a lighter tread than the rest of us, and we live in a better world for their presence. Even my father gave his gift to the world. He played jazz his whole adult life – in bars and restaurants, with combos or alone. His music and his big toothy smile probably lifted the spirits of many an unhappy soul.

FIVE

I try to incorporate my mother into my life whenever possible, but the divide between her world and mine is on the Grand Canyon scale. Once when going through old newspaper clippings about her life, I found a cartoon showing a conductor with raised arms hovering over a prone long-haired individual holding a guitar. Above the drawing there was this quote: "The tight-lipped comment made by musician's musician Rosalind MacEnulty when a fellow conversationalist opined that maybe classical music would come back now that the public had gotten a surfeit of rock 'n' roll: 'It never left.'"

Perhaps she never appreciated rock music, but rock musicians appreciated her when they came into contact with her. On her mantel for many years were four beautiful Fabergé eggs given to her by the drummer of Pink Floyd, so the story goes. Now I have them.

■

One day in the middle of one of our rambling conversations about life, I ask my mother, "Do you feel complete?" I want to know if she's okay about having reached the end of her life. Is there anything else she needs to do?

We're sitting at the round table in her apartment where we always play Scrabble, and she taps her fingers nervously on the wood.

"I don't want the Requiem to die when I do," she answers.

I think of the box of manuscripts in their tattered black folders – that box of poltergeists that follows us everywhere – now sitting on the shelf of her closet. The score needs to be put in computer format if we're ever going to send it to a publisher and that will cost a few thousand dollars. And would anyone publish it?

"Don't worry," I tell her. "It won't."

For my little family, the masterpiece of the era is Harry Potter. Whenever a new Harry Potter book comes out, we clear the deck of all distractions, and each night Celina and I retreat to Hank's lair with a bag of ginger snaps, and I read as many chapters to the two of them as my throat can handle. I have perfected each character's voice so that tag lines aren't even necessary, and we become completely absorbed in the Hogwarts' world. Hank sometimes loses track and insists that we back up, whereupon Celina and I berate him for not paying attention. Sometimes I take a peek at the chapters ahead and, if they catch me, Hank and Celina give me hell. I've done a few cool things in my life and been to some interesting places. But rarely have I been happier than when I am eating ginger snaps and reading Harry Potter to those two enraptured people – my husband and my child.

But this little family scenario is not my mother's idea of fun. She needs an audience and we aren't it. After my first Christmas with Hank's family back in the early 90s, I showed my mother a videotape that Hank had shot of Christmas day with his mother and father, his brother and brother's son and his sister. They were a group of ordinary people, and I liked them in spite of the Republican rhetoric that Hank's father spouted. He was always kind and generous with me and he was knowledgeable about history. Jean, my mother-in-law, was full of family stories, and Hank's brother and sister made me feel accepted. And they all adored Celina.

I had spent so much of my life on my own that I had never expected to have a family. Not like this. When Hank and I broke up during my pregnancy, I thought I'd be a struggling single mom my whole life. Then one day I found myself in the sunny glow of southern California with Ozzie and Harriet.

My mother dismissed the video with a sneer, and at that moment I hated her. I hated her groundless snobbery, her disdain for the ordinary pleasures that might, just might, have kept me from making some of the destructive choices I had made. Her pretensions filled me with rage.

My mother couldn't stand to be ordinary. When I was in my late 20s, I was one of five writers to win the Florida Screenwriting Award. I'd only had a few stories published, no books yet, so this was a big deal to me. And the Florida Film Bureau was treating it like a big deal. To give us our plaques, they had arranged a luncheon with certain state honchos in Tallahassee. I invited my mother to come along with me. She was younger then and firmly attached to her image as an iconoclast, a rebel who didn't need a damn cause.

We were all seated at a round table in a dining room in the capitol. One of the bureaucrats, a nice enough woman in a suit, stood up to say a few words to honor us. My mother was in fine form, poking fun at everything. The speaker was no great orator. These speeches are, by definition, banal. But the food was free and tasty, and they were recognizing me for my writing. I was even in the newspaper and it wasn't for committing a crime! I'd come a long way, baby, from the drug rehab to this fork-clanking event where the Secretary of Commerce, one Jeb Bush, was raising a glass of iced tea in my honor. I'd be getting a plaque, a trip to Hollywood, and a nice line for my resume.

The woman began by saying, "We're here to honor the winners. Well, we're all winners, aren't we?" Then Mom piped up in a fairly loud voice and said, "Not me. I'm not a winner. I'm a loser."

All these years later, it seems innocuous, but at the time I was mortified and angry. This was supposed to be my moment. Couldn't she just give me that?

She immediately looked sheepish, but it was too late. Mom just needed to have the spotlight. It's the smartest-girl-in-the-class syndrome. Usually it wasn't a problem because she was also kind and generous and fun to be around. But as she got older, the need for attention seemed to overwhelm her. If she wasn't getting the attention, she literally couldn't breathe.

This facet of her personality derailed what seemed like a perfect plan. Once she got settled at The Landings, I figured I'd just bring my work over there and then she wouldn't be alone during the day. She always said, "Oh, just a warm body in the house makes all the difference." But it wouldn't be ten minutes before she'd be groaning and then gasping for air and I'd have to turn away from whatever I was doing to find out if she was dying. Sometimes I wondered why she didn't. If life was this difficult, this constantly nightmarish, was it worth the effort?

■

As my mother loses her past, I lose part of mine as well. Aspects of my childhood I simply can't remember. She doesn't remember either.

■

For two weeks at the beginning of July I teach at the Kaleidoscope Arts Camp for creative teenagers on the Winthrop University campus. This is my favorite two weeks of the year, but it's hard on my mother because I am gone all day long and late into the night.

In a way hanging out with these kids with their drama and their problems, their fears and their laughter restores to me my own lost teenage years. Celina comes to the camp, but she is in the drama classes and stays in the dorm with the other kids so I don't see that much of her except in passing.

Each year, I lead a little troop of seven or eight teenage poets around the campus, which is blanketed in the shade of magnanimous oaks. We visit the art museum one day. Another day we go to the dance studio. This year as the dancers rehearse their routines, I remember my own days as a dancer. I was certainly no prodigy but when you truly enjoy something you're bound to get fairly good at it. When I was in the eighth grade, after dancing for eight years, I was given a solo on pointe in the yearly recital. Now watching these young women practicing their pirouettes, I try to remember anything about that solo. I can remember the lighted stage, the cool cavernous dressing rooms and the enormous auditorium, but after that – nothing. I don't remember the music, or my costume. Did my feet hurt? Was I nervous? Was I good?

It's as if it never happened. There's no movie I can go back, rewind, and watch. I think of the stacks and stacks of pictures I have of Celina in her various recitals and performances. There are none of me. I never before thought it odd. In my family, performing was simply expected. Why bother to record it?

I wish there were someone who could tell me, oh, you were so pretty in your satin toe shoes, twirling across the stage. I'm like the tree who fell in the forest and no one heard.

■

When I am not working, I try to get Mom out of her apartment as much as possible. We go to Jason's Deli for the salad bar. We go to see Celina in her choir and theater performances. And there are all those nights of Scrabble playing.

Celina gets jealous of the time I spend with my mother, but I don't know what else to do. She has no one else. Everyone at her retirement community shuts their doors at 7 p.m. to watch "Jeopardy" and then goes to bed when she's ready to party.

"I know I'm not smart like she is and I don't play Scrabble with you, but do you still like me?" Celina finally asks me.

"You are number one," I assure her over and over. But she misses me and she isn't good at hiding her frustration.

■

On Sundays I take my mother to church with us. This turns out to be a disaster.

The church isn't so much a church in the traditional sense as a weekly session in cognitive therapy. The two ministers are a lesbian couple, whom I like a lot. One of them is a singer/songwriter who often plays her guitar during the service and leads us in feel-good folk songs. This is not exactly my mother's idea of church. As unreligious as she is, she is a firm believer in the Episcopal hymnal and the beautiful, complex anthems that she had arranged and/or directed over much of the past century and on into this one. These four-chord guitar songs are simplistic and can hardly be called music in her mind. Unfortunately, she feels the urge to explain this to anyone who cares to listen to her.

We have a friendly bunch of people who come to this church, and a fairly, intelligent, artistic crowd. But Mother can't relate to anyone there except for one of the ministers, whose troubled past has turned her into a deep soul, unafraid of exposing her wounds.

One Sunday morning Celina, my mother and I go to church. Celina has been coming to this church since she was ten years old. She learned guitar from one of the ministers; she is always fussed over by the regulars. I like to hang around afterwards and chat with various people. But my mother usually finds a chair somewhere and sits.

As we leave the church that day, Mother trudging through the crowd on her walker, one of the men jokingly says something to her. Mother spits out of the side of her mouth in fury, "Go to hell!" Then she trudges out the door. Celina and I glance at each other, perplexed.

"What?" I ask. "What happened?" I did not hear the comment which ignited her invective.

Outside, I help my mother in the car. She's crying and won't speak. Celina explains that one of the guys told Mom not to get a speeding ticket with her walker. Could that possibly be the impetus for this tantrum, I'm wondering.

"Tell me what happened," I say as we drive away.

"He was mocking me!" she bursts out. "I'm going to kill myself!" She starts yanking at the door, but the door is locked so she futilely shakes the door handle.

Celina gasps. She's in the back seat in utter shock. I realize that in spite of the occasional spats that Hank and I have, this level of high drama is brand new to her. Betty Davis is in town, kid, so look out.

We manage to get home without my crippled mother throwing herself out of the moving vehicle. But by now I am in a rage. I never forced my mother to come to my church. She wanted to come. Of course, if I were as self-sacrificing as I should be, I could take her to a nice Episcopal service somewhere and suffer through the Nicene Creed and all the kneeling and standing. But the church I go to is where I get my mental health. I can't afford a therapist. "Think about what you want, not about what you don't want. Believe that you are worthy. Love yourself." These are the messages I get every Sunday, and after a lifetime of self-loathing I am finally becoming acceptable to myself.

But here I am with the original self-loather herself, her face gone sour, roiling emotions swirling around her like deranged demons. And she does what the children of alcoholics are all experts at doing: she starts burying the issue as quickly as possible.

I pull in the driveway of my house.

"I don't want to talk about it," she orders as if that is enough.

We go inside, and I make sandwiches for us in the kitchen as Celina watches the two of us warily.

"This," I say, "is why I became a drug addict." I place a cheese and tomato sandwich in front of my mother. I am not sure if what I am saying is true, but it feels true. We bury pain in our family. My mother always said if something bothers you, you put it in a little black box in your mind, you lock the box and then you drop it off an imaginary cliff and it goes away. So why wouldn't I have buried my pain under a blanket of drug-induced oblivion?

I grill a cheese sandwich for Celina and then sit down across from my mother.

"Tell me," I say. "Tell me what is going on with you. No hysterics."

"He was making fun of me," she says. "I hate it. I hate being a cripple." Well, of course she does. And immediately I sympathize. An image forms in my mind: my mother in a tight-fitting red evening gown with a gold dragon design along the skirt, walking on the stage of the Civic Auditorium in Jacksonville. I remember her regal bearing as she sat down at the grand piano and began to play. She looked gorgeous; she looked like power. She had the world under her fingertips.

"Mother, can you see that he wasn't making fun of you, that he was just trying to be friendly. Perhaps rather ineptly, but still . . ."

She acknowledged that was a possibility.

"I'm sorry your feelings were hurt," I tell her.

"I'm just crazy," she says.

"Maybe. A little. Sometimes. But it's okay."

We eat our sandwiches. I smile at Celina who hasn't said a word the whole time. Celina smiles back. It's not the end of the world when someone goes a little crazy.

After that Mom stays at The Landings on Sundays and plays the piano for the "dreadful" church service there, and Celina and I go to church by ourselves until eventually Celina's too busy with her friends and I start seeking my spiritual sustenance elsewhere.

SIX

In 2006, the dice land in my favor. I am offered a teaching job with insurance benefits and a real salary. Not only that, but I have enough freelance writing work over the summer to pay off my old car and put a down payment on my dream car: a gray Prius. A quick search on the Internet and I find the perfect car – right color, right options, right price – just one town over from Charlotte.

A full time teaching job is going to make things difficult. My mother is getting less and less able to take care of herself. With the extra money I make I can afford a little help, but it won't be a lot.

Once school starts I develop a routine. Now every morning Celina takes the Blue Monster to school, and I drive over to my mother's. I scramble eggs with cut up tomato and cheese. I make toast and lightly butter it. We sit at the table and eat. I don't usually want to talk much. I peruse *The New Yorker*, gobbling up the cartoons. Then I pull my mother's compression hose on her, leave out some food for lunch, hug her goodbye and dash off for work. Sometimes she looks at me with desperation before I go. Her depression, when it's on, is like mustard gas filling the room. I'm afraid to breathe it in.

In the evenings while Celina is at rehearsals, I go over to my mother's. When Celina is home, I try to be home as well. Hank spends most of his time working. He occasionally joins me on some obligatory parental outing, and we still go out to eat as a family or watch a movie on the weekends, but increasingly we are isolated units. Our differing political points of view have become sharper in recent years, our arguments a little more bitter. I know it's not healthy, but I don't know how to fix things. I'm doing the old one day at a time trick.

And Celina is growing up. One night I dream of her as a little girl. How I sweep her in my arms, coddle and kiss her, nostalgia flooding my veins. I know even as I dream that she is no toddling child. I know I will never again feel that small body in my arms, heart beating like a rabbit. I ache to remember the way she would turn to face me and drape her small arms over my shoulders. Then I wake from the dream, rise and stumble into my teenager's room, slip under the covers and cradle her long, lanky body in my arms.

"Is everything okay?" she asks.

"Yes," I tell her. "I just want to cherish this moment." But already it is fading like a dream.

■

One night in early November, I am playing Scrabble with my mother at her apartment; I almost have the word VIZIER. Celina has been gone for about ten minutes; the dishes from our spaghetti dinner are still in the sink. When the phone rings, I know it isn't good. I know it is her. I am already standing, looking for my coat, reaching for the phone.

"Mom," her voice shakes. "I'm not hurt." She knows those are the first words she must say. "I've been in an accident. A bad one."

"Is anyone else hurt?" I ask.

"I think so."

"Where are you?"

She tells me, and I fly out the door.

It takes seven or eight minutes to get to the accident site. I keep calling Hank on the way over, but he doesn't answer his phone, so I call the neighbors and ask them to go over and tell him to call me. Red and blue lights pulse through the chilly air, and I can see the Blue Monster in the intersection, front axle broken, wheel turned on its side like a broken leg and another car with a pancaked front end next to it, ambulances on either side. I park my car and dash across the busy four-lane street to get to my child.

"I'm here, baby," I say, but she is surrounded by emergency workers, putting a neck brace on her strapping her to a board. They explain they are taking her to a hospital to have her checked out.

"What about the other driver?" I ask.

"He's going to another hospital. We think he's okay."

The whole night seems to sigh with relief and the air gets a little softer, a little easier on the throat.

"Mom?" Celina says, panic rising in her voice. I reach out and place a hand on her shaking legs.

"Breathe," I tell her.

At the hospital I learn that a couple who stopped right after the accident took care of her and let her use their cell phone to call me since hers was lost in the battered, liquid-leaking car. I also notice that she's wearing my leather jacket. The jacket was given to me when Celina was just a baby by my friend Mike

Gearhart, who had once told me that Celina was the closest thing he'd ever have to a child of his own. I was a single mom and he'd just gotten some insurance money from an accident. He bought Celina baby clothes. He stayed up nights with me when she was sick. Even after Hank and I got back together, he was still a part of our lives. Celina loved him. She was only five years old when he died of heart failure, but she never forgot Mikey.

At the hospital she has the jacket draped over her like a blanket. The x-rays show no broken bones. The CAT-scan shows no internal injuries. We spend about four hours in the emergency room. The other driver turns out to be okay, too. After the doctor signs the release papers, my daughter slips her arms into the leather jacket and we leave the hospital to go home.

Except for briefly visiting my mother in a hospital, I haven't been in one since sixteen years earlier when the doctors had cut me open to remove my daughter from my womb. I have no idea that this environment will become very familiar in the near future.

But tonight I have remained calm as a lily in a summer lake. In the morning, I will lie in bed and weep, thinking about what I might have lost.

■

A week later I hear a yelp and a thud come from Celina's room. She stumbles into my room, ashen-faced, holding her finger. She has just put a sewing machine needle through it.

"Go wash it off," I tell her and rush downstairs to get ice. I find her a few minutes later, passed out on the bathroom floor with Hank lying beside her to keep her warm. We head back to the emergency room, where they remove a half-inch worth of needle from her finger. I am so thankful that she didn't have this pair of accidents back when I didn't have health insurance.

◼

Celina recovers but my mom gets worse. The bad days keep coming. She cannot stand to be alone. She is nearly always in pain. She forgets where the bathroom is. I have become her lifeline. I go over to take care of her seven days a week, once or twice a day and it never seems to be enough. When I am not teaching, I am taking her to doctors or going to the store for her, or just taking her out in my car to get her out of the debilitating depression that swallows her like Jonah whenever she's inside four walls. We can't quite afford assisted living unless we sell the piano that she has had since she was eight or nine years old, and that's something we're not willing to do yet.

On the afternoon of November 27 – my birthday – I check my voice mails. In one of them from earlier in the day, my mother screams "Help me, help me!" over and over. She fell that morning and the paramedics came and lifted her up, but it's my number she called, my recorded voice she begged help from. As I listen to her screaming message, something inside me turns hard and sour. Perhaps, I am thinking of how I had looked forward to this decade in my life. As my child-rearing duties lessened, I thought I would have more time for travel, friends, reconnecting with my husband, writing all those books in my head that are clamoring to be written. But now, I can see no end to this, and my heart feels like a shriveled peach.

But not all days are bad. At Christmas, my mother becomes concerned about all the other residents who have nowhere to go and nothing to do on Christmas Eve.

Perhaps she is remembering that bleak Christmas six or seven years earlier when she was all alone. Since she made her livelihood as a church organist and music director, she'd always worked on Christmas Eve and bah-humbugged the whole thing. That Christmas, however, except for the sparsely attended Christmas Eve service, she found herself with nothing to do, nowhere to go. No one had invited her for Christmas dinner. I was in California with Hank and Celina. Both my brothers were spending the holidays with their own families. I remember calling Mom to wish her Merry Christmas and hearing a lonely pang in her voice when she said, "I haven't seen a soul all day."

When my mother gave up her church job and came to live near me, I wondered how she would function without her identity as a musician. The ideal death for her would have been on a Sunday morning while she sat at her organ during yet another boring sermon. When it was time for the anthem to begin, the choir would look expectantly over at her, but she would not move. She would not lift her hands this time. The grand musical dame would be gone.

Now she is no longer the grand dame; she is just another addled old person on a walker. And yet since she's been at The Landings, she's managed to start a chorus. Of course, at first, the management loved the idea but refused to pay for music or even move the piano around so she could see the singers while she played for them. My mother tried to explain that the piano had wheels on it so you could move it, but our old nemesis – that

136

statuesque blonde in her perilously high heels who had an alarming resemblance to Glenn Close with a dead rabbit on the stove – wouldn't hear of it.

So instead of buying music, my mother hand wrote arrangements for the group of 20 or so singers. Her trusty assistant, Sylvia, took it to the copier to make copies for everyone. When they put on a show every few months, the great room was packed. It wasn't the best singing around town by a long shot, but it was definitely the most appreciated.

My mother's idea for Christmas Eve is a little different. She doesn't want to put on a concert. Instead she decides to throw a big sing-along party. Everyone she mentions the idea to, loves it. Except the management. They tell her she can only do it as long as they don't have to do anything. They won't even publicize the event among the residents.

She asks if it would be okay for Sylvia to deliver flyers to the apartments. Absolutely not. Jeez, I'm thinking. I got better treatment in jail.

Christmas Eve comes. At 6:30 Celina and I go over to help her prepare. Hank is in a huff because we're deserting him on Christmas Eve.

"It's just for a couple of hours," I tell him. "You're welcome to join us."

But Hank doesn't want to come. He doesn't like being around old people. So we go without him, and he stays home and stews.

When we get to my mother's apartment, she is wearing a glittery white vest, looking most festive. By now she can no longer walk as far as the great room, so she gets in her brand new motorized wheelchair, which took weeks of wrangling to get, and we parade behind her, carrying punch and cookies.

We walk into the large room where a crowd of fifty to sixty old folks mingle around the tables laden with drinks, pumpkin bread, cranberry bread, muffins – all brought by a few volunteers. Word of mouth is a fine method of communication in a retirement community.

"Hello, everybody!" my mother yells as she comes in.

The life of the party has arrived. Mom takes command of the evening. Tom, a POW in World War II, sings "Oh, Holy Night." Celina sings "White Christmas." The whole place sings "Jingle Bells" and "Joy to the World." Mom's makeshift chorus sings a few songs. She then whips out a few classical pieces. The happiness in the place is almost palpable, like a cat that leaps unexpectedly onto your lap. As I gaze at my mother in her sparkly holiday sweater, her body coaxing sound from that crummy little piano, hundreds of images of her doing this same thing in different places with different people reverberate through my mind like the infinite reflections you see of yourself when you stand between two mirrors.

My mother's eyes shine as she makes that pitiful little upright roar. I look around at those people. They are having a wonderful time, and I can't remember a better Christmas Eve.

Before we leave, the residents fawn over Celina.

"So lovely, so lovely," they say. My tall, willowy daughter in her pristine youth smiles at them.

As we leave to go mollify my unhappy husband, Celina tucks her arm in mine and says, "Being with Grandma Roz is like being with a rock star."

We can still hear them singing as we walk out the door.

SEVEN

WINTER 2007

The door to my mother's apartment is unlocked, so I enter. The Steinway, silent and black, takes up most of the living room. In the second bedroom – where she keeps her Clavinova, painting supplies and the daybed – the radio plays Chopin. It's nine in the morning, and the blinds have not yet been raised, but there's light enough for me to see my mother lying on her side on the daybed in her ruby-colored robe. She seems to get smaller every day. My mother, I think, will not die. Rather she will float away like an autumn leaf. Her eyes are shut, her face slack; her brown hair with its gray roots is wispy and disheveled. I touch her shoulder, she wakes in confusion.

"It's me," I tell her.

Recognition seeps into her red-rimmed eyes. "Oh."

I sit down at the end of her bed, by her feet, which are covered by a cashmere throw that one of my brothers gave her for Christmas.

"I hurt," she says, matter-of-factly.

"Is there anything I can do?" I ask, rubbing her calf.

She says the rent is on her mind. Will I write the check for it? I find the bills on the counter between the kitchen and the small dining table. She explains that I need to write one check to cover both the rent and the meals, which are on two separate bills.

"I understand," I say as I write. I've been handling her finances for almost three years now.

She wants to know the amount. When I tell her, she looks alarmed. "No, that's not right. That's not enough!"

It takes me several minutes to convince her that I have indeed written the check for the right amount, and my voice acquires an edge in the process.

"Oh, you're right," she says, defeated.

I take the check to the front desk – a 30 to 40-minute round trip for her on her walker, which I manage in about seven minutes. I know she should probably be in assisted living at this point. We'll have to sell the piano and hope that's enough. I don't know how much longer I can go on being her sole caregiver.

When I get back, I ask if she wants me to help put on her compression hose.

"Yes, but will you put some of that ointment on my toe first?"

I smear the antibiotic over her big toe, which is large and red. She winces when I touch the bottom of her foot, then apologizes for the tears that spring to her eyes. I cradle her head and tell her it's okay to cry when you're in pain.

I am not always so understanding of her tears, which sometimes seem manufactured to manipulate me. She becomes frantic over some nebulous concern, and my heart closes up. Maybe I'm feeling guilty that there's so little I can do for her. Maybe I feel I should be a better daughter. No matter what I do, it's never enough. After I've spent two evenings with her, she'll want a third. No, I tell her. Hank and Celina need me, too.

One time when I came to see her, she had the awful expression I've come to dread: lips drooping, head slumping, eyes of a genocide survivor.

"This is not my mother," I said in an irritated voice. "My mother is strong."

"Oh, don't be angry with me," she said, sounding weak and pitiful. I took her for a walk, and she pulled out of her gloom. By the time we returned to the apartment, she was almost her old self.

But as the weeks and months go by, her old self fades in and out. It is not only the fear of death that diminishes her, but also the pain of bones crumbling beneath the skin.

"I'm falling apart," she says. "Can you imagine? . . . Of course, you can't."

"I can sort of imagine it, but not completely." I am on the floor, placing a bin of warm, soapy water under the table so she can soak her feet while we play Scrabble. I once attended a workshop by a spiritual leader who said that it is good soul work to bow at another's feet. I bow regularly at my mother's feet. I wash them. I massage them. I scrape the fungus from under her nails.

"What would I do without you?" she asks.

Truthfully, I don't know. I have managed to bring her back to life for a while, like when you water a thirsty plant. She was never a hugger, but now when I bend down and hold her, she squeezes back and says, "I feel better when you do that, when you hug me." My affection keeps her alive. Perhaps in some small way, I have redeemed myself after all these years.

■

When I was nineteen years old, my mother walked into my bedroom and saw me trying to find a vein for a needle full of heroin. My boyfriend was holding my arm, which was bloody from the punctures in my skin. There was my worried mother trying to stop me from committing slow suicide. Frustrated with my uncooperative veins and mad at my mother for intruding, I raised both of my fists, intending to bring them crashing down on her head. But my boyfriend grabbed my wrists.

"Don't you hurt your momma," he said.

He was right, and I knew it. I never hurt her physically, but over the next three years I dragged her through hell. She paid for the lawyer when I was arrested for robbery. She suffered the indignity of being searched every time she visited me in prison. When I was transferred to the honors camp, she brought me my first free-world food: homemade shrimp salad. It was so rich I threw it up, but I loved that shrimp salad.

◼

"The other residents here all envy me," Mom says now as I dry off her feet. "Because of you."

I don't respond.

"I'm so lucky," she adds. "I'm the luckiest unlucky person I know."

◼

I am broken, and my mother's old age is what's breaking me, I think standing naked in my bathroom, one foot propped up on the sink, clipping my toenails. The bathroom is dirty: hairs everywhere, beads of mold in the corners. Cleaning the bathroom has become a luxury. Someday I will spend one afternoon a week scrubbing my bathroom, but for now I wipe the sink with a dry Noxzema pad, scrape some loose hair from a corner, and hurry out.

My next thought is: It is not a bad thing to be broken. When something's broken you get to see what's inside.

My mother's demands provoke a barrage of arguments with myself: I have a family, and I have a right to spend time with them. Hell, I have a right to spend time alone. I should be able to crawl into bed with a book at 8 P.M. if I want. . . . No, I should be there with her. Imagine if I were in this much pain.

My mother puts on a false happy voice when she calls me. She is the child, afraid her caretaker will abandon her. I am the stern authority figure that she's afraid to cross. She tries to be a good girl, but she also makes sure I see the pain beneath her happy exterior.

Mom has started sleeping in the armchair because she cannot get into and out of bed and she needs to go to the bathroom several times during the night. I buy her a mechanical lift chair so her legs can at least be up at night, but I can't stop the inevitable.

In January, 2007, my mother's legs begin to weep. Such a poetic notion, I think, but the smelly, yellowish fluid oozing from her skin into her shoes is hardly the stuff of lyricism. The medicine the doctor gave a week earlier is not having the desired effect. Now he wants her to go to the hospital.

■

After three days in the hospital, Mom's legs look normal instead of like elephant ankles for the first time in years. What the hospital folks have neglected to notice, however, is that the urine in my mother's Foley bag is dark and full of blood. The catheter has given her an infection. We don't realize this at the time, of course. When I bring her back to her apartment, we find that for some reason, she can't get her legs to move as she wobbles on her walker. How is she going to get to the bathroom alone?

That night I park her in her chair with the incontinence pads beside her, and go home to get a few hours' sleep. First thing the next morning I call the paramedics to come get her. We fear the worst – a stroke.

Back to the hospital we go, first to the emergency room for hours and then to the floor where she was before. New doctors come by. They can't figure out what's wrong. The thousands of tests they administered show no signs of stroke. Mother gets worse. She has a fever. My formerly alert, Scrabble-playing, eighty-eight-year-old mother becomes disoriented and confused. She thinks that she's standing up when she's lying down.

"They're trying to torture me," she tells me.

"Who?"

"Everyone," she whispers.

I cancel my classes. When I dare go home and sleep, I get desperate phone calls from her: "They" weren't letting her lie down. They were making her stand in a closet. They were cruel. I have to come get her, she tells me.

Back at the hospital, I find her in her bed.

"Mom, you're lying down already."

"Really?"

"I promise you. No one has made you stand in a closet."

I am at the hospital so much, people begin to think I work there. The woman at the coffee kiosk downstairs tries to give me an employee discount. My mother isn't quite sure where I work or what I do.

"Are you part of the program?" she asks me.

"What program?"

"The program here. Are you going to a meeting?"

"No," I tell her. "I'm visiting you. That's all."

"Oh, I thought maybe you worked here."

"I practically do," I answer. "I finally know how to operate all this goddamn equipment."

I have mastered the brakes on the hospital bed, learned where to clip the tubes on the IV stand, figured out how to hang the catheter bag. Though it seems a little crazy for my mother to ask whether I work at the hospital, I can understand her confusion. I arrive in the morning, dressed in my teaching clothes and carrying my briefcase full of papers to grade, and the first thing I do is ask the nurse for an update. Then I'm on the phone, making official-sounding calls to the insurance company, the rehab provider, the primary physician. Her physical therapist and case manager consult with me. I am fluent in terms like "CAT scan" and "Foley bag." I come in for eight-hour shifts or longer.

On the one weekday I don't have to teach, I try to get caught up on my freelance writing in the morning. When I show up at the hospital at eleven, my mother looks ghastly, her covers off, her gown hiked up to her thighs, gray hair matted on her skeleton head. The squares of tape from some test are tacked to her chest, IV needles strapped to her arms. I rush over and hold her and say, "It's all right. I'm here."

She gasps and asks, "Where — where were you?"

"I had to go to the bank, and I had an interview to do for a magazine, but now I'm here, and I don't have to leave."

"It's not just for company," she says with a rasp. "This is real."

It takes her a moment to forgive me for not arriving sooner to pull her from this nightmare. It seems as though she may not make it through the day, as if she is thinking of giving up. I debate whether or not to call my brothers and tell them to get on airplanes. Something tells me to wait. There have been many times in the past two and a half years when it has seemed as if my mother were sitting on the precipice and contemplating the other side. Her eyes are closed, and she struggles to breathe in drawn-out gasps. I adjust her head, rub her shoulders, massage her scalp. Finally the antibiotics kick in, and I catch a glimpse of my mother coming back to me. Her breathing slows down and her eyes regain their focus. Nurses and technicians bustle in and out.

"Listen, Mom," I say when we have a moment to ourselves. "You can either let go, or fight to get better."

She ponders the alternatives, her hazel eyes wide and un-blinking.

"Fight," she says.

"Okay then."

At six o'clock Celina calls on my cell phone. "When are you coming home?" she wants to know.

"Soon," I say.

Hearing this, my mother invents tasks for me, trying to delay my inevitable departure. But after another hour or so I leave her and head out through the maze of narrow halls cluttered with computer stations and carts, aiming like a bullet for the glass exit doors. I am both relieved and reluctant to go.

■

On Saturday the fever-inspired dementia has ceased, but the pain medications have my mother in a fog. I step outside her room and find a nurse pounding the keys of a computer, and I ask her to ease up on Mom's pain killers. I need my mother to be pain-free, but more than that, I need her to get her mind back.

When the physical therapist arrives, Mom starts to wimp out.

"I'm too tired," she says.

"I want you to try, Mom," I tell her, giving her a look to remind her of yesterday's decision to fight.

"Okay," she says. Her hands clutch the walker, and the physical therapist and I help her onto her wobbly legs. I hear a noise from her joints, as if her bones are scraping against each other. I cannot imagine her incessant pain or fathom her courage.

"That's good, Mom," I tell her.

She takes a step forward.

■

Sunday morning I drag myself out of bed. The doctor has told me my mother will be released late today. Just as I am about to leave for the hospital, Mom calls.

"I'm doing all right," she assures me.

She still wants me at her side, but more than that, she wants what she has always wanted: for me to be happy. And sometimes that desire is strong enough to override her need to have me with her — at least temporarily.

I never liked the children's book The Giving Tree, by Shel Silverstein, because it reminded me too much of my mother: the way she helped me whenever I needed money; the way she always took my side no matter how wrong I might have been; the way she forgave me, and continues to forgive me, for my sharp tongue. She never put anyone ahead of me. Whatever I needed or wanted, she got for me, if she could. Her generosity has been both a blessing and a source of guilty irritation.

At one point my mother told me that she has reached her life's coda — a musical term for the last section of a composition — and I have made the time bearable for her, sometimes even enjoyable. I wonder if she isn't hanging on for my sake, to give me the chance to ease my conscience for all the years she propped me up with love and money. I wonder, too, if my youthful "troubles," as she calls them, weren't my gift to her: a chance to save someone from self-ruin, as she hadn't been able to do for her father or her husband.

I decide not to go to the hospital right away. Instead I take Merlyn for a walk before the rain comes. The weather is typical of Southern winters, blustery and pregnant with possibility. I feel as if I am seeing the material world in all its splendor after having huddled for weeks in a cave. Standing in the field at the top of my neighborhood, I gaze at the pine trees silhouetted against the cloudy sky. Merlyn scouts the brittle weeds for new scents. I take a breath.

The reprieve is sweet but short-lived. An insistent tug, like the ocean's undertow my mother always feared would sweep her child out to sea, pulls at me with an irresistible force. Soon I am heading back to my house where I will grab the keys to my car and speed to the hospital to be at her side.

■

Instead of sending her home right away, the social worker arranges for Mom to go to a "skilled nursing facility" just down the street from the hospital. It is night time, and I have to enter through the back door. That thick odor of antiseptic and age immediately subsumes me. One seemingly abandoned and shriveled woman, ancient as Egypt, watches from her wheelchair as I look for someone who might be in charge.

The attendant, busy eating her dinner, has no idea where I might find a wheelchair. "Just borrow one from that room over there," she says and points vaguely. I find one, but it doesn't have foot rests, so my mother has to hold her weak legs up. As soon as I wheel her in, I whisper in her ear: "One night. That's it." I leave her on a cot-sized bed in a small, closed-in room with two other invalids, go home and lie in my big comfortable queen bed unable to shut my eyes.

The next day as soon as my classes are over, I head to the nursing home, pack up my mother's belongings and abscond with her back to the apartment – AMA, against medical advice. Using the walker, she is able to get from room to room. The nursing home experience has been enormously restorative. She'll do anything not go back there.

When I finally get home late that night, Hank and Celina ask when they might get a chance to spend some time with me again. I shrug. I've developed a rash right over those deep worry lines between my eyebrows. The rash looks like the letter "A" on my forehead. I'm reminded of Hawthorne's *Scarlet Letter*. Am I an adulteress or does the A merely stand for "Anxiety"?

I sleep deeply that night, hoping that in the dark place I can suckle at the life source and replenish my depleted soul. The next morning when I call my mother, she tells me she is all right.

"I'll be there in a little while," I say. I have some bills to pay, laundry to do: the little things without which our lives spin out of control.

I move slowly, but finally I am ready to leave. Then the phone rings. I pick it up and hear her desperate cry: "Where are you? I'm very sick!"

I cannot help myself. I put the phone down, and a scream escapes from my lungs. And another scream and another.

"Call your brothers, or I will," Hank demands. I call Jo, and 24 hours later I meet him at the Greyhound station and fall crying into his arms.

EIGHT

ONE MONTH LATER

Jo stays for a couple of weeks, and during that time I spend all my time with Hank and Celina. I'm like a starving person at a banquet. I can't get enough of them. But then he goes back to St. Louis, and I start my juggling act all over again.

"If only you could clone yourself," my mother says sympathetically. Though she sometimes seems oblivious, in actuality she is often aware of being burdensome.

About a month after my mother's ordeal at the hospital, I get a phone call.

"Ma'am," a paramedic tells me. "Your mother has fallen, and we're taking her to the hospital. We think she might have broken or twisted her ankle."

It's night, and I'm already in one of Hank's old T-shirts getting ready to crawl into my bed.

"Should I come to the hospital?"

"Ma'am, she's probably going to be in the emergency room for a while. You can wait till the morning when they check her in."

My body is only too ready to comply. I should have known better. I should have gone over to my mother's apartment and stopped them from taking her to the hospital.

Instead I tumble into the comforting embrace of my bed.

After a fitful night, I get up at around six, dress and head to the hospital. Mother has only just then been put in a room. She is dopey from morphine, but there are no broken bones. At least nothing that the x-ray showed. And this is another point at which I could have said, fine, I'll take her home now. But we are conditioned to do what people in scrubs tell us to do.

"We want to do an MRI just to make sure there are no fractures that the x-ray missed," a nurse tells me. "Is your mother claustrophobic?"

"Yes, she is."

"We'll give her something to calm her down."

A half hour later, I'm reaching into the MRI machine clutching my mother's hands as the damn MRI bangs like a berserk bongo drum round our ears. The nurse has asked me to try to keep her from thrashing around in the narrow cylinder or else the pictures won't come right and we'll never get her out of there.

"Help me!" my mother screams over the clattering noise.

"Damn it, you're not being tortured, Mom," I hiss in the brief moment of silence between pictures.

"Please, can we go?" she whimpers.

"No, Mom. It's only a few more minutes."

Back in the room, after the MRI, my mother tries to pull out her catheter and her IV. She tries to get up and walk without a walker. She tells me I need to call Suzy. Who the hell is Suzy?

I stay vigilant, telling her firmly, "You can't get out of bed, don't touch your damn tubes, and no, you can't call Suzy."

Halfway through the hellish afternoon my mother assumes her choir director's voice. She informs the room, empty except for me, that we will perform some wonderful songs and the first one will be "I'll be seeing you."

"Ready, everybody. One, two, three, four . . ." Silence. She grimaces. "Come on, everybody, now. One, two, three, four, one, two, three, four . . ."

So I pipe up in my wobbly soprano, "I'll be seeing you in all the old, familiar places. Dadadadadadadada." My voice fades. My mother smiles indulgently and says, "That won't do."

■

Finally the nurses put an alarm on Mom's bed and promise to watch so I can go home and get some sleep. She calls me at 5:30 the next morning. "They're so cruel here. They won't feed me," she wails. The hard edge of my voice cuts through the dim morning as I observe that it isn't time for breakfast yet.

"You are cruel, too," she says and hangs up.

An hour later when I arrive at the hospital, she is happily eating breakfast.

The doctors find nothing wrong with my mother – no breaks or fractures, but these couple of days in the hospital have completely debilitated her and now they want her to go back into a "skilled nursing facility." This time I spend the day investigating my options. I find a place that is decent, but there's no getting around the horror of these places – the abandoned people consigned to their wheelchairs, drool dripping down their chins as they wait for death.

■

Mom is situated in the rehab wing on a plastic-mattressed bed near a window. I hook up her Bose radio for some entertainment, put her name in all her clothes and slip her a couple of pain pills before I leave. I hate to leave her there, but I am tired as hell. On the way home, as I pass the dark fields, I cry. I am missing my boon companion, my bosom buddy, my best friend, my kid.

When I get home, Celina isn't there. I call her cell phone and find she is having dinner with a friend. I suggest that I pick her up from the restaurant and we go to Target to get a bathing suit for her trip to the beach the next day.

"Sure," she says.

I find her by the fountain in front of the restaurant with her friend.

"Are you telling her about the time you fell in?" I ask, remembering the dripping wet child who came to find me in the restaurant one day eons ago.

"Yes," she says with a laugh. She hugs her friend goodbye.

We head over to Target where the collection of suits is especially NOT cute this year, but we don't have time to go anywhere else. My daughter holds up a bathing suit top covered with ruffles and says, "I *so* want ruffles." This causes us to laugh so hard that she collapses to the floor and I am doubled over, wiping tears from eyes.

And as we laugh, something inside me that is stiff and black begins to soften and glow again. This is my life, I realize, I have no choice but to let it sweep me out to its dark waters. Acceptance equals mercy. Even if it's only temporary.

■

In her bleak little room in the nursing home, my mother draws an O from the bag. I get a U, so she goes first. The word she puts down is CODAS. We are seated across a rolling bed table. My mother has often told me that this part of her life is her coda. I have discovered that she is not having one coda but several.

I have just put down the word NEWS on a triple word score, tacking the s on to the word TOUGH when I hear a faint, plaintive cry: "Help me. Please someone, help me!" In the nursing facility, you will find odd lumps of bruised flesh with dull eyes parked in wheelchairs in the hallways. Occasionally, one of them will ask you, "Will you please tell me where we are?"

I am afraid to answer that call, afraid I will be confronted with my own helplessness. But I can't stop myself. I have to find the source of that plea. I get up and look down the hallway as Mom searches for a word among her seven letters. The hallway is empty. So I peek in the bathroom my mother shares with the two women in the room next door and find a white haired lady in a wheelchair facing the toilet, desperate to get her rear end across the chasm and onto the toilet. My fear dissipates.

"Let me help you," I tell her. Perhaps I shouldn't help. After all, I'm not a professional here. What if the woman gets hurt? But although the staff here is generally competent, they have many patients and little time. It seems more expedient and frankly kinder just to help her myself. Besides, I have learned in recent years how to get an old woman onto and off of a toilet.

So I help the woman, lifting her under the arm, the way I lift my own mother, helping her maneuver around.

"It hurts," she says.

"I know it does," I tell her.

A strong, vile odor lets me know that the woman has already messed her diaper. (They all wear diapers in the nursing home.) But I am unprepared for the stench as she lowers her diaper to her knees and drops clumsily onto the toilet seat. I am unprepared for the black tarry mess filling the cup of the diaper. I help her remove the soiled garment, deposit it in the trash can and quickly leave the room to get another diaper. I also have to stop my stomach from hurling up the vegetable lo mein I have just shared with my mom because the nursing home food is so bad she won't eat it. I suck in some air from my mother's room as she looks at me, wonderingly.

"Be right back," I tell her and grab a diaper from her own bag. In the bathroom, the toilet is filled with black goo. I wonder how anyone can have that in their body and still be alive. But with my queasiness under control, I use wet paper towels to wipe between the soft jiggling buttocks of the old woman, trying to get the sticky black shit off her pale skin.

"You are such a kind person," she says to me over and over. I don't know about that, but I do find that these small acts of kindness I get to perform add a certain dimension to my life that had not been there before.

■

On Sunday, Celina and I go to see Mom. We take her outside to sit in the courtyard sun. Mom wants to go home. She is scheduled to stay until Thursday, which is as long as the insurance will pay for.

"How about Tuesday?" I ask her.

"That's fine."

"I'll make the arrangements."

On Tuesday, March 20, my mother's 89th birthday, I go to Harris Teeter to buy a cake and ice cream. A drunk woman in front of me is trying to buy a six-pack of Smirnoff Ice. Martha, the cashier, leans over and asks in her kindest voice, "Are you sure you want to get this now?"

The woman, a blond with disheveled hair, an expensive purse and cute shoes, mumbles that she knows she has the money for it. Martha exhales in relief when it turns out the woman doesn't have a wallet. She pats her on the hand and says, "You can come back later, honey."

The woman leaves, confused and disappointed. As I watch her wander away with her eyes cast downward, I feel a sense of my own remembered shame – the years when I took pills, drank tequila, injected myself with almost anything I could cram into the barrel of a needle.

Martha turns her attention to me and says, "The Good Lord is watching out for that lady today. I sure didn't want to sell her any liquor."

I nod, pay for my things, and tell Martha that today is my mother's birthday, and that makes Martha smile.

When I go to pick up my mother, she's sitting up in her wheelchair, hair combed, lips sticked, and eyes bright. When my mother is happy, she radiates it. She's all packed and ready to go like a kid coming home from a dreadful summer camp. She's made friends, of course, and they hate to see her go.

"Your mama is one smart lady," the woman from the room next door tells me. To my mother, "You be good, okay. Don't get in any trouble."

When I get her home, Sylvia (who I finally realize was the "Suzy" she needed to call at the hospital) comes by. I had called her the night before and said we'd be having some cake and ice cream. She promised to spread the word. By seven o'clock the small living room is filled with my mother's friends all eating Harris Teeter's finest red velvet cake with vanilla ice cream. Mom plays "Happy Birthday" on the black Steinway in a variety of styles from classical to boogie-woogie to a solemn "church" style, making everyone laugh. Then they tell church jokes. Mom tells one about the little girl who was making noise at church until her older sister told her to be quiet: "Can't you see people are trying to sleep?"

Then she tells a story. "During high school I was playing the organ – for money! and conducting a choir, and was the accompanist for the New Haven Light Opera Guild. It could have been one of their rehearsal nights, and they served orange blossoms after the rehearsals. I just thought it was the best orange juice I ever had and took two glasses, and promptly went to sleep. They had forgotten that I was just a child, really, and there were multiple abject apologies when my mother came to get me. However, it did not lead to a life of drinking," she says.

Her friends laugh and tell stories of their own.

There aren't many night owls at her place, so by about the time the vernal equinox has passed at 8:37, most everyone has gone home. After Bill and Nancy, Art, and Mark straggle out, my mother looks at me and says, "I don't know when I've been so happy."

I lean down and wrap my arms around her tiny frame.

"Goodnight, Mom," I tell her. "I'll see you in the morning."

NINE

In spite of its painful beginning, a few small miracles occur in 2007. The first is that the marital intimacy I thought was dead and buried rolls the stone from the tomb and shows up in my doorway wearing her Easter Sunday frock. I'm not sure how it happens. For several years now, Hank's pals – you know them: Bill, Sean and Rush – have been warning Hank from their cable news thrones about the commie in the house. Every couple of years I go to the polls and single-handedly corrupt America's youth, undermine the principles of liberty, and seek to force millionaires to give up their hard-earned money and hand it over to shiftless welfare mothers. And like all other traitorous Democrats, I am secretly hoping that every pregnant woman will run out and have an abortion even if she's eight and a half months along. But at some point, Hank turns off his television and decides that I may be a commie, but I'm his commie. Throughout the years of conflict we still maintained an affectionate relationship, but now, we're spending time together again, and for the first time in years, I think that we might make it. We're laughing again. Dare I say, we're happy.

The other thing that happens is that my spiritual life takes a new direction. Early in the year a woman named Cheryl comes to me with a book she wants edited; it's about her experiences with a spiritual teacher called Sadhguru. The story is fascinating. All my life I've wanted to meet an enlightened being and it looks like I might soon have my chance. But what really piques my interest is the story Cheryl tells me of Sadhguru's wife who simply chose to leave life behind. She wanted transcendence all the time and she made it happen. That's what I want – a key to unlock the door that keeps us here. I do not want to live as long as my mother has lived. The Etruscans believed that the perfect life lasts 84 years. That's long enough for me, I'm thinking. I mean, maybe with technology they'll be able to have us feeling like we're 30 when we're 90, but I'm not counting on that. What I don't want is to wind up in one of those nursing homes in a fetal position unable to walk or read a book or laugh. So after I edit the book, I decide I'll take one of this man's workshops. I'll see if there's anything to this yoga practice he teaches.

■

But first we have a pressing issue. Celina is a junior in high school, and college is looming ahead of us. The college search freaks me out. When do we start looking? Where? The college advisors warn that Celina's top picks might not be achievable because of her inconsistent grades. She never could get the hang of that get-the-homework-in-on-time thing. Teachers couldn't get a handle on her: *Was she ADD? Did she harbor a buried genius that made periodic eruptions? Was she lazy?* Her photography teacher, however, knew. He said she was talented and smart and would eventually be fine.

One weekend, Celina and I drive west to check out the colleges that are within a three-hour radius. The trip is fun. We sneak away from one college tour because it's so boring it makes us want to weep. After ruling out a couple of possibilities and keeping one option open, we are traveling back home under a bruised sky when my cell phone rings.

It's my mother.

"Where are you?" she wants to know.

"I'm on the road, Mom, with Celina. We've just been to look at some colleges."

"Then you won't be coming over tonight?"

"No, I'm almost two hours away, and I've been driving all day."

Then she starts to cry.

After I hang up, Celina is practically apoplectic.

"I'm the kid! You're my mother! Can't she even let us go look at colleges?"

I reach over and run a hand along her arm.

"I know, baby. I know. It's just that she's lonely."

Celina crosses her arms and stares out the window as Simon and Garfunkel sing us back home.

■

Like all the good middle class folk, we go to the college fairs and that's where Celina and I make a fabulous discovery. North Carolina has an Arts University with a drama program for high school seniors, and it's free for North Carolina residents.

A month later, Celina and I sit nervously in a waiting area at the North Carolina School of the Arts with other parents and their teenaged sons and daughters. For days Celina has worked on her monologues with me and the drama teacher from Kaleidoscope. One of the monologues comes from the play *Proof*, and the other comes from my favorite, *Medea*. I played Medea myself when I was a teenager. I slid easily into the persona of that crazy, vengeful murderess, and sometimes channel her even today when the need arises.

A beautiful woman with short dark brown hair and bright brown eyes sits across from us with an equally beautiful daughter. Something about the two of them radiates confidence and kindness. So Celina and I sit up a little straighter in an attempt to look a little sharper ourselves.

I try not to put any stock into anything at all today. We're just here with no expectations. Don't make any friendships, I'm telling myself. Don't picture Celina strolling across campus. Celina has adopted the same attitude. We refuse to admit that she wants this.

The brown-eyed woman and I strike up a casual conversation, but we can barely breathe. She's nervous, too. It hurts so much to see our girls might not get something they really want. Celina and the girl quickly learn they have a mutual friend from Celina's school. Don't make friends, I'm thinking. We're just passing through.

Then it's Celina's turn to go in. We've been here all day what with one meeting or another, nervously chatting with other parents and students, sizing up the competition. This is the final audition. Celina is not quite the last one but almost. Will she make it? Will she spend her senior year of high school on a college campus, attending what is arguably the best arts school in the country? It depends on which Celina goes in there – the knock-your-socks-off Celina or the lose-your-backpack-and-total-your-mother's-car Celina.

Fifteen minutes later and it's over. We won't know anything for a few weeks. Neither of us has much to say, but I have this sick feeling in my stomach like I've been on a small boat in ten-foot waves. My gut is saying "bad news." I take Celina to Greensboro to stay with a friend and to get a closer look at the state college there.

After I've dropped her off, I drive back to the Interstate for the hour and forty minute drive home. The sick feeling has not gone away. It has only turned into a deeper feeling of dread. As I pull into the 70-mile-an-hour traffic, I have an epiphany. I realize I am not feeling sick because Celina is not going to get into that school. I'm sick because I suddenly know that she will.

When she gets the acceptance letter a couple of weeks later, she screams so loudly that her friend a few houses down calls to find out what happened.

■

A woman at my Religious Science church who has just lost her mother tells me how lucky I am to still have mine. She's right. And yet, I am so unhappy. I have no life. I feel like I'm somehow back in prison. I pray to that ineffable something. I ask for guidance. I know there's got to be a way that I can be a good, loving daughter and yet still have something left over for myself. I keep looking for someone who might need a place to live and who might be willing to stay in my mother's extra bedroom in exchange for taking some of the load off my shoulders. There must be someone who needs a place to sleep and is not psychotic and wouldn't mind fixing scrambled eggs each morning.

When a longtime friend calls me one morning to complain because she's broken her wrist and has no one to help her, I simply respond, "This, too, shall pass."

"I don't need platitudes," she says angrily. I hang up the phone and decide to let go of this friendship of 20-something years. I cannot add anyone or anything to this cart that I am toting. It's a year before that rift is repaired.

Help comes from places I'd never suspect. Sylvia, who has been assisting Mother with her chorus at The Landings, was a nurse in her former life. She's one of those saints who loves to help others. She's self-effacing and kind. She offers to take off my mother's compression hose at night and sometimes even puts them on for her in the mornings. Thank God I can sleep in once in a while!

I realize I've got to do something or this love I have for my mother will fester into something rotten. My brother Jo comes down and stays with her for a few days in May while I go to a conference in New York. Celina has come with me and as a birthday present, I buy two tickets to *Wicked*, a damned pricey show. On my 19th or 20th birthday, my mother took me to New York and we saw the American Ballet Theater at Lincoln Center. I don't remember which ballet they performed, just that I felt glamorous and excited to be in that beautiful place with those beautiful people. And I remember thinking that I was so lucky to have a mother sophisticated enough to give me such a wonderful gift.

Celina brings up some clothes that she made (a prom dress and a pair of patch-work pants) and shows them to a friend of my brother's who works at the Fashion Institute of Technology, and before we know it she's scheduled to take some fashion design classes in New York that summer. I decide I will escape from my life and join her for a few days. No work, just fun.

So after Kaleidoscope Camp that year, I hire some helpers for my mother and take a trip to be with Celina in New York – just the two of us. Except that it's not really just the two of us. There's my brother and his girlfriend and other family members who live there and several of Celina's friends (from Charlotte and Florida) who all decide that this would be a great time to go to New York. Her best friend from Charlotte is there when I arrive.

So here I am two days into my visit with two teenage girls and not a whole lot of money. What recreation we choose will have to be easy. And fun. And different. Then I find the ideal thing in *The Village Voice*: The Siren Music Festival, free, on Coney Island. In all my trips to New York, I've never been to Coney Island, and Celina hasn't even heard of it.

"It's famous," I tell her. "There's a hot dog named after it."

It's not hard to convince the girls. The previous year Celina and I and her friend Evan went to the Bonnaroo Music Festival in Tennessee. By the time we left, I'd lost so much water I looked like a mummy. It was devastatingly hot, especially for a meno-pausal woman; it didn't help that I was in Rottweiler mode so that two sixteen year old girls could enjoy the music unmolested. No one much bothered them in the daytime, so I let them wan-der around while I hunkered down in the shade of the smaller field, digging on Buddy Guy or Ziggy Marley and observing the mating rituals of the species. But at night I kept a tight reign. When we wandered the fringes of the main concert, more than one valiant young drunkard spotted my two wards, advanced and then backed off quickly, saying, "Oh, wow. And this is your mom. What a cool mom." When they started hitting on me, we knew it was time to listen to the music from the comfort of our lounge chairs at the tent.

But Bonnaroo had been worth it, worth the seven-hour drive, the heat, the money, the horrible macaroni I tried to make on a borrowed Coleman stove, the moments of panic when the cell phones wouldn't work and I was standing in a heaving throng of 80,000 half-naked totally drunk or stoned partiers, clueless as to where the girls were. It was worth suffering through

Death Cab for Cutie so that Celina could hear Conor Oberst, and so she'd have some bragging rights like I did (and still do) by the fact I saw Jimi Hendrix play at the Atlanta Pop Festival in Byron, Georgia, on July 4, 1971, when I was 14 years old. I had, in fact, been trying to relive those halcyon days by this journey – minus the purple microdot, of course. But it hadn't been the same. Not at all. I wanted that sense of peace and blissed out freedom that I'd gotten a taste of when I was 14. I didn't find it at Bonnaroo.

But today I get more than a taste of it. For this one day my mystic thirst is quenched.

It starts out with breakfast at a sidewalk cafe by Union Square: eggs Florentine for me and French toast for the girls. Then we head to the subway station. The swaying motion of the train lulls us as if we are newborn babies. We chug out of the dark underground world into the warm light. Other people dressed in beach attire join us on the way. Then at some point the train stops and we figure this must be our stop.

The ocean, a bright azure beacon, calls. Soon we are crossing the wide yellow beach, making our way through a maze of blankets like a giant patchwork quilt. Children splash in the meager waves. The water looks inviting. I take off my flip-flops and stick my feet in the water. At this point the screeching violins from Hitchcock's *Psycho* suddenly erupt in my brain and I leap out of the freezing water.

"Refreshing," I say to the girls. "Now where's the festival?"

Following a thread of bass beats, we work our way through the Boardwalk area and along a fenced off street. A stage has been set up at the end of the street nearest the Boardwalk. We listen to a band called White Rabbit, and I love them. I can hear a little Island influence, and a breeze seems to have floated up from the Caribbean, darting in and out to cool off the swaying crowd. A crystal blue sky shimmers above us.

In between bands we stroll through the sleazy carnival atmosphere. I don't know if it's the music, the seductive weather or the fact that I am 643 miles from my mother and my husband, but I can barely keep from levitating as I partake of the communal moment.

The last act we see before we leave is Lavender Diamond. Becky Stark comes flouncing out in a 1950s dress with her thick straight hair hanging on her shoulders, pulled back from her face with a wide headband. She is wholesomely quirky.

"Woo hoo," she yells, "let's hear it for world peace!"

Celina and I lock eyes.

"I love her," Celina says.

"Me, too," I say.

Anymore perfection and we'd dissolve. Somehow all the good feelings of a past era are resurrected inside me. And this time I can be high as a puffy white cloud without having to ingest anything other than my dollar-bottle of cold water. The odd thing is that the ubiquitous blanket of sweet smoke combined with the smell of spilled beer is absent here. I wonder if everyone is as happy as I am.

The mystics tell us that we're all filled with the same light. Most of the time, I'm blind to it. Sometimes I can barely muster contempt for my fellow humans. But today with Becky Stark singing like ambrosia, the sun heaving a sigh of contentment above us, and my laughing daughter and her friend dancing around me, I can feel those invisible connecting threads thrumming with life.

If only I could hold onto this, lock it into my heart forever. But I cannot.

TEN

FALL 2007

Hank and I drive Celina to her new school. We stock her room with a microwave and bags of snacks. We linger, not wanting to leave. Hank was vociferously against this idea last summer, but now he has become reconciled to it.

The dreaded "gone-child-grief" doesn't attack me like I thought it would. My mother needs more care than ever, and I'm excited about the Isha Yoga class I'm going to take in late September. Excited and worried. The class is seven days long and in Atlanta, and I don't know how my mother is going to survive without me, but Cheryl keeps pushing me. If I take the class in September, then I can take the next class with Sadhguru himself in October. I will finally get to meet a real live realized being. I've been waiting my whole life for that experience.

■

I was curious about the world beyond my senses from a young age. When I was five years old, we lived in a small brick house in Jacksonville. One afternoon there was a terrible thunderstorm, a Wizard of Oz type wind with cows and bicycles flying by. The entire Atlantic Ocean had been sucked up into the clouds and was now falling down on us.

I'd had enough so I went outside with my little twirling baton, stood on the porch waving the baton, and called out in my booming child's voice: "Oh, wind! Oh, rain! I command you to stop. Stop! Stop now!" Nothing happened, so I commanded once again, "Stop, rain! Right this instant!"

The rain continued to tumble down. The wind laughed at me, wrapped my hair around my face, and sloshed a bucketful of water all over me. Drenched, I went back inside and turned on "Let's Make a Deal." I had thought I was God until that day.

And yet life so often seemed to have a magical quality. It was as if there were a constant whisper that I could almost but not quite hear. I suppose that I was searching for that magic when I started taking drugs at the age of fourteen. Those adventures took me to another realm. But what at first seemed like heaven fairly quickly turned into hell. Even so, I was amazed at the way we junkies could connect with each other and by that extra sense we had that kept us out of jail up until it didn't.

I guess I always figured in jail I'd read the Bible and finally discover that peace which passeth all understanding. That didn't happen. The Bible part anyway. Instead I read literature and found God was there, of all places, incognito, of course. But I could discern Him or Her or It, whatever you want to call it, in Dostoyevsky's words and Grass's images, even there hiding in Conrad's *Heart of Darkness*. And then one Easter Sunday the choir members got to take a field trip to a church in Ocala, Florida. The congregation held our hands, and the preacher called on Jesus and something happened. I'm sure scientists could come along and offer some chemical explanation, but that something was like the big bang right in my own body. Drugs could never replicate this feeling. I'd been ruined.

After that I was on the prowl. I wanted Nirvana, Samadhi, Heaven, Godhead. But no matter what books I read or how much I meditated, I only got tiny moments of grace. Slowly I began to slough off lifetimes of pain. And still there was more. More sadness, more judgment, more unforgiveness.

■

In preparation for the yoga program, I watch videos of Sadhguru on YouTube, and am hypnotized by his laughter. I want to see him for myself; I want to see if I can see in his eyes what I once felt. I can't let the chance pass me by.

So in September I go to Atlanta, leaving my mother in Sylvia's care. I've hired a caregiver to come in the mornings, and hired the girl who lives next door to us to visit her a couple of times.

In Atlanta I stay with an Indian family. I go to the local library and work on my computer during the day. I go to the class every night. I learn the practice, called Shambavi Maha Mudra, that the teacher says comes from an ancient science. It entails some breathing, chanting, and exercises. One day they feed us a banquet of raw foods. The other participants and I gobble it down. We have homework, we watch videos of Sadhguru, we sit cross-legged, our backs aching and listen. One day we play games like a bunch of kids. I'm not a great athlete, but an odd thing happens during a game of dodge ball. I have the sudden sure sense that I am going to win the game. I will be the last one in the circle. It's like I'm invincible. And that's exactly what happens.

A week or so after the first program, I leave home again for three days to take another more advanced program at the ashram in Tennessee. Whenever possible I sit right up front and stare at the Master as he speaks. He laughs, he cries, he is certainly brilliant. Is he enlightened? I cannot say. All I know for sure is that

I've found an adventure that I've been waiting for a long time. And I've gained a spiritual practice that will be helpful in the face of the brutal days that are charging fast at me like a pack of rabid dogs.

■

We have to miss Parents' Weekend at Celina's school because we are going to California for the weekend. Beth's cancer has moved into her brain. And Hank's dad also has a brain tumor. Jean is not sure Beth will be around for Thanksgiving so there is no time to lose.

In the airport we sit together, Celina between Hank and me. I'm explaining to Celina the meaning of the word *Zeitgeist* when Hank says to her, "Babe, that woman's pants are so tight, I bet her farts have to squeeze out the bottom like cockroaches under the kitchen door." Hank is a connoisseur of fart lore, and of course, there's someone sitting right behind us who can hear him; Celina and I are mortified and laughing in embarrassment at the same time.

"Sir, please don't talk to my daughter," I lean over and say in a loud voice. He laughs his wicked little boy laugh.

On the airplane, a man sitting in the row in front of us has a snore like a buzz saw, and Hank periodically jolts the man's seat to get him to stop and giggles maniacally every time he does it. Again, Celina and I can't help but laugh when he does. It's viral.

When we get to Hank's parents' house, Jean is waiting for us as she always is. But she has been diminished by half. Taking care of her dying daughter and her sick husband has carved up her soul. Her strength in the face of this adversity makes me feel like a welterweight. I know anti-depressants are helping her deal with it all, but for God's sake, she's 80 years old, and she's got rheumatoid arthritis. Yet, she's ever stalwart.

"One time we were at the hospital to see about Beth, and I turned around and Hank Senior had passed out," she says to me. "They had to check him in right then and there. So there I was with both of them in the hospital, running from one floor to the other."

"How do you do it?" I ask.

"I don't have a choice, Trish," she says. "What else can I do?"

She could turn into a raving lunatic, I think. But she doesn't. She finds whatever helps her whether it's the serenity prayer or a bridge game with friends, and she copes.

Fortunately, Hank's brother Steve has been there to help her. He reconnoiters with us at the house, and we pile into his Blazer to visit Beth. Beth is tall and gaunt. She hugs us fiercely. I've noticed that the dying tend to express love with reckless abandon. Hank is aghast at the sight of his bald sister with a black line of stitches across her skull.

"Ya look like Beetlejuice," he says.

Hank's family is not renowned for tenderness, but they're a loyal bunch. Steve has shown his true mettle, captaining the ship of this beleaguered family. Generous and handsome, with a big laugh almost as infectious as Hank's, Steve is now figuring out the next step for Beth. He thinks she's ready to come home, and he's also found a hospice down the street from his parents' house for that inevitable step.

Hank notices a pretty nurse and whispers to Steve, "You should ask that nurse out. She could take care of the whole family. I think she's hot for you."

But Hank doesn't know how to whisper, and I'm sure the nurse has heard him, so I look at him wide-eyed and Celina joins me, and soon we're all cracking up there in the hospital room at Hank's faux pas.

The next day Beth comes home. She needs help getting her long white compression hose on, and since this is something I'm fairly experienced at, I go into help her. In order to have something to say other than how awful her situation is, I bitch about Hank.

"He didn't even want Celina to go to that arts school," I complain.

She sucks her teeth in disgust. We're the same age, and ragging on Hank has been one thing we could agree on, as if we're both the younger siblings. She doesn't sleep well. Neither do I, and in the early morning the two of us are alone in the quiet light of the living room enjoying the hush before everyone else wakes up. She eats a donut and drinks her coffee. Since the return of her cancer, she loves sweets. She's not exactly watching her weight. In some ways she reminds me of my mother. A lot of things don't matter when you're on the precipice. She can't remember much. She's not interested in much. She's become an aficionado of silence.

When we leave there's still a miniscule thread of hope, but in December Beth dies. Hank Senior has lung cancer and a brain tumor. We stay home that Christmas.

FOUR ANTHEM

What need have you of further demons?
Figures from your own hells are enough.
(Save us from our minds!)
Dry papers flutter about your feet,
Lifted by poisonous dust.
(Save us from our words!)
Your monsters devour the hills,
The forests are laid low.
The oceans are slowly dying.
(Save us from our works!)
Traced deep in each man's being
Are the tracks of his transgressions.
For as soon as the wind goeth over it,
It is gone, and the place thereof shall know it no more.

Rosalind MacEnulty
An American Requiem

ONE

The year 2008 came down on my little family like the Four Horsemen on a rampage. It started all right. I was in my second year of a full time teaching job. My third novel had just been published, and it was getting good reviews, though, of course, not raking in the big bucks. All my life my dream had been to publish a novel. Now I had three of them and a short story collection. This was the time of my life I needed to be doing whatever it was that writers do to promote their work. I needed to "get out there" and do readings and workshops – something I hadn't really done for my previous books. So I had two trips scheduled for the spring – one to a conference in San Miguel de Allende in Mexico and another to New England.

In the back of my head I knew that it was risky – planning these trips – but I'd gotten a local grant to fund both, and I was determined to go. I let my brothers know that I had made my plans and that nothing would stop me from going. Nothing, I insisted. Even if Mom wound up on her death bed (which I was sure was exactly what was going to happen) I would not alter my plans. I had sacrificed enough. So I bought my airline tickets and waited for the inevitable disaster to strike.

It did, of course. In February.

Mother's belly had blown up to the size of a basketball, and she constantly complained of constipation. Over the years, I had given her enemas and plied her with laxatives recommended by the doctor, but her large intestine simply didn't have the power to do its job. This time she was backed up so badly that Roto-Rooter couldn't have helped us out. And the doctor wasn't sure what was going on with that enormous pregnant-looking belly. So it was time to go back in the hospital.

At first she charms everyone there. One of the doctors, an elderly Jamaican man, is smitten and tells me what an intelligent woman she is, how much he enjoys chatting with her. But this little honeymoon ends soon.

They are going to flush my mother out. They need me to stay there and make sure she drinks several gallons of Drano. Already my mother's fabled intelligence is getting murky. Hospitals have that effect on old people, I am told. I sit at her side and say, "Drink up, Mom." Mother balks, of course. Who wouldn't? But she has to drink it all, and I keep after her for several hours till it's all gone. Then we wait for the inevitable eruption.

I won't go into the details. Suffice to say the toilet is never as close as it needs to be, and not only do I become a medical professional, but I also serve as janitor.

That should be the end, right? But it isn't. My mother makes the mistake of letting the nurses know that she is in pain. Well, she's always in pain. Because the doctor nicked a nerve in her back during her spinal operation, now her brain has gotten locked onto the idea of pain. This is a trick that brains do though I don't fully understand how. So my mother is in constant pain. In hospitals they don't like pain. I understand this. Why should anyone be in pain if it's unnecessary? We have the technology to get rid of it. A little visit from Sister Morphine and all your cares slide under the table to sing about dead roses. And they always think they're doing you a favor by giving you just a little extra bump. Oh, wouldn't the junkie I once was have loved these folks?

So they start to give her morphine, which does not put her to sleep. Instead my mother goes from being an outspoken witty old woman to a deranged madwoman. I must be looney myself because I actually go home one night to try to get some sleep.

The phone rings at 2:30 in the morning.

"Will you come do something about your mother? We can't handle her," the nurse says.

I roll out of bed, put on my jeans and shirt and head out the door.

In my mother's hospital room, I settle on a little plastic covered reclining chair and try to drift back to sleep, but she won't be quiet. She's babbling about how guilty she feels and how sorry she is and not really meaning it because she's out of her head, and finally I growl at her, "Would you shut up! Just shut up!"

A nurse walks in at this very instant and stares at me in horror. I am rather notorious among those few who have heard this particular verbalization come from deep in the back of my throat. Celina says, with a touch of admiration, that it is the scariest sound she's ever heard. I used it once to quiet some unruly girls on a choir trip, and she has never forgotten it. Just as it worked on the choir girls, it works on my mother, but I'm sure the nurse thinks I am an awful daughter. Yes, damn it, sometimes I am.

At least I get a little bit of peace. Finally it's 6:30 a.m. and I can head to the cafeteria for something to eat. My mother is finally out of it. The food offerings in a hospital cafeteria are not particularly appetizing; I get some scrambled eggs and a biscuit and sink down in a booth in the deserted room. I'm mechanically ingesting the food when my cell phone buzzes. It's Hank.

"Hello?" I say.

"Yeah, I've called the paramedics and need to know which hospital to go to," he says.

"Come again?"

"My blood pressure has skyrocketed, and I feel bad. I'm all shaky. The paramedics are on their way and I'm probably going to have to go into the hospital. Which one do I go to?"

"Good Lord. Go to the one in Pineville," I tell him. It's not the same hospital where my mother is, but she has a different insurance policy than we do. "I'll come by on my way to school." I spend the day bouncing from one hospital to the other and somehow manage to teach my classes as well.

Hank comes home that night with a list of different doctors to see. My mother, on the other hand, spends ten days in the hospital and she is much worse at the end of those ten days than when she went in. She's had a colonoscopy and every kind of test known to humankind, but they can find nothing seriously wrong with her. She is simply old and the plumbing doesn't work anymore. But now she's gotten infections and something has gone really wrong with her brain. She can't understand why she is still alive. And I am helpless to do anything for her.

"This is so awful," she says over and over.

One of the nurses insists that he has to give her the full dose of morphine that the doctor has prescribed, which is nuts. The morphine has sent her into another dimension. She doesn't need that much, I try to tell him. You can give less than the doctor orders, just not more. This isn't penicillin, for God's sake. It's morphine. I manage to win this battle but something bad has happened to my mother's brain.

She is somehow still alive at the end of this ordeal. The hospital, however, is through with her. They've done their worst, and now it is time for her to leave. She is heading back to the nursing home where she was last year. But now the insurance rules have changed and I'm looking at the possibility of a bill that will make me a pauper. Still, there is no choice. And no matter what, I'm going to Mexico in another week.

I visit her every day at the nursing home and stay for hours. She has infections. She can no longer create complete sentences. She spends a half hour trying to tell me about her problem with the telephone. There is no phone. In spite of her condition, I am determined not to cancel my trip to Mexico. My brother Jo and his girlfriend come to Charlotte to relieve me of my duties. I get on a plane and I am gone.

■

In Mexico I sleep a lot. Hal and Lynda live in a beautiful five story apartment. Each story consists of a single room. I am ensconced on the bottom floor on a futon mattress. It's comfortable. I am surrounded by books, and I lose myself for hours in someone else's words, someone else's woes.

In San Miguel Vitamin D is plentiful, church bells ring often and randomly, dogs bay, pigeons worry about the sheen of their feathers, and bread smells slide over the balcony ledge to place a calming hand on my shoulder.

In Charlotte my life is a litany of despair. Hank and I lie next to each other trading our tales of woe, calculating the calories of grief in our daily diet. My mother can no longer defecate, I tell him. Hank counters, my father's brain is riddled with cancer like Swiss cheese. And then we list the others gone or going – his

179

sister, my friends, his co-worker, my professor. We are paralyzed, and only our tongues can move obsessively tolling the bad news.

In San Miguel de Allende I don't tell Lynda the details of my life. This is not a conscious decision, but simply a response to the unwritten code of Paradise. Leave those shit-filled diapers back in the nursing home. Do not defile the sanctity of this crystalline dream with the tales of your endless tears.

In Charlotte my colleagues at school wheel toward me, their faces compositions of concern when I enter our wing of cubicles. They know that I am an embattled solder. I don't volunteer a lot but I am not prone to lying either. "Fine" is no longer part of my vocabulary. I keep the bulletins short. My coworkers nod sympathetically, realizing that sympathy is pointless. It does nothing, and "talking about it" provides no relief.

Lynda is my mentor/soul sister/friend and literary mother. Hal is her cranky but kind poet husband, who adores her. Lynda and I talk only about books. A salve on my blistered psyche. This is what sympathy would enviously love to be. I realize in a rare moment of self-satisfaction that I have chosen my friends well. This kind of friendship is not earned. It is a kind of grace. This friendship helps me become light, light as that vermillion flycatcher tossing about on the currents of air, barely clinging with its clawed toes to the topmost cedar branch. I want to be lighter still like the quiet haze resting on the hills pale and almost empty, absorbing smoke, filtering sunlight, nestling an insubstantial cheek on a warm white wall.

San Miguel de Allende is every gringa's dream: cobblestone streets, galleries, parks, crimson birds flitting about in branches of gargantuan trees. I eat well, I read voraciously, I watch the Oscars with Lynda and Hal and their friends. We meet writers and artists. At a lovely outdoor garden restaurant while an insipid musician croons Jimmy Buffet songs, a poet flirts with me, and I flirt back. We meet a sculptor and his painter wife, who invite us to come by for drinks and marijuana, of all things. We decline. Once as we are walking, Lynda and I stop to read a sign listing upcoming 12-step meetings. One is for sex and love addicts.

"That used to be me but not anymore," Lynda says. "Disgusting."

And we laugh till the tears stream down our cheeks. Our sex-filled stories and voracious concupiscent characters bound us together when we first met. But things change, don't they? And we can't help but lapse into hilarity at the notion of our old voracious selves.

I could stay here, I'm thinking, and never go back. Then my cell phone rings insistently. It's Hank.

"I'm in the hospital in Atlanta," he says.

I'm silent.

"I was in the airport waiting for my connection, and my blood pressure spiked again. I don't think I can handle this thing with my parents."

Hank is supposed to be going to California to work with a TV company on the LA Marathon and then stay and take care of his dad while his mother goes into the hospital for a perforated colon.

"Call me when you get to California," I tell him.

The next day he calls again.

"You need to come to California. My blood pressure is hitting the roof. My dad is probably dying and my mother has got to go to the hospital. Dad refuses to go to hospice."

No, I'm thinking, I need to go home. I need to get back to my own mother. She can't be alone in that place after my brother leaves. But really, there is no question, no debate here. Hank has not asked for a lot these past years. And now he needs me. My heart is resolute. My mother will have to cope without me. I am going to California. The company that hired Hank has offered to pay for my ticket.

The next day I am flying into Los Angeles with Arlo Guthrie's voice in my head: "bringing in a couple of keys." Yeah, I'm thinking, a key to my house and one to my mom's. That's all the keys I've got.

When Hank picks me up at LAX, we have a short reprieve. His mother is not going into the hospital for a couple of days and the company he works for has booked him a room at the Sheraton Universal. That night we wander over to Universal City in search of food. What a culture shock after the sweet naturalness of San Miguel. It's like a sensory rape, like entering a comic book world, like a funhouse on steroids. IMAX cinemas! Mechanical bull riding! Bungee dives! Fun dining!

We get out as quickly as possible to head to downtown Burbank, which has, of late, become the trendiest place on the planet. Throngs of teenagers and tourists spill over the streets. But it's downright mellow after Universal City. We wind up in a Thai restaurant where the plates are square and black and the food is, let's face it, superb.

It's comforting to be with him. We don't talk much. We don't need to. We know each other so well. Somehow my presence helps settle his blood pressure, and I feel calmer around him, too. Though we have our fights over money and politics, we also enjoy each other's company. Briefly we can forget about everything else and be the same two people we were 25 years ago when our biggest worry was where would we eat dinner that night and what kind of wine should we get.

■

The next day we head down behind the Orange Curtain to La Brea. We enter into the maw of homogeneous corporate America and find a world of identical chain stores and restaurants, beckoning us to eat and buy. Hank's parents live in a ranch house in a manicured subdivision. His father retired in his 40s and spent his days playing golf, watching television and listening to talk radio. That life is over.

Hank Senior is back in the bedroom when we get there. When I see him, I am floored. His head is swollen with fluid and he cannot stand without a walker. The last time I saw – six months earlier – he looked the same as he always had, same trim compact body and head full of dark hair. He didn't look like he was approaching 80. He looked like he'd just qualified for social security.

"It's the chemo," Jean tells us.

The next day she has to check into the hospital and she's worried about the "prep" medicines she has to take – with good reason. They wipe her out. No way can she help Hank Senior to the bathroom. Suddenly my Hank is their caretaker, helping one parent and then the other. The look on his face is of a man in a war zone, and I'm reminded of one time we went to Nicaragua. We were exploring Managua, which was not such a smart thing to do after dark, and we realized a car was slowly following us as we walked along the darkened streets. We knew we were in danger, but we didn't panic. We headed straight for the hotel like we were on a mission and somehow we made it back to our lonesome bottles of rum unscathed.

I try to help, but mostly I'm there for moral support.

The next day, Hank's duties have changed. Hank and his brother have finally convinced Hank Senior he needs to go to hospice. They take him to the same house where their sister died just a few months earlier. Jean is now in the hospital, getting ready for surgery. And with the immediate care-giving crisis over, Hank and I find ourselves alone in the house.

And this time we panic. We are not supposed to be alone in this house. This house is supposed to be filled with people, with the smell of cooking foods, with the sounds of television and radio. We aren't even supposed to be in this house at this time of year. Where are the two children? Where is the dog we usually bring? Neither of us can swallow. Breathing becomes difficult.

I'm remembering one Christmas before Beth got sick. On Christmas Eve I sat down with Jean as she opened up the cupboards of the past and hauled out one family member after another, showing me pictures and mementos. She told me about the six children from Russia, the eight who were born here, the aunt who was a dwarf and the uncle who died of rheumatic fever when he was seventeen.

The next day after the ritual gorging on gifts and before the ritual gorging on food, Hank and I left the house for a walk. We cut down an alley behind perfectly landscaped lawns and up a hill into a meadow.

"This is the old way to the high school," Hank said. We wandered along a fence beside the football field and into the woody edge of a golf course. We cut over and wound up inside a cemetery where we lingered, reading rows of plaques bearing remote dates: 1844 - 1910 and 1851 - 1904. I found myself reading the first names as we walked down the long rows – Margaret, Stella, Effie, Walter, Grazella, Charles and John. Above the names were the words: father, mother, husband or sister.

As I gazed over the grounds at the hundreds of simple plaques on the ground, I felt as if I were watching a parade that had been going on forever. All these people, I thought. All these laughing, loving, lying, hating, working, eating and finally dying minds and bodies. All those souls, all those now silent voices. My mother has often said she wonders where the music goes when we can no longer hear it. Those vibrations are still traveling somewhere.

It's an old, old truth that seems to lie in wait for us like the tree we never notice until it falls down in our path. It seems that we must acknowledge every once in a while that we are only visiting here and briefly at that.

Now Beth's ashes are lodged in that same cemetery, and Hank Senior's time is short. Hank and I stare at each other in the empty house like two lost and abandoned children.

"We have to get out of here," I tell him. Everything about this house, the couch where we're sitting, the coffee table where we played Clue, the two recliners where his parents always sat, the dry black hole of the fireplace, everything is a reminder of all we once had. And it wasn't long enough. There just wasn't enough time.

"Here take this," Hank says, handing me a half a Xanax. So I do. The grief lifts briefly, and we get on about our business, visiting one parent and then the other, eating dinner with Steve, and then back to visit a parent.

The most poignant moment is when Jean in the hospital is talking to her husband, her high school sweetheart, on the phone while he is at hospice.

"You take care of yourself," he tells her.

"I will," she says. "I'll see you soon."

At the hospice house, I sometimes pick an orange from the tree in the backyard. Hank Senior is not the only one dying here. A few very quiet people sit in the living room or stay in their beds. The women work hard, cleaning these broken bodies, feeding them, making them comfortable. Their activity keeps the place from feeling morose. Business as usual, people living, people dying.

Jean's surgery goes well, and she comes back home. It's time for me to go home as well. While I was gone, Celina was sick with the flu and I was not there to take care of her. My mother was alone in the nursing home and I wasn't there for her either. But they both survived without me.

I hug Hank goodbye at the airport. He is staying with his mother for a while as she recovers. The sky picks me up from the ground and tosses me over the continent.

■

Morning. I drive to the nursing home where my mom is in rehab. Her body is a crumbling house. Her mind is worse. It is 9:30 when I walk through the corridor to her room. I find her lying in bed whimpering.

"What's wrong, Mom?" I ask. "What's wrong?"

She has no answer, and I realize I am once again asking the wrong question. Somehow I assumed there was something I could fix if only she'd tell me what. But it is obvious I have misstepped. I should not ask questions. I need to bring answers.

"There's nothing wrong," I tell her. "There's nothing wrong, Mom."

I turn to lower the volume on the TV, which I had brought from her apartment. She keeps whimpering as I fiddle with the controls. The whimpering is an insistent tug on my consciousness, making it impossible to focus.

"Stop it," I say, glancing back at her, but my voice is gentle. She closes her mouth in compliance.

"Now, why aren't you dressed yet, I wonder? Do you want to get dressed, Mom?"

"I don't know. I don't know what I want to do," she says, clutching her hospital robe. "I can't tell if it's day or night."

I glance at her rolling table and see that her breakfast is mostly gone.

"Mom, look out the window. See, it's daylight, and you've just had breakfast, so it must be morning, right?" An azalea bush waves a meager bloom on the grounds outside.

"Yes, yes. You're right." Her voice relaxes. She lets go of the gown.

Actually, she is far more coherent than she was before I left. And the infection she had earlier is gone. Her breathing is better. Once again, she has peeked into the abyss and beat a retreat.

"I wonder if I should dress you. Maybe they're going to clean you up first."

I go out to find a nurse's assistant.

"Has my mother been cleaned up?"

"No, not yet," she says. She's headed into someone else's room.

"Then I'll do it," I answer. She directs me to the clean towels and washcloths, but the closet is empty so I get some clean ones out of the laundry room. It doesn't take long to know where everything is, to feel like one of the staff.

Back in my mother's room, I gently wash her back with the warm, soapy washcloth. I wipe down her arms and armpits and bring the washcloth under her soft shapeless breasts. Neither of us is self-conscious about it. I once nursed at those breasts. Can there be a more intimate bond?

I dress my mother in a green dress with long sleeves, but then I discover that her diaper has not been changed. It is thick and musty with pee, so I change the diaper, promising myself I will be more vigilant about the care she gets in this place.

■

I am lodged on twin peaks of grief. Celina is away at school, growing up, growing away from me, on her way to a new life. And my mother has taken one step closer to death. I know I have to empty out her apartment. She'll never come back to this place. I have no idea where she'll go, but in the meantime I need to pack her things for storage. Alone in her apartment with the piano like a black accusation, a claustrophobic agony slips a pair of thick hands around my rib cage. I rush outside, gasping for air. I find the shelter of my car but the sobs are shaking me like an angry parent. I call my brother, Jo, and I cry and can't stop for a long time.

TWO

We celebrate my mother's 90th birthday in the nursing home: Celina, who is home for spring break, my two brothers and me. We sit at a little square table in the dining room. It's a shabby place, but we have it to ourselves except for the occasional staff person who walks through to the kitchen. I think the last time we were all together was when I was four months pregnant with Celina. We had all gone to spend Christmas at my mother's house in Edenton. For some reason she was living in the parish house and it was big enough for all of us and then some. What I remember is snow on the ground and tromping through the small town with Jo after David and his family left. Funny how families form and reform little alliances. That year David was constantly bickering with his wife, and Mom was a bag of worry. As a music director and orchestra conductor she was used to being in control, but we rolled out of her reach like marbles on a polished floor. Not to mention that I was pregnant and unmarried.

"I'm tired of being the mother," she said.

Today we are all in alliance. I've brought a cake. David takes pictures with a fancy new digital camera, Jo smiles his beatific smile, and Celina brings that light laughter with her as always. Our mother is so happy to be surrounded by her children. The

189

scrambled jigsaw pieces of my mother's mind now seem to be able to form half a picture of the world. I have taken her to a neurologist, who treated her like she was moron instead of a brilliant woman with brain damage. We still don't know if she's had a stroke – or if her mental state is just the result of the effects of the medicine. What I don't know yet is just how long it takes for medicine to leave an old person's system. When I was a young druggie, I needed a fix every day.

■

Early the next morning Hank calls me.

"My dad is gone," he says.

"Are you okay?" I ask.

"I've been to the hospital twice to try to get this blood pressure under control," he says.

"I'm sorry about your dad. Is your mom okay?"

"Yeah. Yeah, we'll be fine." I take this to mean they've gone into coping mode.

There will be no funeral for Hank Senior. He will be cremated and his ashes placed in the cemetery next to Beth. We will each need to grieve in our own way. How am I going to tell Celina? For a moment I feel sorry for myself that I have to be the bearer of the bad news – once again. She'll know, of course, by the sound of my voice. And she can read my face like a text message. Besides she's had practice in bad news. When I had to tell her that her godmother Kitty died, she wailed in agony and shook for hours. Grief like that stunned me. I suppose I had learned at an early age to zip up my feelings. But Celina never did that, and she's better off for it.

Later that morning I am in my office at the computer. Celina comes in and sits on the floor.

190

"Hi!" she says, cheerful as a little goldfinch.

I wheel around and look at her.

"I have to tell you something."

Her smile drops. Her eyes darken. She is on high alert.

"What?"

"It's Grampa," I tell her. There's no way to do this gently. "He died this morning."

She is not expecting this. We probably should have told her how serious things were, but she was away at school and we didn't want her to burden her with that heartache without one of us there.

Her sorrow floods the house as she sinks down and sobs.

Her Grampa had been her biggest fan.

"That girl is as smart and talented as anyone you'll ever meet," he would pronounce in his stentorious voice. Her face was on his screensaver. As a child it was her job to muss his dark hair and provoke his ersatz wrath. With Grampa she knew without any doubt she was golden.

I hang onto her, but in truth, we can't stay like this for long. While my brothers are still here, we need to pack up my mother's apartment and get everything we can into storage. My mother has been approved for Medicaid, which means she will move to a nursing home as soon as I can find a decent place with a "Medicaid bed." In the meantime if we don't want to pay April's rent I have to get her place emptied and cleaned out now. Once the Medicaid kicks in, Mother's social security will be gone.

So the four of us converge on my mother's apartment. I've already given away a lot of her things to other residents. Now we are packing and throwing away and cleaning.

Tears stream down Celina's face as she packs. When we take a lunch break, Celina cannot eat. She puts her head in my lap right there in the restaurant and weeps.

Her tears seem to speak for all of us.

■

The storage unit is packed to the brim with furniture, art supplies and those old moth-eaten copies of the Requiem stuffed into a box. Her Requiem is the one thing I'm supposed to keep alive for her, but I've no idea how. It's one more thing that makes me feel guilty and inadequate.

My brothers are gone. Celina's grief has abated and she's gone back to school. In the meantime, I have cleaned every millimeter of my mother's apartment. I scrub the bathrooms, wipe down the refrigerator inside and out, sweep the kitchen and steam clean the carpet. I am stupidly under the impression that she can get her deposit back. Technically, she's not breaking her lease if she leaves for medical reasons, but technically, they've still managed to construct the lease so no one ever gets a deposit back. In fact, they send me a bill for sixteen hundred dollars for some stains on their cheap-ass carpets. The evil that I wish upon those people is ugly. My Medea alter-ego wants to send them lovely dresses, the kind that turn the skin to flame. Instead I throw their stupid bill in the trash and never hear from them again.

The perfect solution we thought we had found for Mom is not even close to perfect because I cannot find a "Medicaid bed" anywhere. The only option is a private-pay assisted living facility that we had checked out a few times over the years. But even though the marketing manager agrees to give us a room at the incredibly reasonable price they had offered it to me a few years earlier, Mom's social security check is still about $600 short then there are all her other expenses. In the past few years I've been

192

paying her credit card bills and taking care of things like eye-glasses, a new television, help three mornings a week, and medicine. According to an article in *The Charlotte Observer,* the average cost of taking care of an elderly parent was approximately $5,500 a year in 2007, which is about what I've been spending. David was putting two kids through college and helped out when he could. Jo was on disability from his cancer and didn't have anything extra. Now, I've got to get Celina through college and so an extra 600 a month, plus another 300 or so for extras (phone, medicine, incontinence products, snacks, etc.) is just not doable.

The one ace I thought I had up my sleeve is gone. I always figured we could sell the piano, but David is adamant. That piano is not leaving the family. My father's piano was firmly lodged in his wife's condo. It is eventually supposed to come to us, but we all doubt that would ever happen. Another family piano was sold when my grandmother died. David is not going to let the Steinway go.

"I'm going to learn how to play the piano," he said after I'd already found a purchaser – a man with a ten-year-old girl who would have loved that piano as my own mother had. We went round and round, but in the end he wanted to keep it more than I wanted to sell it. And so I relented. I mollified myself with the fact that I had kept the bird-of-paradise plates and I wouldn't have given them up for any amount of money (not that they're worth all that much). Besides, I thought our financial problems were solved. I thought Medicaid was going to provide. I was wrong.

If it's this hard for the middle class to take care of their elderly, I can't help but wonder and worry about the poor. Because my mother worked till she was 86, she has a pretty good social security check, but I imagine there must be many out there who just can't make it. One woman I know had to quit her job to take care of her mother and they both barely subsisted on the mother's social security. How many people are out there who have given up their jobs or who are working two or three jobs to take care of their parents? What does someone without siblings or with crazy, unhelpful siblings do? A woman I work with said her sister stole $20,000 from their mother. I can't imagine. It would be so much easier if we could subsidize assisted living. We subsidize agribusiness and education and all sorts of things. But this is America, land of the 5.4-million-dollar tobacco CEO and the 86-billion-dollar invasion. What am I thinking? I should be grateful we have social security.

I call my brothers with my news. Although the financial situation isn't good, I think we're all relieved that Mom isn't going to a nursing home. Even the nicest ones are pretty bad. And to my surprise, my mother's brain, after six weeks in rehab, seems to be functioning again. She no longer frets about whether it is day or night. She can make complete sentences. Her eyes, which had been dull and empty, now contain a spark of light. One day at the nursing home, I wheeled her to a little crummy upright they had. As she sat in front of it, someone came by and asked if she could play Rachmaninoff. She lifted her hands, placed them on the keys, and magic happened. Rachmaninoff, Moonlight Sonata, Debussy poured from her fingers. I bit my lip to keep from crying.

One of David's kids has graduated from college, and Jo's symphony pension has finally kicked in, so between the three of us we figure out that we can do it. We can afford to keep Mom in assisted living instead of a nursing home. Hallelujah.

Between Mom's troubles and Hank going to the emergency room every couple of weeks, I decide not to teach for the spring term. This isn't the brightest idea I have ever had. For one thing, I need the money. For another thing, I am now faced with "gone child grief," which I'd been hiding from since September.

Empty nest syndrome. What a ridiculous idea. And yet this grief that hounds me, that sits on my chest and turns a crank, wringing my heart dry is the direct result of Celina's absence. I'm still not used to this adjustment in my life. Every day a new realization of something I'll never do again hits me. I'll never take her to choir practice or theater rehearsal again. She's not there to go on a walk with me and Merlyn. In the super market I drag myself like a bag of bowling balls down the aisles. My stomach is an empty well. How do parents whose children have died ever survive, I wonder. I feel guilty, ashamed of this pain. My daughter has only grown up. A joyous event. But now I feel like I have no business in a supermarket, no reason to pluck a frozen Amy's spinach pizza from the frosty caverns, no heart to pick up a package of her favorite pasta.

Mom is now safely ensconced in an assisted living facility. I don't have to go over every morning or every night. But I am not used to other people taking care of her, so I make daily visits. In my loneliness for Celina, I am slowly beginning to understand my mother's constant yearning for my company.

Thursday morning I must go with Hank to the cardiologist. He's been to a sleep clinic and found out he has sleep apnea; he's also been to an endocrinologist. We're still playing with the blood pressure medication trying to get him on an even keel.

"Stop drinking diet soda. Take more walks," I tell him, but I'm not the kind of doctor he listens to.

■

Then the weekend comes. Hank and I drive halfway across town to find the movie "Double Indemnity." Then we drive up to Winston-Salem to pick up Celina. Everything is good. This time there are no boys kissing each other in front of the building – a sight which burned the corneas of my homophobic husband – there is only our girl with her long thick hair and her wide smile as she bounds out of the building and into our arms. Suddenly it's as if I've never been sad or lonely in my life.

Back home, Hank cooks refried beans and tortillas. Celina grates the cheese and sets the table. I cut up the onions, lettuce and tomatoes and chop cilantro. Celina makes the guacamole the way her dad taught her to with cilantro, cumin, salt and tomatoes. After we eat, we all clean the kitchen and then sit down to watch the movie. My mother is left to her own devices. I am with my family, and I'm thinking of the rainbow Hank and I saw in California when I was a couple months pregnant – one of those arching textbook rainbows. Our kid was the pot of gold.

■

"Your mother's wheelchair has got to go," The head nurse at The Sanctuary tells me. My heart sinks and my spirit turns a sickly yellow color.

"Are you sure?" I ask.

"Yes, the other residents are complaining. They're afraid of her," she says. "Not only that, she knocked the glass door at the front of the building off its rail. We've ordered a manual wheelchair for her."

I'm trying not to imagine a glass door shattering over my mother's head.

The next day I head up to her room on the third floor. She's got that frantic confused look on her face that is so common to her now. She's in a small black, manual wheelchair, and I'm shoving the motorized wheelchair into her closet.

"I don't know why you have to take it away from me. I've been very careful, very careful," Mom says.

"Because you knocked the glass doors at the front of the building off the track and cracked one of them. Because you dragged a chair out of the activities room all the way to your bedroom, clearing everything in your path. Because the other residents are terrified of getting run over by you. Which you may recall happened to me not that long ago when you pinned me against a car," I tell her.

"But I've gotten better. I really have." My mother is frustrated to the brink of tears.

"This one is so hard. It's so hard to push it with my arms. Can't we move somewhere else?"

"No."

"No?"

Now I am frustrated to the brink of tears. I want my mother. My real mother.

"Where did they take it? Will I get it back? When do you think I'll get it back?" she queries.

"Mom, it's here in your closet. I don't know when you can use it again."

Right then, in my imagination, my real mother, handsome and vibrant, enters the room.

"Hello. Who are you?" my 50-year-old mother asks.

I feel such relief. I want to fall into her arms, but she doesn't know who I am.

"It's me, Trish. Your daughter."

"Trish? What are you doing here?"

"Taking care of you."

"Taking care of me? Are you still taking heroin?"

"No, Mom. I cleaned up more than 25 years ago. I'm a mother. I'm a college teacher. But I had to take a leave of absence when you went in the hospital. When you got out of the hospital, I had to bring you here."

"Well, that's wonderful. I thought you'd be dead by now. You made it. I won!"

"Yes, you did. And now you are exacting your revenge. You're whacked out on pain medication most of the time. You whine and complain constantly. You call me three, four, five times a day. No, Mother, I'm not dead, and you aren't either."

"God, how awful. How old am I?"

"Ninety."

"Ninety? Impossible."

Reality breaks in on my imagined conversation with my mother. My real mother.

"I have to go to the bathroom," my impostor mother says, "but I don't know what I'm supposed to do. It's in there, isn't it?"

I miss my 50-year-old mother right now. I miss her so much. She never complained about anything. She was the life of the party. We talked almost every day. We laughed even when things were awful. She always said she felt so lucky that she didn't just love her children, she liked us, too.

I allow myself a moment of bitterness, thinking of my two brothers, far away with their new girlfriends.

"I really need help. I can't figure out how to move my feet. I need to go to the bathroom. Trish, what are you doing?"

"Talking to you," I tell her.

She was always afraid that I would die. Now I understand why it was so important to keep me alive. She must have known.

I get the walker and help my mother transfer from the wheelchair to the walker. Then I pull up her dress and pull down the disposable underpants while she balances precariously before falling backwards onto the toilet. I go into the bedroom and wait for her to call me when she's done. My phantom mother waits for me by the window, looking out into the parking lot below.

"I'm sorry about all this," she says. "Terribly sorry. But I do love you."

"I know. I love you, too," I tell her. "I always love you even when I think I don't."

Then she's gone, and I hear my mother calling from the bathroom.

"Trish? Trish? I'm ready."

THREE

The biggest favor the universe has done me is for my mother to be at The Sanctuary, where there are people to help her, listen to her play the piano, talk to her and eat meals with her. My life is about to crack wide open.

Celina has decided she won't go to college right after high school. She wants to work with an experimental theater company for a few months and defer college for a semester. I like this plan. I was never in favor of going straight into college. As a university professor, I've watched many 18-year-olds flounder in their first year, taking pointless classes, flunking out, getting depressed, getting drunk, spinning around completely clueless. At the theater company she'll be working with adults on a professional level, and when she isn't doing theater, she'll be doing farm work.

But when Hank hears about this scheme, he explodes. Hank is not a halfway kind of guy. He's the sort to pull out the canons when a water pistol might do.

I start throwing things in a suitcase. My M.O. is always to disappear. When I was about three years old and my drunken father came home, I took off for the woods behind my house. My brothers had to go out and find me. I may have been just three years old, but I knew danger when I saw it.

But Hank knows this about me, and he reins in his anger enough that we don't bolt. It's only a temporary truce, however. This is a fight to the death. It isn't about whether or not Celina goes to college in the fall or sometime later. There's something deeper, more fundamental going on. Twenty years' worth of resentments and disagreements boil to the surface.

Hank and I battle like Titans.

"Why can't you be on my side?" he asks.

"Because I think your side is wrong," I tell him.

No matter how many times we get in the ring to duke it out, neither of us wins. We just get bloodier.

Celina has become a zombie. Neither of us can eat. We live on smoothies. I decide she's got to get out of this toxic atmosphere while I figure out what to do, so I send her to New York to visit a friend.

■

That night I lie in my bed in the dark and push into the pliant flesh below the curve of my belly, an inch or so above the ridge of my right hip bone. My body reports back to me in a language I don't understand. What is it telling me? Hank is in his room asleep. Now that he has a machine for his sleep apnea and a prescription for Ambien, he sleeps at night like the rest of the world.

I contemplate the demise of my marriage as I lie in bed. Most marriages break up because of infidelity, substance abuse, someone going wild with the credit cards or just plain boredom. But in our case none of the above apply. Are we really breaking up because of an 18-year-old's possible career choice? I can't help but wish he'd had me for a kid. Then he'd have something to be pissed off about.

"I'd rather see her be a prostitute than an actress," Hank says bitterly.

When Hank thinks "actress," he thinks bankruptcy, drugs, suicide. But Celina is not even sure she wants to act. She has no cotton-candy movie-star dreams. She's interested in theater as a means of communication. And she's interested in a lot of other things, too – politics, art, music, history. But Hank won't hear of it. In his narrative, I have corrupted his child, infusing her with illusions of glory to make up for my own rotten childhood.

History is filled with such stories. St. Francis' father rejected him when he became a monk. Gay friends tell me of being turned out of their parents' homes. My own father preferred a mediocre piano student to his own children.

As I lie there poking around my belly at the source of this mysterious pain, I wonder if there's more at work here than this eruption over Celina and her desire to live her own life. I realize I've been living in a comfortable cage for a long while, and now suddenly it looks like the door is open. And maybe that's what Hank is thinking, too, deep in the far reaches of his subconscious. We are both so dependent in this relationship. We have become each other's drug. And we are stagnating. I wonder, is Celina the sacrificial lamb that allows us to break free of each other? The one point on which neither of us will budge?

■

The next day the "gone child grief" overwhelms me.

"Let's go to the beach," I tell Hank. I've got to get out of this house with all its memories cascading over me. Maybe at the beach, Hank and I can talk. Maybe we can find a way out of this hole we've dug for ourselves.

We pack up some things and throw them in the car.

Just as I'm pulling out of the garage, I notice that odd little phrase coming from inside my body. What the hell is it?

I turn to Hank and ask, "Where is the appendix located?"

"In your lower right abdomen," he says. "Why?"

"I have a pain there. In fact, I've had a pain there for a few days."

"It could be appendicitis," he says.

"It could be gas," I reply, remembering once when I was a child, my aunt taking me to the doctor because I had stomach pains which were nothing more than gas. Besides, I don't get things like appendicitis. I'm the healthy one here, the non-smoking vegetarian yogi who doesn't drink alcohol or caffeine.

But we decide not to take a chance. So instead of going to the beach, we wind up in the emergency room for eight hours. At one point I have to drink a few gallons of some orange crap and go into a little room where they inject me with stuff that makes me feel like I have to pee and then we wait some more. Fortunately, I have brought along a copy of *War and Peace*, which I read aloud to him while we await the results of my CAT-scan. We don't mention Celina or the on-going battle. Instead we're friends again. But I get tired of reading and tired of waiting.

"Fuck this," I say. I get off the gurney and demand a nurse come unhook me from their diabolical machines. I hate hospitals. I am determined never to be like my mother, never to obey these people who act like demi-gods. They barely manage to placate me until a friendly doctor with a gray beard comes into the curtained room where we wait.

"It's not appendicitis," he tells us. "You have a tumor on your appendix."

He shows us the CAT scan, which Hank is able to read but which looks like abstract art to me. "You'll need to have an operation to remove it. The surgeon will probably want to take out a third of your colon as well to check the lymph nodes for cancer."

There it is: the C-word. Hank and I look at each other. His heavy eyebrows are raised as if to say, *I knew it. I knew the worst was yet to come.* He has lost his sister and his father, and now they say that his wife might have cancer. I want to hold him, comfort him, but we've crossed some invisible boundary in our relationship. We can be friends, but we can't be lovers. We cannot touch each other.

■

I don't tell my mother that I might have cancer. I simply tell her that I have to get my appendix removed.

Celina comes back home. At this point, she's like a refugee. She's numb to the news. She's lost her father and now she might lose her mother. She finds a little summer job and mostly stays with friends at night. I worry about her being at loose ends, not having a place where she feels safe, a place to call home. I think about moving out, getting an apartment somewhere, but now is obviously not a good time.

■

A few days before the operation I dream that I am in the ocean. My body is rigid like a piece of driftwood as I twirl out to sea. I am just past the breakers when I hear Hank's voice calling me back to the shallow water. So I begin twirling back, back through the waves toward the sound of Hank's voice. When I get to shore, I climb a set of stone steps and sit next to Celina.

On June 24, Hank takes me to the hospital. I am put into a hospital gown, laid on a gurney and told to start counting. The next thing I know I am floating, pleasantly drifting. I am conscious of worried voices, but I am not worried. I hear the voices as if they are on the other side of a thick curtain of fog.

"She should have come back by now. She's not breathing."

Then I hear Hank's voice. I don't know what he's saying. I am utterly at peace until suddenly I am not at peace. Instead a violent upheaval wracks my belly. Pain sears my abdomen. Now the voices are explaining something to me: "We had to give you Narcan. You were under too long. You had a bad reaction to the Dilaudid. Your respiration . . ."

"Stop!" I scream at the blurry faces now sharply coming into focus. "Stop giving it to me. It's making me puke."

I would not normally say the word "puke" to people I don't know or any vulgarity for that matter, but after I relentlessly vomit the thimbleful of fluid in my stomach into a small plastic pan, I collapse against the plastic side of the hospital bed and whimper, "fuck."

"That doesn't look comfortable," Hank says. "Should we move her?"

"No," I croak. I equate the least movement with staggering pain.

The irony is not lost on me even in this crumpled state. Dilaudid had been my drug of choice in my early 20s, when I had helped my boyfriend break into drugstores to get pills. I had done time for the love of this synthetic narcotic. Then I met Hank, who, for whatever reason, was the first person to be more important to me than a drug. He was an engineer who could fix anything, including me. He was my anchor.

Because of my reaction to the Dilaudid, the doctor switches me to morphine and the nurse hands me a button to click whenever I need more. At first I don't click it all, but the pain after three and a half hours of abdominal surgery feels like the knife is still stuck inside me, so I start clicking and the pain eases and then almost disappears.

That night Hank sleeps in the chair by my bed with his sleep apnea machine quietly chugging fresh air through his mask. A small plastic tube pumps oxygen to my nose, and I doze off into a drugged sleep. Hank's presence soothes me, and I imagine our dreams blending together like blood with blood. Here we are at the end of our relationship, and Hank and I are finally sleeping in the same room. I have never loved or needed him more.

After a while I notice I am forgetting to breathe. I let go of the button and force myself to stay awake until the morphine wears off a bit. These drugs that I loved so much as a teenager – I hate them now. How could I ever have enjoyed that feeling, I wonder. Of course, back then I had a death wish. Now, I'd rather live with the pain. Now I want to be awake. Now I want life.

Not only do I hate the drugs, I hate the hospital. I hate the hard, plastic bed; the stiff, uncomfortable chair; the catheter that makes me feel as if I constantly have to pee; the tasteless food. The thing I hate the most is the chemical stench that emanates from my body. I reek. When they finally take out the catheter, the disgusting odor of my own urine makes me wilt. The blessed bowel movement that signals I am ready to leave the hospital is a toxic tar.

As the days pass, Hank, who is generally fairly antisocial, makes friends with the nurses. He learns about their families, where they went to school, all sorts of things that hold no interest for me. He chats pleasantly with my friends when they come to visit. He examines my scar and helps me get out of bed and walk around. He monitors what I eat and how much. He tells the nurse when my Foley bag is full.

He does not, however, speak to Celina once during the whole ordeal. He manages to leave long enough each day for her to visit me. The truce he and I have achieved does not include her.

■

Four days after entering the hospital, I am able to go home. We still haven't learned whether or not the tumor was cancerous.

At home I spend my days on the couch or in the recliner. Once when I can't make the recliner work I wind up screaming at it and crying until Celina rushes in to help me. When my brain finally starts functioning again, I spend my time reading magazines several years old. Celina stays nearby, and Hank locks himself in his room. He still refuses to speak to her. He thinks he can "win" if he takes a hard line. He is willing to go to whatever lengths are necessary to get her to do what he thinks is right. But he is going to lose us both.

At night Celina and I watch movies. Our favorite comfort movie is "101 Dalmatians." She huddles next to me on the couch.

"I miss him," she tells me. "He doesn't love me anymore."

"He loves you," I reply, an answer I know to be true. I am sure that in spite of all the evidence to the contrary that he does love her. "He just doesn't know how to let you go."

"Are you going to be okay?" she asks.

"Yes," I answer, but of this I am not so sure.

Pongo and Purdy dash through the snow to find their puppies.

■

The next week Hank and I go back to see the surgeon. By now I am eating and shitting regularly, and I realize that all the things I thought were more important than those two vital functions are practically meaningless. Otherwise, I'm still not feeling great. I walk slowly, a little hunched over, skinnier than I've been in decades.

Hank has studied appendix cancer on the Internet. If I have cancer, then my survival chances are 50/50 according to the data. Having lost his sister and father to cancer in the past six months, Hank looks at me with wary eyes.

Before the surgeon comes into the small white examination room, Hank asks, "Am I going to have to carry you out of here?"

Sitting on the table, I smirk at him and then pretend to get hysterical over my impending death. We both laugh. We can't help it. We may be in battle, but I am grateful for his presence in these cold, boring little rooms with their walls decorated by pictures of wormy intestines.

The surgeon enters. He's a handsome, matter-of-fact fellow.

"The tumor was cancerous," he tells us. Hank inhales sharply. "But we got 24 lymph nodes when we took out the portion of the colon, and none of them showed any signs of cancer."

I sit and listen. Hank asks the questions. The surgeon believes they got all the cancer in the surgery.

"But is it possible that a few microscopic cells escaped?" Hank asks.

"It's possible," the surgeon says. Then he turns to me. "I'm sending you to an oncologist. You may need to get some chemo as a precautionary measure."

I am already resigned to the idea.

After our visit to the surgeon, Hank and I stop for lunch at an Indian restaurant. I load up my plate with palak paneer, dahl and nan. We eat quietly, comfortably. I know that while my chances of survival are only 50/50, my marriage's chances are much worse. And yet today there is no one else I want to be with.

My mother called constantly while I was in the hospital. But I didn't want to talk to her. I couldn't even muster the energy to be around Celina for very long when she came to see me after the surgery. Even now, Hank is the only person in the world that I can be with in my utterly joyless condition. He is simply a part of me, and we are dreamers, sleepwalking toward the end of our life together.

FOUR

LATE SUMMER 2008

With our differences irreconcilable, Hank and I decide to sell the house. Aside from repainting the bedrooms, the house hasn't been updated once since we moved into it ten years earlier, and in upscale Charlotte no one is going to buy a house with linoleum kitchen counters. It needs so much work – new flooring, new bathrooms, and new paint, at the very least – before we can expect to sell it.

Fortunately, my mother has grown accustomed to her new surroundings, and I am more free than I have been in years. Which is a good thing because my life is divided now between helping Hank repair the house and escaping that house with Celina.

Celina leaves to visit a friend. She'll be gone for a couple of days, which means Hank will venture out of his room and we might get some work done on the house. We're going to repaint the living room and he wants to order a new bathtub for his bathroom.

At Home Depot, I follow Hank around listlessly and watch as he loads the flat cart with varnish, paint, 2 x 4s and 2 x 10s. There's some rotted wood on the front of the house that needs to be replaced. So much work to be done. We've neglected the house the way we neglected our marriage.

Hank grabs a strange ladder contraption that can transform from a regular step ladder to an extension ladder like those weird toys that boys love so much. I don't help load a single thing. I can't because of the operation. The nurse told me no heavy lifting for six weeks or I'd regret it. No exercise. No house cleaning. All I can do is read and watch movies. I even stopped doing my yoga practices that I had been doing faithfully since last September.

I feel guilty for not helping Hank load the stuff onto the cart and then into the car, but I also realize he doesn't have to be doing this by himself. He could have gotten Celina to help with all of this, but the few times she offered, he simply shook his head and pointed for her to get out.

We haven't discussed the future; our only goal is to get the house in shape in order to sell it. Then we'll have another bridge to cross. But today we aren't talking about that.

■

Later I drive over to see my mother. I've just gotten there when Mom tells me she needs to go to the bathroom.

"I don't know if I can do it with my shoes on," she says.

"Your shoes?" I ask, grabbing the walker and bringing it over to her wheelchair. She can still walk a little. She can take a few steps from the wheelchair to the toilet. "I don't think your shoes will be a problem."

"Well, they're up."

She means, I think, that her feet are on the footrests of the wheelchair and they need to be moved. She knows at some level she's not making sense, but we pretend that this is a normal conversation. In some ways, it is.

After her trip to the bathroom, she looks at me and says, "I love that dress. It's so pleasing to look at."

Then we go downstairs, she in her hand-pushed wheelchair, and I walking beside her. I'm not allowed to push her yet.

When we get to the dining room, she takes my hand and brings it to her cheek.

"You can do no wrong," she says.

"I'm glad you think so," I answer dryly and bend down to kiss her cheek.

■

Celina and I decide to take our annual trip to Florida. This year it is especially important for us to get away. Before we leave I stand in my bedroom and look down at my finger. My diamond shines as brightly as ever. How often have I gazed at this ring, happy to have it on my finger? Happy to be married. But Hank has not kissed me since Celina's birthday. I feel more like a younger brother than a wife. I don't see the point in wearing it anymore. I put it in a small cloth bag, and stash it in a drawer.

"It's the divorce tour," I tell Celina as we drive out of town, Celina's iPod playing through the radio. Our hearts weigh as much as a bag of bricks, but we will manage to have fun anyway. We will sing along to our music at the top of our lungs. We will drink champagne with friends in Tallahassee. We will drive to St. Pete and stay with my dear old friend, who did time with me back before I ever thought of being a mom. We will meet Sadhguru in person. I've got a new green notebook, ready for work.

I'm scheduled to have an interview with Sadhguru at Cheryl's house. Cheryl is the author of the book that I edited, and we both think that an interview will help get the word out.

On the drive down, Celina seems so sad and lost.

"Maybe I should just give in," she says. "I don't want Dad to hate me anymore."

I don't say anything. I don't want to influence her one way or the other, but if she doesn't follow her dream, I know I will never forgive him.

At precisely 10 o'clock, we enter Cheryl's well-appointed new house, overlooking a golf course. Instead of his usual robe, Sadhguru is dressed in jeans.

Still sitting he bows to me as if he knows me quite well and then he reaches for my hand as I awkwardly drop my purse on her glass coffee table. I've never been star struck. I wouldn't recognize most celebrities if they came up and kissed me on the cheek. But when he holds my hands for that brief moment I feel light-headed.

"What have you got in there?" he asks with a laugh as my purse clunks on the table. "Sounds like something heavy."

"It's a present for you," I stammer. "Oh, and this is my daughter."

He smiles at Celina. I feel completely ill at ease, like someone on a blind date. I hand him the jar of raw honey that I've brought and explain that I was inspired by the story he told in one of the programs of some incredibly healthy beekeepers in India who live almost exclusively on honey. I have decided to start using it myself because raw honey has anti-oxidants and (as he already knows) I'd just had surgery to remove a cancerous tumor on my appendix.

"The honey is my chemo," I tell him and sit down on the couch. My oncologist just a week earlier changed her mind about giving me chemo treatments. It seems that my cancer is so rare they have no data that chemo actually helps. So they're going to monitor me and hope for the best. The truth is I'm not too worried about it.

Sadhguru is intrigued with Celina, who sits on the other couch. I'm glad I have brought her along. For one thing, she exudes a purity of heart that I haven't had since I was four years old. I knew that he would see that. More importantly, I'm hoping he might say something that will help her gain some clarity.

Sadhguru asks Celina what does she do, is she a student?

"What?" she stammers.

"A student? Do you study?"

"I just graduated from high school," she says. "And I'm going to take a semester to go to Massachusetts . . ."

"A semester?" he asks. He laughs heartily. "I don't think it takes a semester to get to Massachusetts."

She laughs and blushes. "No, I mean I'm going to spend a semester in Massachusetts, maybe, I'm not sure. But I'm going up there to work with a theater company. I'm very interested in social and political justice, and this company does a lot of plays that have been performed in prisons and battered women's shelters. I'm going to work with them for a while. Then I'm going to college and probably study history."

"Oh, that's good," Sadhguru says approvingly. "So many young people, you know, they are only interested in making money. My daughter is going to take four years of dance. Not because she wants to be a dancer but for the discipline."

Sadhguru hands her a book that he had been reading called *The War of Wealth*.

"You will find out a lot about justice in that book," he says.

Because I'm drawn to issues of social and political justice my-self, I ask Sadhguru about his views on the United States. Sadhguru is careful not to publicly criticize this country or its government, and I can understand why. He is focused on one thing – offering a spiritual process to people who want to explore their spiritual potential.

This is not to say that Sadhguru doesn't speak his mind. He is quick to point out that the lives we are leading right now in the U.S. are not sustainable.

"When you can't get what you need, then you have to go to war with someone," he said. "It's simply not a sustainable life."

"What about the planet? Are we doomed? Is it hopeless?" I want to know.

"No, the planet will be fine. People may be in trouble but the planet will take care of itself. Nature will correct our mistakes if we don't correct them first. That may become very painful."

"Do we have the will and the ability to do that?" I ask.

"The ability, yes. The will? Not yet, but when it becomes painful enough, we will have the will," he says.

No matter how dire his words, amusement plays on his face. His eyes shift from serious to mirthful in a moment. I've never met anyone so clearly authentic. He is the same man – in the book, on the dais, in videos, and sitting on a white sofa in Flor-ida.

I ask him my interview questions. He answers them pa-tiently.

Sadhguru's message is clear: "There is an endless longing to expand. At the same time there is an instinct for self-preservation which is constantly wanting to build walls of safety and comfort. These things seem to be a contradiction. This confusion has arisen in our minds because we are too identified with our physical bodies. The instinct for self-preservation and longing to expand are opposed to each other. They're not really opposed to each other. The boundaries of our body need to be preserved. Everything else within us longs to expand."

We continue to talk about a range of subjects; his humor and wisdom are playful. When Sadhguru has answered all the questions I have for him, he turns his attention once again to Celina.

"I like this girl, Trish," he says laughing.

"Her father disapproves of her plans. Mightily," I tell him. Celina shrugs to indicate she doesn't know what to do about it.

"He's supposed to disapprove!" Sadhguru tells her. "How else will you know that you really want to do it?"

Celina thinks about it for a moment. Then she smiles that bright, happy smile. Our visit ends and we're back on the road, heading to our next destination. We're listening to the stereo and singing, "Cruel, Cruel Summer." The Florida sky arches over us like a big blue tent. The highway unfurls like a decision made a lifetime ago.

A couple of weeks later I put Celina on a plane for Massachusetts.

FIVE

AUTUMN 2008

In autumn our dog, Merlyn, who is only seven, becomes suddenly old and feeble. The veterinarian says he has an auto-immune disease. In other words, his immune system has decided to wage war on his body. The vet also says it will eventually go away. He is wrong.

When the dog first gets sick in October, he whimpers in pain and later howls in agony. I never realized a dog could cry, nor did I know that the sound could rip you in two. It comes on quickly though he's acted punky for a couple of days. Monday night, after the vet's office is closed, we realize the severity of the condition and that waiting until morning is not an option. We get him into the back seat of the car. I drive to the emergency vet (not daring to calculate the cost) while Hank tries to comfort our frightened pup.

At the emergency vet they tell us to sit and wait in one of the examination rooms. Hank doesn't like to sit in doctor's offices. He prefers to stand or pace. That's what he did during my cancer ordeal. When my follow-up CAT scan, three months after the removal of my appendix, came back clear of any malignancies, I thought we could get back to the complicated business of dismantling our marriage, but now October has arrived and our dog has begun shrieking.

A day after our first trip to the emergency vet, Hank and I are hopping around him in panic as the pain pills and antibiotics apparently provide little or no relief. He whimpers and whines, and we are beside ourselves.

For the first time in months Hank and I cleave to each other while we weep, sure that we are going to have put him down. We make five trips to the emergency vet in two weeks, spending hours on top of hours, waiting for some kind of information. After one of those trips, we leave him there for tests and an MRI. For the cost of the MRI, we could get and maintain ten healthy dogs from the pound, I'm thinking. But Merlyn is not a dog in the abstract. He is a being in the concrete – a dog whose face I know, a dog whose eyes have looked into mine with total under-standing, a dog with whom communication has become second nature. Besides, Hank will not be deterred.

The MRI shows a mysterious inflammation of the muscles. Not deadly, we are told. And yet even after we know what's wrong, we still have to bring him back again and again. The pain is not being managed.

I spend my days downstairs with my computer on my lap, working and watching over the dog. We give him pain pills and sleeping pills along with a variety of antibiotics and high doses of steroids. He wears a narcotic patch; we consider using it our-selves. Hank spends his nights with the dog. One night he stays on the living room floor holding the whimpering, shaking dog. Hank often carries all 70 pounds of the dog outside several times a day.

After two weeks, we can take it no longer. Nothing seems to help him. This is no way for an animal or a human to live. Every time the dog cries, we want to puncture our own ear drums.

"We have to do it," I tell Hank. "He's not getting better."

"He has to get the shot," Hank agrees.

We are numb as I back the car to the front door and Hank carries Merlyn out and places him on the comforter that is now a permanent fixture of my car. We drive in silence up to the freeway.

"Hank," I ask, "what is that dog doing?" I am looking in the rear view mirror at Merlyn sitting up, gazing outside the window, his pink tongue hanging like a bell from his black mouth.

"He seems to be enjoying the ride," Hank says.

"That's weird."

We pull up in front of the emergency vet; we're old hands at this by now and Hank goes to get the rolling crib. I step out of the car and open the back door. Merlyn rolls his head to the side, smiles and thumps his tail.

When Hank comes back out, I tell him, "Put him on the ground and see if he'll walk."

"He won't walk," Hank says.

"Let's just see."

So Hank puts Merlyn on the ground, and the dog stands up and begins tracking the pee of other dogs with his noisy snuffling nose. He looks just like any other dog wandering around a yard full of dog smells.

"I don't think this is the day," I say.

"No," Hank answers, "today is definitely not the day."

The vet tells us the steroids must have finally kicked in.

"Give him some time," he says.

■

We bring the dog home and for a month or so we pretend to be okay. We work on the house, replacing an old moldy shower with a gigantic whirlpool bath, which we both land in when it's finished, bubbles bursting over the sides, our slick legs rubbing together like happy fish. And wouldn't this be a nice place to roll credits? The theme of the story would be that the trials and trauma of our sick dog somehow repaired our sick relationship, that Merlyn had lived up to his name and created some Hollywood-movie magic. Sometimes it really does work out that way. But not for us, not this time.

Soon our words are tiny missiles as we hide behind a stockpile of accusations: the car I had bought without consulting him, his last name that I had never taken as my own, his refusal to allow overnight visits from my friends and family, the abortion twenty years earlier. We are no longer screaming about Celina and my support of her decision to go away for three months to study with an experimental theater company. We have worn that issue to a rag.

Finally as Christmas and Celina's inevitable return approaches, Hanks decides to go stay with his family in California for a while.

I drive him to the train station. As he leaves we're somehow back to being friendly with each other. I figure when he comes back, we'll continue to work on the house. As much work as it needs, we may never split up. He and Celina will eventually reconcile. Of this, I am sure.

◼

Celina comes home from her adventures, and the two of us spend the Christmas break, feeding pills to a feeble old dog, who pees on the carpet and hobbles from one resting spot to another. My mother and my friend Darryl join us for dinner on Christmas Eve. Celina and I miss Hank, but even if we're not getting "peace on earth," at least we have "peace at home."

Merlyn gets worse.

On January 14th Celina and I go to the Original Pancake House for breakfast, but the food sits like cement on our bellies.

"Today is the day," I say.

I call the veterinarian's office and make the appointment for two o'clock.

That afternoon I drive the car across the lawn to the front steps. Celina gets Merlyn into the backseat. She has been his extra set of legs for a week now, picking him up when he fell in his own pee, bathing him, carrying him when he couldn't make it up the steps. He is a heavy dog, and he growls in pain but the two of them work together with his failing body as best they can.

We drive to the vet's office where they are waiting for him.

Celina waits outside, sobbing. I call Hank and put him on the phone with her. "Comfort her," I tell him. He manages to squeeze out a few civil words – the first words he's spoken to her in eight months.

I go into the little room with Merlyn. As I wait for the veterinarian to come with her shot, Merlyn licks my hand thoughtfully, gently, lovingly. He is too young to die, but he seems grateful to be going. My arms encircle his neck as she gives him the shot. Then slowly his head drops between his forepaws, eyes closed. He looks like a sleeping puppy.

"It's over," I whisper.

Hank does not return.

FIVE REQUIEM

O Lamb of God who takest away the sins of the world,
Have mercy upon us.
Give them peace, O Lord,
And grant to us also that grace which comes from thee,
That peace which only you can give,
The peace of accepting,
The peace of forgiving,
The peace of knowing the oneness of God, the greatness of
God.

Rosalind MacEnulty
An American Requiem

ONE

Celina and I stare at the dorm room with its blood-dripping horror movie posters covering bleak cinderblock walls, tiny metal-framed bed crammed into the corner, and junky furniture piled in the middle of the small room. The first inhabitant, who is nowhere to be seen, has already commandeered the window.

At this moment, Celina could pass as a model for an Edvard Munch painting.

"I'm thinking you would need a shit-load of antidepressants to stay here, honey," I tell her. "And I'm not sure we can afford the therapy."

A few hours later, we're looking at a studio apartment a couple of blocks from campus. A few days later, we've finished emptying the storage unit where the last of my mother's things have been kept since she entered the assisted living place last April. The boxes of music, the distressed copies of the Requiem, and a stack of her books are now in my office. The daybed, love seat, and bookcase have been moved to Celina's new apartment. She's decided she'd like to take the wicker chest, too. So we're sitting on the living room floor, the wicker chest beside us with the lid gaping open, and I'm slowly extracting the contents – envelopes filled with pictures and newspaper clippings, a scrap book, old literary magazines where poems and stories of mine were published, a photo album and framed publicity shots of my two brothers from their days as a conductor and an actor.

The arrangement of the photos in the album is a haphazard affair: a few pictures of me as a child, of my brothers and their kids, of my godmother and even a couple of my father and one of my stepfather. Celina and I look through the photos, remarking on each one in turn. Celina is entranced with one large studio portrait of my mother, her sister and two brothers as children. My mother is the eldest. She has a pixie haircut and is smiling at the camera. The youngest has a large picture book on his lap. When they were very young, the Field kids all had blond hair, and my mother's father, Lewis, remarked that they looked like a bunch of Swedish immigrants.

"It was the worst thing to be called an immigrant," my mother once explained. "He didn't like children very much." Conversely, my mother never cared for him either. He was a powerful judge, involved in dirty politics, and a drunk, who left his family to fend for themselves during the Great Depression. She says she first discovered the truth about politics when she overheard him on the phone telling someone that he would "fix" everything with a certain judge.

Now my mother is the last of the "Field kids." Her two younger brothers and younger sister are all dead. Her dearest friends are dead. Her ex-husbands are dead. Even her piano has been carted away and put in storage.

In the scrapbook a newspaper clipping catches my eye: it says that 12-year-old Rosalind Field has been chosen to be the accompanist for the Girl Scout Chorale.

"Her first job," I say, shaking my head in wonder.

Then there is increasing evidence of the jobs and accolades to come: an article about "the musical family" – my mother and two brothers – putting on a performance for the Friday Musicale; programs from concerts where she was the composer, the conductor and/or the pianist; a brochure from The Lost Colony, an outdoor drama, where she was musical director for a quarter of a century. There is also a program for "An American Requiem."

I put it aside to show her. I'm remembering that request she made that we not let the Requiem die when she dies. I hope my brothers and I can find a way.

I stuff these relics from my mother's long and productive life into another box and notice that old dog Grief sniffing around my heart. Sometimes it feels as if the last four years have been a series of small deaths.

■

With Celina gone to school, Hank missing in action, and the dog dead, I spend more and more time at The Sanctuary with my mom. Her memory plays tricks on both of us.

One time when I come over, her hair has just been cut and styled. It's a gorgeous thick silver halo.

"Your hair looks lovely this color," I tell her.

"Well, I never did dye it," she says.

I laugh and say, "Yes, you did, Mom. In fact, sometimes I dyed it for you. You've never been fully gray before you lived here."

She looks at me in surprise.

"Really? Well, I suppose if I were to write my memoirs, it would be mostly fiction."

One night I go over to The Sanctuary about 6:45 to spend some time with Mom. She hates that the evenings are so dull – almost everyone else goes right to bed after they eat dinner – so I try to get there after dinner and play a game of Scrabble with her. This night I help her go to the bathroom first, then get her back in her wheelchair and put her feet on the metal footrests. I push her into the hallway and wait for the elevator.

Without fail, my mother says, "It's so convenient having this elevator right here."

"Yes, it is," I answer and rub her shoulders as we wait.

Downstairs we head inside the parlor to play our game. A woman named Jane asks to join us, and so I put out a third rack. Mother and I stopped keeping score several months ago. It had gotten to the point that I couldn't play with her anymore because she made such seemingly stupid moves. It was annoying to beat her by hundreds of points, and it would infuriate me when she would make a play for four points that with one simple adjustment could be 14 points. Finally I realized that if we played without keeping score, we could both still enjoy the game.

Jane, however, wants to keep score. I can tell she's a bit competitive. I am, too. So I make sure I get a 50-point lead and then I relax for the rest of the game. Jane's husband is in the hospital. He has Alzheimer's and when he returns from the hospital, he'll be moved from their apartment to the memory care unit.

"I'll still be able to eat with him," she says with a smile. Then she tells me that she's taken care of him for 64 years, the last six with Alzheimer's.

"That must have been hard," I say.

"Not when you do it out of love, it isn't hard," she says.

We finish the game at ten minutes till eight. I like to get out of the place by eight. Otherwise, the door will be locked and I'll have to hunt around to find someone to let me out. So I hurriedly wheel my mother upstairs. This is where I make my mistake. She has to go to the bathroom, and instead of pushing her call button, I decide to help her myself, but quickly so I can get downstairs before they lock the door. Only you can't do anything quickly with an elderly person.

Once she's done, I try to get her into her reclining chair, but panic hits her. I don't know why, it just does. And I'm just trying to get out of there. But she's suddenly incoherent. She needs or wants something but she can't say what it is. She stammers and waves her hand and looks terrified. And the saintly person I was just a few minutes earlier is replaced by the demon daughter from hell.

"God damn it," I growl through clenched teeth, my face within inches of hers. "What the hell is wrong with you?"

Then she cries, and I get angrier. And I'm angry about everything. Angry about my guilt for treating her badly, angry about the fact that she's gotten old, angry that she's always in pain and no longer the tough cookie who used to be my mother, angry that I'm no longer young either, angry that I'm not out with some cute guy in a fast car with a cold bottle of beer in my hand, angry that I'm not rich and successful or poor and holy or some damn thing, angry that my daughter has grown up and left me, that my dog is dead and my husband has gone AWOL, leaving me in a half-finished house where the squirrels and raccoons can nest unmolested. And don't get me started on the Republicans or the Taliban.

One of the caretakers enters. She can see that she's walked into a bad situation. She can see that I'm not being a good, loving daughter. She can see that I'm a snarling demon bitch.

I leave immediately.

The next day I go over to see my mother. I bring chocolates. She is happy to see me. I wheel her outside to get some fresh air. You'd never know the night before even happened.

■

My mother complains that she never got to travel enough. There had been a trip to Bermuda with her mother when she was just a child. The trip had been to help Skipper recover from the nervous breakdown she'd had as a result of her husband's drunken escapades. Then there was a trip to Europe in her early 20s, funded by Skipper, to help my own mother cope with the strain of being married to her drunk husband.

Other than that, she devoted her life to working. She was at the church on Sundays and Wednesdays and in the theater on Tuesdays, Thursdays, Fridays, and Saturdays. When in her 80s she had finally planned a trip to Heidelberg, a vertebra in her back needed attention. She went in for surgery. Not only did she not go to Heidelberg, she did not walk unassisted ever again.

The lessons of 2008 and my mother's regrets have not been lost on me. I have decided to go to India and take a program at Sadhguru's ashram. Because of the economic "downturn," airline tickets are cheaper than ever, staying at the ashram is ridiculously inexpensive, and I've got a break between terms. The only reason for me not to go is that Hank doesn't want me to. And Hank is on the other side of the country and shows no inclination to return, so his opinion is of little weight.

"You should go," my mother says. "You will never regret it."

"Will you be okay?" I ask.

"I'm terrified of you leaving for that long. But you must do it."

She's right. I do not want to be sitting around spilling my regrets to Celina some day.

TWO

FEB. 2009, SOUTH INDIA

The thick woolly heat of the late February afternoon has finally released its tentacles from around our necks as Margit from Germany and I pick our way through the crowd of Indians in front of the Temple. Dust rises around our sandaled feet but does not settle on our pristine Indian outfits. I am in borrowed silk (from my Indian neighbor back in Charlotte) – cobalt blue with gold flowers on the tunic and the pants. Margit wears linen, a little more comfortable for the daylight hours, but by the middle of the night, I'll be glad I'm in something heavier.

We wind our way through throngs of the devoted outside the Temple and pass a giant statue of a kneeling black bull to meet up with a striking blond woman named Anya, whose job it is to help us find the bus. Anya is wearing a turquoise tunic and pants with linen trim. A few other westerners gather around her with us. We're all dressed so beautifully. Have I ever been to a rock concert in anything but jeans and a t-shirt, I wonder? Have any of us?

We leave the Temple grounds, which are located on the edge of the sprawling Isha yoga ashram, and walk past long rows of towering coconut trees to the bus. We crowd in and soon bang down the dirt road to the concert grounds where we will celebrate Mahashivratri with live music, dancing, and chanting with more than 100,000 other happy, dancing people. The bus chugs through swarms of motorcycles and deposits us in a veritable ocean of people: old folks, children, parents, teenagers. At the edge of the grounds a giant Ferris wheel spins, lights twinkling. We wander into an enormous white tent. Our section is close to the front along the side of the tent. We have a great view of the stage where the bands will play.

About 500 of us non-Indians are staying at the Ashram, preparing for the meditation program. Tonight, however, we are going to kick out the jams Indian-style from six p.m. to six a.m. Why are we doing this and without the benefit of wakefulness-inducing drugs? (Most of us haven't had caffeine for the past forty days.) We are here because Sadhguru has invited us to be here, and generally when Sadhguru wants you to do something there is a certain amount of fun involved, not to mention the spiritual sparks. And always music.

Mahashivratri means "The Great Night of Shiva." It is celebrated all over India on the fourteenth night of the new moon that occurs in February or March. Shiva is the destroyer – the original yogi.

The program starts with music, but my new friend Ginny and I decide to wander around the grounds. I notice a fashionably dressed woman I thought was a friend, who is busy impressing richer and prettier people than me. In a way it feels like high school.

When we get back to our spots in the bleachers, Sadhguru is sitting on the stage in his robe. He explains to the throngs that there are several legends attached to Mahashivratri, which make it an ideal night to honor Shiva since you get to decide the reason.

"For one, it is the day that Shiva attained his ultimate stillness. For another, a day of absolute inclusiveness. For another, it's a wedding. For another, it is conquest, and for another it is the day of the weird." Then Sadhguru gives that characteristic hearty laugh of his.

Weird it is, but in a somehow familiar way. Woodstock without the mud. Bonnaroo without the hangover. Bliss without blowback. I thought I might have a hard time staying awake, and there were a couple of moments early on when my head lolled forward, but pretty soon the energy in the place starts crackling. It's like a fire. There is that first lick of flame, a few inquiring tentacles, and then the sudden bursting forth of yellow pitchforks and searing heat. The enormous crowd is chanting, calling "Shambo, Shambo," which is another name for Shiva. The sound beating from a hundred thousand throats mesmerizes me.

As the night rolls forward, serious dance music ratchets up. A band called Indian Ocean roars into the wee hours, and the night turns wilder and wilder. Finally, the house band, Sounds of Isha, comes on. A supernatural ecstasy permeates the tent. By this time we are on the chairs, gyrating madly, hands in the air. It goes on and on. Tribal. Primal. The Destroyer has demolished all inhibition. We are marionettes and the musicians pull the strings.

And then it ends. Six a.m. has arrived, and we have not slept or even wanted to. We file out of the great tent into the delicate morning air at the foothills of the White Mountains. Those rosy fingers of dawn creep over the mountains as we jostle our way onto the bus. No one is tired yet. We're all high, but we're not stoned. This may be what I've been looking for all my life.

I cannot describe the experience of a program like Samyama – the seven day silent meditation program created by Sadhguru. I won't even try. But I will say that for seven days I finally paid attention to myself and I discovered some things I had kept hidden in the storage chest of my head. I took a good, hard look at my marriage, and I realized that it had run its course. When I emerged, I was a subtly different person. I was free in a way I had not been before.

Before I leave the ashram, a large group of us takes a trek into the mountains. This is supposed to be the "easy" trek, the one for the ladies. I'm in fairly good shape, but I'm glad I didn't take the hard trek because that might just kill me. We walk through a village – a few small plaster houses with chickens and roosters strutting around dirt yards, curious children watching, incurious monkeys not watching, just swinging in the trees nearby. We climb along a steep path. We can smell elephant dung but we don't see elephants. The trek up takes a couple of hours of steady walking. We take periodic rests. We've been given a picnic lunch and we stop to munch an apple or raisins. Our goal is to reach a sacred cave where Sadhguru once meditated. How did he ever manage to find it, I wonder.

Then we reach the brook running down the mountain beside the cave. And I finally understand what is meant by the word paradise. The few men who are with us peel off and go down river. When they are out of sight, we women strip down to our bras and panties and jump into the freezing waters. Waterfalls shock our senses. The sunlight bends into blues and reds in the tiny drops. We lounge on the huge boulders and eat our lunches. And as we do so, thousands of butterflies of every color and design imaginable hover in the air and dart about. I feel like a kaleidoscope has broken over me. Pieces of sky and sun have come to life and are dancing before our eyes.

The next day I am flying home, back to my mundane life, and I'm feeling so grateful to my mother for insisting that I go on this adventure. I'm not sure if I'm any closer to enlightenment. I doubt it, but she was right: I would never regret this trip. My gratitude extends beyond my mother as well. Celina had promised not to have any emergencies while I was incommunicado, and she didn't. Even Hank contributed in his own way by vacating my life.

■

The day I get home, I drive over to The Sanctuary. When I walk inside I hear my mother playing improvisations on the piano. Unaware that I am watching, she drifts into that world where I can never follow except on the backs of the notes she plays. While I was in India, Sadhguru told us about a guru who became wise through loving attention to his elderly parents. I begin to realize that the years I gave to my mother were really a gift to me.

THREE

SPRING 2009

It may seem absurdly obvious to say that ending a 25-year marriage is not easy. But you never know until you try to do it. Sometimes I feel as if I am trying to amputate my own arm.

Since he left, Hank and I rarely communicate, but when we do, I feel like I'm in a Quentin Tarantino movie. One afternoon, we have it out. He's angry about everything, and his rage is like a sledge hammer, shattering my psyche. Me, I'm too tired to be angry. I'm tired of defending actions that I don't believe are wrong. But I pull out any ammunition I think I have. He pulls out his. We aim, fire. We take no prisoners. Finally, I tell him I can't talk to him anymore. I hang up the phone and refuse to think about what has just happened. I refuse to acknowledge the fact that my best friend is no longer that. I go to bed as if everything is the same as it ever was.

But in the morning, I find I cannot get out of bed. My blood has been replaced with some kind of thick sludge. I'm sure that glue has been affixed to my skin. I roll this way and that, but I am effectively paralyzed. What am I going to do, I wonder. I could reach for the phone, call a friend, and ask her to come help me get out of bed, but how would she get in the door? I ponder my situation. I am like a three-quarters dead woman. I will have to get up. I will have to go to the bathroom. I will have to eat something. It takes a long time, but eventually I push the lavender comforter off me, and I coax my recalcitrant body, my crushed spirit, my noodle spine into an erect position.

Without allowing myself to think, I move forward, stumble into the hall, into the bathroom, go through the morning motions, and then find I am downstairs where I fall into the couch, the same place where the phone call took place. And then I cry like a wounded animal. How long? I don't know. I crawl across the floor to the windows that look out upon the spring day. There are three of them – floor to ceiling windows. After five days of steady rain, the sun is beaming its godly face onto the brilliant wet green of the woods outside my window. And in the midst of this hellish pain I feel a warmth, a weird, totally inappropriate joy. The birds outside are going nuts. A woodpecker taps on the trees. Cardinals streak by like red comets. Blue jays are on the prowl, and a tiny yellow bird comes flitting over the back deck, and it occurs to me as the yellow bird flits past me that I'm going to be okay. I repeat the thought: I'm going to be okay. And the bird flits past me once again. So one more time, I say it – this time out loud.

"I'm going to be okay."

The bird flits by one more time.

I get the message. I know it will be hard as hell but I get it. I will be okay.

Still I can't help thinking of all the times I wasn't there for someone, a friend, when they may have been wounded. I think of how selfishly I live my life, wrapped up in my world of mothering, daughtering and writing. Okay, perhaps those aren't the most selfish activities. The point is that when my friends have been grieving I have not always recognized the depth of their pain. Sometimes it seems that it's only about me, my pain, my drama.

I vow right then that I will be more sensitive to the needs of others—and not just those who are related to me by blood. I stand up, feeling I have resolved something, my tears dried, a sense of having been washed ashore after a wicked storm.

■

I've been invited to give some workshops at the Tallahassee Writers Conference that April. I'm delighted. My university is paying to fly me down, and I'll have a chance to see my oldest and dearest friends in the college town I'll always consider home.

It's Tallahassee in the spring, and the azaleas are blooming. I stay with my friends Pam and Gary in their A-frame in the woods by a pond where otters occasionally visit. In some essential way Pam reminds me of my mother. It is her combination of kindness and wide-ranging intelligence. She knows books, art, cooking, movies, different cultures. And somehow she manages not to make other people feel stupid.

Other friends join us and we laugh and toast to nothing as we salivate over Pam's delicious dinner made with crushed mushrooms from her backyard.

The next day at the conference, I'm seated between two writers. They want to know what I've written lately. That's always the question.

"Not much," I answer. "I've been taking care of my elderly mother for the past few years. It's not so bad now that she's in assisted living, but still . . ."

I don't have to tell them. Soon both of them are weeping over their pasta primavera, talking about their fathers, how these men they loved got sick, what their mothers could or could not do, and the wrenching loss.

"Jesus," I say. "I'm so sorry." The three of us sit there, morosely recounting our parents' demises the way we once would have sat and gossiped about the boys we liked or later about our children.

The second day of the conference I find vendors in the lobby of the hotel selling hand-made soaps, imported clothing, and jewelry. I'm trying to conserve my cash and so I propel myself past the shiny objects, but a carousel of greeting cards lands a hook in me, and I stop to look at a card with a picture of a bright, blue butterfly on the front.

"I made the card from my photographs," the eager seller says.

I can't think of any reason I need this card, but I do like butterflies.

"How much?" I ask.

"Four dollars."

A lot for a card, but not much for a work of art. I buy the card.

The conference ends, and I leave, wondering what to do with my time. Pam and Gary are at the beach with friends from Scotland. I've already been down to the water the night before and had dinner with my friend Dean. We spent most of it talking about the death of his wife, our beloved poet Wendy Bishop. I remembered the love poems she had written for him, and how happy he was when they finally got together. I was sad that Dean had lost her, but also envious that he had gotten to know such unequivocal love. It seemed that Hank and I had always held something back from each other. What would it be like to give yourself wholly to another person the way Dean and Wendy had?

Since I've got some time, I decide I will go see Kitty's mother, Cathy. Kitty of breast cancer in 2001, and I try to visit Cathy whenever I am in Tallahassee. I think Cathy likes to have someone to talk with about Kitty.

To my surprise, Kitty's sister Martha, who lives in California, stands on the porch leaning against the wrought-iron trellis. Her red hair is pulled back from her thin, pretty face, and I can see shades of Kitty in her features.

"Mom is in the hospital," Martha says.

"Oh, I'm sorry to hear that." Martha and I have not always been on the best of terms, but today she treats me like an old friend.

"You don't know what happened, do you?" she asks after apologizing for her unfriendliness the last time we met.

I shake my head and follow her inside the red brick ranch house.

Through Kitty I had met Martha, but there was another sister that I'd never met. This sister, according to Martha, had swooped in one night with her husband, both of them in the military, and in a domestic coup they had deposed the matriarch of the house. They took her to a place that Martha described as a "locked ward" and cleaned out her house.

"They couldn't sell the house because unbeknownst to me, Mother had put it in my name as well as hers," Martha confides. By now we are sitting in the living room which had once been quite comfortable with overstuffed couches and chairs. Now Martha is perched on a spindly looking white settee, holding Cathy's poodle on her lap. Her eyes are weary, and her mouth held tight against a storm of betrayal.

"They destroyed all the books," she says and indicates the barren shelves. My God, I'm thinking, they were like Nazis getting ready for a book-burning. "And pried those antique mirrors off the wall." I see the two blank spots I hadn't noticed before.

This story seems incredible to me. How could someone do this?

"They took all the china and silver, too," Martha says. I get up and go into the dining room where once upon a time I ate blueberry pancakes with Kitty and her mother and Celina. I look in the china cabinet where I had often stopped to admire Cathy's collection. I liked those plates and cups and saucers so much because they were the same pattern that I had chosen when I was 17 and embarked on a misguided marital adventure with the heroin addict next door. The marriage ended soon after the wedding, but to this day I still own one beautiful blue and gold-trimmed plate.

The china cabinet is empty. I sit back down, stunned. Martha continues.

"They put her in a locked ward," she reiterates. "With crazy people screaming all night. She wasn't out of her mind. She knew exactly where she was. She called me every day and said if she didn't get out, she'd kill herself. I spent every cent I had on lawyers and finally got a court order to have her released. "

My disbelief turns into horror and sorrow.

"I don't remember meeting your other sister," I say to her. "Was she at Kitty's funeral?"

"No," Martha answers. "She took her kids to Disney World instead."

We sit quietly for a moment while I absorb that piece of information.

"Where is Cathy now?" I ask.

"In the cardiac intensive care unit at the hospital. Six months in that place broke her, Trish," she says.

"Will they let me see her?"

"Yes, she'd like to see you, I'm sure."

On the way to the hospital I think about getting some flowers but I don't want to take the time. Martha had mentioned that the doctors were talking about getting her into hospice, which was where we watched Kitty die. Then I remember the card in my briefcase.

■

I place the butterfly card on the rolling table at Cathy's bedside where she can look at it. She looks so frail, with her bruised arm and the bandage wrapped around the IV needle. It takes a moment for her to recognize me. I can tell the state of her health is not the best topic so I tell her about Celina.

"She's in college now, taking honors courses, and she has a cute little apartment near campus." Cathy's eyes light up.

"Oh, that's so wonderful," she says in her soft, lilting voice.

A nurse comes in to draw blood. He's gentle and friendly. Cathy seems tired, and I'm not sure how long I should stay. I clasp her hand. Her hair is a white crown surrounding her lovely face. Kitty always said, "Isn't she precious?"

Yes, I'm thinking now, our precious mothers.

■

Before I leave Tallahassee, a few of us go over to our friend Joe's house, which is tucked under enormous Spanish-moss laden live oaks. I've known Joe since graduate school, where he was admired for his dry wit and whiskey. I remember his wedding. I even remember scouring the local antique stores for a wedding present and finding a soup tureen that seemed like a weird enough gift to give the two coolest people I knew. We hadn't seen each other much over the years and so I had only just recently learned that Joe's wife left him about a week before Hank got on that train to California. We commiserate a bit about how odd it is to be suddenly single after years of marriage.

Lately, I'm wondering if I'll ever be attractive to anyone again. A sociologist named Sara Lawrence-Lightfoot describes the years between 50 and 75 as the third chapter. She says these years are transformative and regenerative, a time for passion, risk, and adventure. But to me, it's looking scary and sad. It's looking like years of going to bed at 9:30 with a book and my cat. It's looking like maybe being alone and sometimes screaming out loud just to see if anyone hears.

Everyone but me is drinking wine, but I might as well be drunk as I show off the scar from my surgery. I've become rather proud of my brief fling with cancer, and my friends are dutifully impressed. Then we're winding down. Gary, Amy, and Mark are talking music. Pam falls asleep on the couch. I am sitting on the other end of the couch bundled up in a paisley blanket. When I look up, Joe is smiling at me, and it occurs to me that the third chapter of my life might not be so bleak after all.

FOUR

Back in Charlotte, I sit at the Caribou coffee shop with my friends for our biweekly writer's get-together. As we're waiting for everyone to arrive and eat a quick lunch, I notice Tamara's big, boxy emerald ring with two diamonds on either side.

"Wow, that's beautiful," I remark.

"Thank you," she says. "It's my engagement ring. I love emeralds." Tamara's husband is a doctor and makes a pretty decent salary – a lot of which gets donated to various causes that Tamara believes in, but I guess he gets to spoil her a little when she'll let him.

"I gave Celina an emerald ring for Christmas a couple years ago," I tell her. I had bought it at the jewelry store in this same shopping center.

"That's right," she says. "I remember that."

"She lost it," I say. We both laugh. Celina is notorious for being unable to hold on to things – her cell phone which she left at a bus stop in the Bronx, her lilac winter coat (brand new) that she left in a Taco Bell when she was 11, her backpack and keys in high school. The list is long.

"Someday," Tamara says. "You should give her a map with a red pinpoint of everywhere she's lost something."

After I leave the coffee shop, I head over to The Sanctuary to see Mom. The manager takes me aside as soon as I walk in. I'm worried he's going to tell me that they've decided to raise her rent. But instead he asks if I've heard that Mom has lost her ring. My heart sinks. It's a beautiful amethyst ring in a big gold setting that my brother David gave her. How could she have been so careless, I wonder. She knows that there are always people around who will lift what you leave behind. She never locks her apartment, of course, and has even complained that people come in and take her cookies, which I'm pretty sure doesn't happen. Still, it would seem if she thinks there are cookie thieves out there, she would surely guard the one thing she has of any value.

When I find my mother in her room, she's distraught. I do an exhaustive search, but no ring. Overall, I'm pretty sure the employees here are an honest bunch, but the economy is bad right now and one of them might have been unable to resist the temptation or maybe my mother managed to drop it in such an obscure place it will never again be found. Regardless, she's going to have to suck it up.

"Let it go, Mom," I tell her. "There are worse things than losing a ring."

"I just feel so guilty," she says.

"Please don't. It happens," I say. I want to chastise her the way I chastise the forever-losing-something Celina, but it serves no more purpose than her purposeless guilt.

I push her wheelchair outside and we sit on the little patio area in the sun, facing the parking lot. I relish the spring sunshine and this moment free from grief and worry. I am filled with gratitude and not a little relief that I can be here with her today, and because today the worst thing that has happened to us is the loss of a ring.

Celina comes home from college for a short visit. I was thinking we'd spread out the comforters in front of the TV and get
reacquainted with Woody Allen. But she can't stay for a second
night. She has four papers to write and decides to go back to
school to finish them. It has begun to happen. This house is
more storage, more of a way station for her. In a different course
of events, Hank and I would be rekindling our love life about
now. I would not be living in this big empty house alone without
even a dog. But Hank is gone, Merlyn is dead, and my next new
ship hasn't come sailing over the horizon.

So instead of watching Woody Allen, I'm visiting my mom.
When I walk in her room, she's got a helpless look on her face.
She's just rung her pendant for someone to come help her get to
the bathroom.

"I'll help you, Mom," I say. As often happens she has a big
wet spot on the back of her dress. So I help her change into
something else.

Mom is in good spirits today. She doesn't complain of pain.
I wheel her into the courtyard where we slowly circumnavigate,
stopping to admire the flowers. She's always liked flowers, but
now she seems to derive a special delight in them.

After we've toured the small courtyard, I park her wheelchair
catty-corner to one of the mesh chairs and sit down. I tell her
about a movie I've recently seen. She likes to hear about what's
going on out there, but it doesn't hold her interest for long. Soon
her conversation veers to the past.

Somehow we get on the topic of "The War." Both of her
brothers served. Bob went out and shot a rabbit before enlisting
and realized he simply couldn't kill a person, so he joined the

Merchant Marines. Dave was in the Navy and served in the Pacific. He made one cryptic and pained comment that Mother never forgot: "All the terrible things that they say the Japanese did to us are true. But we were no better to them."

"Daddy never served in the military," I say.

"No, he got out of it because of his eyes," she replies.

"So after Yale, the two of you went to Vermont?"

"Yes," she says and smiles. Her teeth are stained yellow, but she still has a great smile. "Vermont was wonderful." She has told me many stories of the boys' school where my father taught right after college. They had no electricity and the winters were brutal. But she loved the adventure of it.

"Driving up there, I saw a house with smoke pouring out of it, and I thought it was on fire. I told him we had to stop and help whoever was inside, but he just drove on and said, 'Oh, those people know what they are doing.' I was so frustrated, but he was right. It was some sort of cooking house for the maple syrup."

She has often told me that my father was the only man she ever loved. I hope this is not a genetic disorder. I hope that Hank will not be the one great love of my life.

"It must been a culture shock when you wound up in Jacksonville."

"That's right," she says. "At the time there were still separate water fountains, marked white and colored." She pauses and then remembers. "We had some friends who were black. Musicians."

"Mitch and Ruff?" I ask. I have a book about them and remember hearing that my parents knew them – jazz musicians from the south.

"It's possible. Anyway, they were on tour, and we had them over for dinner. I distinctly remember having to pull down the shades so we wouldn't wake up with a cross burning in our yard. It was a scary time." She pauses again, remembering. "I'm sure I've told you about the trip we took up north with our colored maid."

She has, but I don't stop her from telling it again.

"We had to bring food out to her in the car when we were in the south because they wouldn't let her eat inside the restaurants where we stopped. I felt awful. I couldn't let her go hungry, or put her through that humiliation."

The lines were clear cut in the south during the 50s and 60s. My mother was berated by her neighbors in Spartanburg for paying her maid too much. One time she tried to sit down and eat lunch with "the help," and the woman immediately got up and said that wasn't the way things were done. We weren't the sort of people to always have a maid. But she was a working woman with two young boys and it wasn't abnormal to hire help. They didn't have daycare back then.

"It's quite different now. We've seen such a big change in our lifetime," she says. It's true but I can't help but notice that most of the CNAs (certified nursing assistants) here and at the nursing homes we've been to are women of color, and most (though not all) of the residents and the supervisors are white. My favorite care givers at The Sanctuary are Charlene and Lam. They've shown me that the work they do, which I thought was hard and demeaning, is as rewarding as anything I do.

"You learn so much from the residents," Lam once told me.

"Not everybody can do this kind of work," Charlene informed me on another occasion. "It takes a lot of love. You have to love these people."

The conversation with my mother changes course.

"I've always wanted to write something, and I think I should write my autobiography. Not for publication but because the grandchildren might be interested someday," she says. This is a familiar path. Just do it, I always tell her, and a few scraps get written here or there. Then she begins again, "The worst piece of advice I ever got . . ."

I know exactly where this is leading. This is one of her dominant themes. Her mother told her not to bother to learn how to type because "you'll always have someone to type for you." Eventually my mother did type on a computer but never with any confidence. It's no wonder that the summer after my eighth-grade year, my mother signed me up for typing lessons at Jones Business College. I was the youngest in the class and not very good at it, but I learned how to type passably well. Later when I took typing in high school, I still wasn't very fast and I could never do it without errors. The "quick brown fox" was often a "wuck brown foz." But my mother's insistence that I learn to type was prescient, I suppose. We had no way of knowing that one day these magic machines would be invented and it wouldn't matter how many errors I made.

At around 5:45 Mom starts to get anxious. Dinnertime is six, and she is never, ever late for dinner. At five minutes till six, I wheel her into the dining room. While Mom is eating, I get into a long conversation with Charlene. Charlene tells me she started working with the elderly when she was sixteen years old. She's my age now. Her eyes are so bright they dazzle.

"Why do you do it?" I ask her.

"I love being able to take care of somebody who can't do for themselves," she says.

It's true that when Charlene is on my mom's floor, Mom's care is impeccable. Lam joins us and the three of us hang out for a bit in the library, chatting.

One thing I've been curious about is how much the CNAs make. I remember a technician at the hospital telling me she couldn't survive on her paycheck. And it rankles me that these people who work so incredibly hard don't get paid what they should.

"How much would someone make as a CNA just starting out?" I ask.

"Starting out maybe $8.50 an hour. People with more experience can make about $12 an hour," Lam says.

"Do you get benefits?"

"Benefits are offered, but they're too expensive," Lam says.

"So you don't have health insurance?"

Lam shakes her head.

"It's a lot better up north," Lam says. "The health insurance is good up there. Here it just costs too much."

At this point, my mother wheels herself into the library.

"Still I love this job," Lam says.

"Me, too," Charlene agrees. "These people are so interesting. Your mother told me all about working with Andy Griffith. And she said Aunt Bee isn't really as nice as she seems on TV. Ain't that right, Roz?"

"Oh, stay away from Aunt Bee," my mother says. Charlene bursts out laughing.

■

In early June the management at The Sanctuary sends me a letter saying they are going to raise her rent by a thousand dollars a month. In truth that would be about in line with what any other place would charge, but we cannot afford it. I panic. I can move in her with me for the summer and cancel any plans for travel – or sleep. Then I can move her to my brother's house in

St. Louis, and he and his girlfriend can try to take care of her. But I don't want to move her. She's found some semblance of stability here, if not necessarily happiness. There are always people about. She plays the piano, Scrabble and bingo. A couple of days after the letter, the director calls me and makes a deal. He'll raise the rent by $200. I figure I'll just have to work more. I'll have to come up with it.

But I have other money troubles. Over the years I used my mother's credit card to pay for some of the bigger things she needed that I couldn't quite manage – the lift chair, some hospital bills, medicine whenever the Medicare gap hit and the drug costs skyrocketed. I dutifully paid the minimum each month, but you know how credit cards work. You can pay and pay and never pay it off. At some point the low-interest period was over and boom, the minimum was beyond my reach. So I stopped paying it. Now, they've tracked me down. The truth is, I don't have to pay this. The credit card is not in my name, and they can't squeeze any money out of my mom. But I have this bad feeling about letting her die in debt. So when they offer me a fairly reasonable payoff deal, I accept. It makes things tight as hell and there's plenty of other things I'd like to do with that money, like start my own retirement account, but I agree to pony up.

■

I don't have any teaching work during the summer, and Celina is taking summer classes to make up for missing the fall term. I spend huge chunks of my time alone. I believe this is good for me. Time for a slow settling of all the upheavals of the past. I do my yoga every morning outside on the deck with a flock of leafy trees for company. I listen to Vivaldi and Bach. It feels as if my spirit is reconnecting the wires that got loose or ripped off in the storms. I am getting reacquainted with myself.

I also spend time with my mother, and I begin to catalog what happens when your parent grows old. I sit with her in the courtyard and search her face as she explains to me once again the beauty of her recent circumstances is that she doesn't have to worry about food – no preparing, no cleaning. It's just there. This is a marvelous thing. She says this often. Very often. As I listen to her, I'm trying to remember the woman I once knew and I'm angry with myself that I didn't know her better. I look back and see how we ignored her aging. She was always the same, and then she wasn't.

At home I look at my own face. I barely recognize it. Those lines on my forehead can't belong to me. And what is that? A shadow? Some kind of strange lumpy formation on my forehead? I rub extra virgin olive oil into my skin, trying to lubricate it. Who the hell are you, I ask my reflection. I've heard that our cells replace themselves every seven years. Like my mother I am not the person I used to be. My cells are different. I don't know my own face. When I look at it, I usually see what I've always seen – not what is really there.

One evening I find my mother in the courtyard with four other residents. One of the women is my age. She has early onset Alzheimer's. She's very sweet and often visits with my mother, but my mother says, "She's not very bright." The poor woman can't remember anything. The women in the courtyard are all listening to a woman with a heavy French accent. Her name is Jacqueline. She has thinning red hair and an interesting ruddy face full of character.

"It was June," she is saying, "June of 1944. And the Germans had taken all of the grand hotels and turned them into hospitals. We were students at the time and the Red Cross advertised for help. Well, school was out so we thought it would be a good idea."

She tells us about the German nurse yelling at her: "Oust! Oust!" and finding an amputated leg covered in maggots in the bathroom. She tells us about the handsome American G.I. she met after the war. How he managed to find her house although all the street signs and landmarks were gone. How she married him.

"I was very thin because we had no food most of the time," she says. "Oh, I was lovely." She laughs.

Like Lam says, you can learn a lot from these people.

FIVE

Celina gets a phone call from her landlord Tuesday morning, saying that they've found a renter for her apartment in Greensboro. If we can clean out the apartment that day we won't have to pay rent for July. Hallelujah, I think. She won't be returning since she's transferred to another university about forty miles away.

I borrow a truck from a guy I know and then we head up the highway for the two-hour drive to her apartment. When we walk in, my spirits drop. She's done nothing as far as packing and I'd forgotten just how much stuff she has accumulated in a few months.

"There's no way we're gonna do this in one trip," I say. "No way."

"Yes, we will," Celina says. Right-brainers like Celina are better at spatial visualization than linear thinkers like me.

While she goes to the courthouse to try to keep herself off death row for the heinous crime of making an illegal left turn, I start packing. Celina is supposed to bring a sheet of paper proving she had undergone some driver education, but of course that piece of paper is in the glove compartment of her car, which is sitting in Shawn's driveway.

"Are they gonna send me to jail?" Celina asks.

"Maybe," I answer. "But probably not. Just ask for a new court date."

I am halfway through Celina's closet when the cell phone in my pocket begins to vibrate, causing me to jump.

"They gave me a new date," Celina whines, "but it's when I'm going to be in New York."

"Why didn't you tell them that date wouldn't work?"

"Because that woman is mean and scary!"

"Oh, sweetheart, this is all the power that woman has. Just find someone to give you a new court date."

Thirty minutes later, I have most of the kitchen done. My phone vibrates again.

"Mom, they told me to get a lawyer!"

Jesus, this is going to be the most expensive left turn in history.

"Did you talk to the scary woman?"

"No."

"Go back and talk to the scary woman, babe."

An hour later Celina is back with a new court date, and I'm trying to figure out how to open the back of Shawn's truck.

"That woman looked at me like I was a child murderer," Celina says.

Celina manages to get that truck filled to the brim. All the while her piano-playing next-door neighbor Julian smokes cigarettes on the porch and watches mournfully.

"Julian, help yourself to anything in the refrigerator," I tell him. He does. Then we sweep and mop and throw away bags and bags of stuff. Sweating, aching, and exhausted, we start the drive home. Celina topples over and sleeps while I enjoy the tunes on Shawn's satellite radio, looking down on the little cars from my rumbling throne.

Shawn calls me about halfway through the trip home and says he needs the truck early the next morning. He tells me he'll help us unload it tonight.

"Great, Shawn. Thank you so much," I tell him even though I've been planning to go to bed and unload tomorrow. "I'll pick you up in about an hour."

"Noooo," Celina moans.

We pull into my driveway about 11:30, and the three of us unload that truck into the garage in about 20 minutes flat. The back of the truck is empty.

I stare at that great empty space that just a few minutes earlier had housed a love seat, day bed, two bookcases, five or so suitcases, two boxes of kitchen items, a record player, two big bags of nonperishables, comforters, sheets, towels, everything except the garbage can and the shower curtain. We left those things behind.

I think of the empty truck as a metaphor for my life, which was so recently overflowing and now is not. Now more than ever, I understand my mother's deep well of loneliness. It's my loneliness, too. I'm all she has, really. And in a sense, she is all I have, too.

■

An idea has been tunneling through my head. As Celina and I prepare for our annual trip to Florida, the idea begins scratching at the door.

Thursday morning we do our last minute errands. Celina makes CD mixes for the car ride. Our road trip music must be perfectly calibrated in order for the trip to be a success. I'm trying to complete a few loose ends on a freelance project. Also I decide to dye my hair at the last minute, pay some bills and write down instructions for the neighbor girls about taking care of the cat who now requires fish oil and some kind of paste for cat-viruses added to her food to stop the damn sneezing.

After this we have to return a movie, go to the bank, get gas, and stop by The Sanctuary to pay Mother's rent and hairdresser bill. And I have to reassure her that I'm not going to be gone forever. The night before we stopped by to see her on our way to see the touring version of *Phantom of the Opera* because one of Celina's friends was a dancer in the show. And I was feeling a little guilty because I hadn't been a frequent visitor this week.

So that night when we went to see Mom she was still eating dinner. Her hearing had gone almost completely from her left ear. She took a few bites of her dessert and then we paraded into the lobby. She seemed more distressed than usual, probably be-cause we were going away for a few days. When we explained we had moved Celina out of her apartment the day before, she wanted to know where we would be staying tonight.

"Um, at my house," I said.

■

On Thursday when we come by, she is much more lucid.

"You're going to Jacksonville?" she says. "I really would like to hear the organ again." She means the organ at Good Shep-herd. Her organ. Though not hers anymore.

The idea grows a little bigger.

Finally we are on the road, heading south, where the air will be thick and soft, the trees juicy, the sun harsh and the sleeping arrangements questionable.

As soon as we cross the Florida border, Celina slams the R.E.M. CD into the CD player and we stick our hands outside to feel the silky sheets of air running through our fingers.

Thursday night we pull into the driveway behind Jim and Dale's house. The back door opens and my lean, handsome 74-year-old godfather comes out to greet us. If my own father represents everything dark and heedless in the masculine, my godfather represents all that is bright and good. He is the quintessential white knight – gentle, strong, funny and wise. Like my father, he once succumbed to his generation's penchant for three-martini lunches and after-work cocktails. Unlike my father who continued to drink and bluster in his egomaniacal manner until that fine mind of which he was so proud was drained and all that was left was a jumble of fears and odd compulsions, Jim turned in humility to the 12-steps long before he destroyed the lives of the ones he loved. A die-hard liberal, a baritone in the church choir, a banker who helped small businesses get loans, he became my godfather when I was six years old and realized that I had not been baptized as a baby. After all, the church was our second home, and if I wasn't baptized I couldn't get confirmed with everyone else and go to communion and have the priest deliver the bitter tasting wine onto my young tongue to wash down the papery wafer that was poor Jesus' desiccated body.

So my mother said I could choose my own godparents. I chose wisely at the age of six. My two godparents took their roles quite seriously. While my godmother Elise loved me and fawned over me while I was young, my godfather Jim was the stalwart figure in the background of my life who emerged in my later years as the salve to heal my father issues once and for all. Every time he said that he loved me or spoke admiringly of some accomplishment of mine, an old hurt disappeared. Though he is not technically my father and there are four people who can lay legitimate claim to him, in my head and heart he has replaced that bitter old man who ignored my existence, who belittled my mother, and who engaged in fistfights with the husbands of his lovers.

So Thursday night we are in the Florida room of Jim and Dale's house, Jim sitting in a chair by the stereo system, Dale at the other end of the small room, and Celina and I on the couch in the middle, scarfing up potato chips and clam dip. I mention to Jim that my mother has said several times that she wanted to hear the church organ again.

"Do you think it would be possible," I ask, hesitantly, "for someone to do her Requiem again?"

I can see the thought registering. His clear blue eyes light up. Soon we are figuring out whom to contact. Jim digs through his old cassettes. He finds the original recording of the Requiem when it was performed back in 1982. After some fast-forwarding and rewinding, he manages to get it to play. I am stunned. First of all, I recognize it. But what I hadn't realized until now is just how really wonderful a piece of music it is. Powerful and strange and haunting.

"The times have caught up with it," Jim says with a gentle smile playing on his lips.

"You're right," I say.

An American Requiem's time has come.

■

In late July, my brothers Jo and David arrive like a couple of Viking warriors. Jo shows up Tuesday around midnight with his drum and his flutes. We spend the next day with Mom and then on Thursday we all pile into my car to go to the airport to retrieve David. But Thursday is not a good day for me. These days happen. I wake up tired and cranky, off kilter. I don't know what it is. It's like having bipolar energy levels though not so extreme.

How do I explain myself on these days? Usually I don't. Usually, I hunker down and wait it out. It only takes a day and then I'm okay again, but for that day I can't think, can't pretend to be friendly, outgoing, and happy.

When we get to Mom's place, David tells me he hasn't brought the movie.

"What?" I wheel around, my cranky shrew level ratcheted up ten knots. Mostly I'm annoyed with myself for not reminding him to bring it. There is much buzz at The Sanctuary about the movie event: David is going to be showing "Knights of the South Bronx," an A&E movie starring Ted Danson that is actually about David's work teaching chess to children at a school in the poorest congressional district in the country. The activities director has been asking for months for a copy and I've provided something better—David in person. But now we don't have a movie.

"Where are we going to get it?" I ask in full tilt whine.

"Netflix?" David asks.

I decide to calm down. Getting upset is taking way too much energy, and it turns out they have the movie at Blockbuster.

The three of us eat dinner with Mother at The Sanctuary. The food isn't bad. In fact, she never complains about it. Then we go upstairs to the media room. Not for David's movie. That's not until Friday night. But Jo has brought a copy of a video recording from the 1980s of a performance of "An American Requiem" by the Lost Colony Choir. I've told him about my plan to resurrect the Requiem, and he's all for it. In fact, somewhere he's got the orchestration for it, and he promises to find it.

The four of us commandeer the media room and Charlene helps us figure out how to get the video started. She stays to watch with us for a while. I close the curtains to shut out the light and on the large screen comes a picture of a choir as they begin to sing, "Requiem." Rest. My mother's Requiem uses the Latin words and mixes them with English. It begins, "Requiem æternam dona eis, Domine." Meaning "Grant them eternal rest, O Lord." Is that what death is? Eternal rest?

My two brothers are riveted. Here it is, our mother's masterwork. Mom falls asleep. She doesn't really care that much anymore. I gaze over at the three of them in profile. Jo's head punctuates the musical score. He is, after all, conducting the piece in the video. David holds his chin and thoughtfully gazes at the screen. Mother's chin rests on her chest. Three pairs of eyeglasses reflect the flickering light of the screen. And I am watching them, as always. They are the musicians. I'm the one trying to tell the story.

Before we leave The Sanctuary, David and Jo want to hear Mom play the piano. No one else is around. Th place is like a mausoleum at night. So we have the parlor to ourselves. I am still wanting a little requiem myself so I stretch out on the couch and shut my eyes. Mother plays "The Moonlight Sonata." God, it's beautiful. She doesn't finish it. I don't think she remembers the whole thing. She tries to play other pieces with that amazing manual dexterity she once had, but the speed is gone.

"Slow down," David says. "You don't have to play it fast. You know that skater Peggy Fleming? She never had the technique of other skaters but she had so much grace that they couldn't hold a candle to her."

David convinces Mother to play one of Bach's Inventions very slowly, and the effect, I must say, is haunting. David and Jo fawn over Mother in a way I never do. But they understand music better than I do. They talk about her musicality. She has something that not many people have. And I'm remembering someone once saying they knew the instant when my mother took over from another accompanist. Suddenly the beat was exactly there, where it was supposed to be. But to me her piano playing is like air – just always there, always a part of my world. I'm afraid that after she dies there are certain pieces of music I'll never be able to listen to again. Goodbye, "Moonlight Sonata."

Afterwards, we leave mother with promises to return the next day before lunch. We have to see about getting her $3,500 bed that David bought three years ago fixed. You'd think a bed that cost that much would hold up longer than three years, but it has gotten stuck in the head up position and won't move, so it is useless. The staff at The Sanctuary is worried that Mother will get open wounds from the constant pressure on her back and buttocks from always sitting. Mother, on the other hand, doesn't even want to sleep on the bed. Her recliner feels more secure. But we have no choice. The bed must be fixed or gotten rid of.

(I know a woman who works for an HMO. She didn't really want to take the job because an HMO's reputation is about as good as the CIA's when it comes to people's rights. But she has been able to do good there. She told me one story of an elderly woman who had no family and nowhere to go. The woman was in a nursing home where she developed open wounds that simply couldn't be healed. My friend signed lifelong hospitalization for the woman. "We had to. I insisted. She had no family. This was the only way she'd be taken care of." Well, there was one answer to my nagging question – what happens to people with no money and no family. They wind up with open wounds in a hospital bed or nursing home for the rest of their lives.)

My brothers and I go back to my house where we stay up late into the night and talk about spiritual experiences we've had. This is a conversation I've never had with David who is so rational he makes Mr. Spock look giddy. But it seems almost everyone has had some experience that involves something more than our five meager senses. Jo talks about the experiences he's had with sweat lodges and the time it got so hot he became like a crazed animal and rushed outside, followed by about nine other people. David mentions a reiki session he had and visions that seemed to have come from past lives, visions of being killed and then morphing into the killer. I talk about those moments I've had of perfect awareness like the time we were playing dodge ball at my first Isha workshop and no one could hit me.

■

Friday night we show "The Knights of the South Bronx" in the media room at The Sanctuary. By the time the movie starts, we have a full house including two of my colleagues from school, Darryl and Bill. Everyone in the room is transfixed by the movie. Tears slowly leak from my eyes somewhere near the beginning and continue to flow all the way to the end. I remember when they held the premiere for the movie in New York at the Fashion Institute of Technology School. David flew Mom, Celina, and me up to see it. This was in December of 2005, and Mom was a little more mobile and a lot more awake than she is these days. David also got us a hotel room since the one other time I'd brought her up to New York for a Thanksgiving visit she went berserk with claustrophobia in his apartment. But this trip would be a triumph for my mother. Ted Danson may have been the star of the movie, but David's star was shining just as bright that night. It was his success and the success of the children he worked with that we were all celebrating. After eight years of long hard work, paying for tournaments out of his own pocket, buying the kids food and clothes when they didn't have any, he saw his kids earn the national championship and a trip to the

White House. The movie is a fictional documentation of that feat, and David has a cameo role.

Unfortunately, the theater was down a long set of winding steps and I didn't know how I'd get Mother down them. Someone who worked there volunteered to take her by wheelchair down the elevator and through the kitchen. I reluctantly let the person take the wheelchair from me, and Celina and I went downstairs where a huge crowd of people milled around. Ted Danson was there. People from the chess world were there. David's ex-wife and current girlfriend were there along with his two kids. I kept looking around for my mother, who had vanished. I waited. I looked. I went back upstairs. I found the elevator. I took the elevator. I wandered through the kitchen. I went back into the party area. My mother was not anywhere. Panic set in. Was she freaking out somewhere? Alone in a hallway, screaming right about now? I clawed my way through the crowd and finally got my hands on my brother.

"I can't find Mom," I said breathlessly.

David swiveled his head in all directions before being seized upon by someone else and dragged off to make another speech. I began my search once again. And then finally she just showed up, smiling and thrilled to be here, basking in the attention. David's mother. "Yes, he was always wonderful," she told everyone. I wiped the sweat from my brow and proceeded to enjoy the rest of the evening.

Tonight I am crying as I watch the movie again, but Mom doesn't watch it. Her head drifts down toward her chest. At one point in the movie, she screams. I suppose she dreams she is falling when that happens. She jolts awake and has no idea where she is. Jo reaches over and reassures her. The rest of us continue to watch the movie.

Afterwards, David and Jo and I and my mother and Jacqueline, the 85-year-old French woman, and Bill and Darryl sit in a circle and talk politics. We can't believe the W years are finally over.

"I refuse to remember them," I say. "It's like they never happened."

Mother then pipes up, "I went to Yale, you know," she begins and I'm thinking, here she goes again with the Yale thing, which didn't matter so much in the old days but now it's her claim to former greatness. But then she cracks everyone up when she adds, "But after Bush became president, I thought about returning the degree."

■

At The Sanctuary the next day Jo performs a concert of Native American flute music. He explains he got interested in the Native American flute when our mother needed some authentic music for "The Lost Colony." When he couldn't find a performer, he learned the instrument and recorded the music for the show himself. Ever since then he's been hooked on it. Jo intersperses his music with stories from Native American lore and from his own life. I'm sure these people have never heard of a sweat lodge and cannot imagine anyone playing a song on a flute for "Brother Rock," but Jo's music casts a spell over them.

We spend the rest of the day with my mother, but she has become sour and unhappy. I think it's been too much for her. Too much stimulation. Too much attention, for once. Instead of eating at The Sanctuary David and I go get Thai food and bring it back. But Mom hates the seafood salad we get for her and frowns and acts like she is being tortured until the cook sends over some chocolate cream pie that the rest of us find inedible and she gobbles up. Then Jo fixes her some coffee and ice cream and she gets happier. But the pain in her leg has become her main focus, and so we take her upstairs where I put down some hot soapy water for a foot soak for her. Then finally the night comes to an end. And we leave. The whirlwind tour is almost over.

■

I wheel Mom outside to the parking lot, following my two brothers. Jo is a big guy, his feet damaged by the chemo treatments of nearly 20 years ago. David is lithe and quick-moving as if he's always trying to catch the subway. His vertigo is hidden in the canal of his inner ear. They are both still handsome to me – Jo with his nicely trimmed beard, bushy eyebrows, hair in a ponytail. He looks like a happy Buddha, but you'd never mistake that happiness for simpleness. He'll raise an eyebrow and shoot you with his green eyes. David is not one to show anger, the cool and collected chess player, except on rare occasions and then, don't fuck with him.

I push Mom into the shade of a truck, and we watch as Jo checks the oil in his Honda. There is always the sound of conversation when my brothers are present. They are not laconic in the least. They are full of jokes and stories. This time Jo is talking about this car and how he bought it for a thousand bucks from a friend of his and it still runs like a dream even as it edges up to the 300,000 mile mark. He never drives it over 63 miles per hour.

Before they leave, each one of them leans over to hug Mom in her wheelchair, and although I've already hugged them goodbye, I insist on one more embrace from each of them. David, who was born under the sign of Leo, makes a little growling purr when he hugs. Jo's hug is all bear.

But as they pull out of the parking lot, and we roll over to the rocking chairs in the shade, I realize that this is an old familiar feeling: my brothers leaving to go on an adventure while my mother and I stay behind. It occurs to me that this moment's sorrow is a replica of the sorrow we felt forty years ago. And now that I've felt the grief of my own child leaving, I can only imagine how it was for my mother when her two boys became men and packed up their instruments – Jo with his tuba off to the Eastman School of Music, and David with his trombone to the Navy Band.

I have always been aware of how deeply I missed them, how I longed for each return visit, greedy for every minute I could spend with them. But I've never really considered how that must have been for my mother to lose these two laughing, joking, story-telling heroes. Not only sons but fellow musicians. It seems a shadow swept across our lives at that time, and although we eventually grew used to their absence, that lonely darkness would return now and again. Sometimes back in Edenton and even at The Landings, I couldn't wait to flee her presence and the oppressive sense of misery that engulfed me. Here at The Sanctuary, surrounded by other people, it can't seem to get to us. Until today, as we sit together in the shade while birds zoom around us. I don't want to go home. And I realize that the worst thing about her life must be the empty days. There is nothing she has to do. No errands to run. No projects to finish. The enormity of that vast emptiness swallows me.

I am despondent for days, but my new obsession eventually drives out the despondency. I take one of the old battered copies of "An American Requiem" over to Kinko's and make a fresh new copy and put it in a bright red folder. Then I mail it to

Mom's friend Karen in Jacksonville. Jim has enlisted her help for getting the production underway. So far we've had no luck finding a choir, but Karen has a hot lead; an old friend of Mom's happens to direct the choir at a college in Jacksonville. I'm not sure this is really going to happen, but maybe it will, and maybe this way I can fulfill that promise I made to my mother to keep it alive

■

Celina comes home from New York, and the rain is falling just like it did on the day when she was born, ending the long drought that had gripped Florida for months.

"Tell me about your workshop," I say. I want to hear everything. I was disappointed I hadn't been able to go up and see her performance of Antigone. Antigone is another of my favorite Greek plays. I admire the way she defies Creon when he orders her not to bury her brother. And, of course, it resonates with our situation.

For Celina's production, the actors each began by describing how they wanted their own deaths to be recognized.

"I said that I wanted my life to be celebrated and that I wanted my ashes to be scattered on the beach in Florida because that is where your friends all made their wishes for me."

The wishes! She remembered the story of the wishes and remembered my telling her about that evening in the summer of 1990 when she was a tiny infant. Four of my women friends and I took her to the beach, and in the light of the moon we sprinkled ocean water on her forehead and spoke aloud our wishes for her future. I don't even remember what we wished, but I have a feeling they have all come true.

Then on August, 3, 2009, with Celina at her new house in Chapel Hill, getting ready for her new college, I realize my 19-year project is complete. I'll always be Celina's mother. I will be around for advice and to help pay the rent. But my parental goal has been accomplished. She has gotten into a great college; found a house and negotiated with roommates, realtors and landlords; registered for classes, and found a job – all without any help from me. That was the aim – for her to become a self-sufficient adult, able to make her own decisions and manage her own life. My job is effectively over.

I go to my mother's place to play a long game of Scrabble.

SIX

My heart has been a lonely hunter, searching for something this long, empty summer. When Celina is with me, we are a couple of merry pranksters, but when she's gone I might as well be on the moon. It's cold and barren. Should I get another dog, I wonder. A bird? Or a hobby? I need to learn a musical instrument, the cello maybe. I tried pottery earlier in the year. That was good for a while, but it's not enough. Visiting my mother occupies me, but there's only so much time I can spend with the old folks. I walk. A lot. And sometimes that's enough. Sometimes it isn't. Hank and I are no longer screaming at each other on the phone. Silence stretches between us like the desert.

Then one day an email pops up. A desperate plea: "Help. I'm losing my apartment. I'm going to have to live in a shelter or in my truck. I'm disabled and I lost my job, but I can pet sit. Please, if you need someone to take care of your pets, let me know."

"Who are you?" I typed.

"Lorri. A friend of Colin's."

My friend Colin had forwarded the email to everyone on his list, and I was the one who responded. Darryl is going to Paris and needs someone to look after his German Shepherd, so I set them up. Three weeks later, Lorri moves in with me. During the day we sit outside on my front porch with our laptops and work.

Lorri, it turns out, can make websites, and I happen to need a new website. We like the same TV shows. We make salads every day and drink smoothies. I decide not to get a bird right now. The cello can also wait.

■

I want to get away. Mom seems to be fairly stable. School doesn't start for a couple of weeks. Celina is happy and working at a bookstore, waiting for the semester to begin. As far as I can tell, Hank has no intention of returning, and I don't know what to do about the back of the house where he ripped off the rotted siding but didn't replace it. The master bathroom has no shower now and a hole in the ceiling. I don't have the money to fix it. Now seems like a good time to get out of town. Lorri can take care of the cat while I'm gone and even go check on my mother once in a while.

So I head down to Tallahassee where I fill my time, drinking decaf at the Black Dog Cafe, eating lunch at Cabo's, hanging out with friends, catching up on stories. I visit Joe, eat French cheese at Pam's, and buy Celina some fabric from an imported clothing store.

Thursday afternoon I need to go see Dean, the hermit. I love the beach house where he used to live with Wendy. It's still a shrine to her with her books displayed on the living room shelves, and pictures of the two of them. Dean and I walk the beach, talking of sea turtles, guitars, old friends.

"Tell me the name of those again," I say, pointing to tiny clams that disappear bottoms up in the brown wet sand.

"Donax," he says.

"That's right," I say and laugh. "I always want to say 'gonads'." I'm sure that Wendy once wrote a poem about them.

Returning to the thin arm of sand, stretched before the low beach house, Dean sits on the towel while I wade into warm water, my joy meter ticking upwards as the waves canter toward me. And I dive into the murky Gulf, thick with salt and seaweed. Far across the water, the horizon stretches in a long flat line.

"It always changes," Dean had said. And he's right. It used to be you had to walk miles for the water to reach your shoulders. And now I'm just twenty or so yards out and it's plenty deep enough. And yet it's always the same, too, I think, laying my body on the surface as waves jostle and knead and tease me like a cat with a toy mouse.

Yes, this is why I came, for this. And a voice in my head says, this would make a nice poem. Not my voice, of course. It is Wendy whispering, not wondering why I turn up like a bad penny. She never scolded me when she was alive, just gave me that look sometimes that said, "Simmer down." Now she exhorts me to clutch the seaweed, the long water grass, to breathe in the pungent, ancient scent, to stop simmering now, and live life at a full boil.

Feeling refreshed and happy, I am driving back to Tallahassee when my cell phone rings. It's a nurse from the Sanctuary. She's afraid my mother has had a stroke, and she's called the paramedics to come get her. I begin to calculate the hours it will take me to get back home.

■

"No morphine," I tell the emergency room doctor who calls me as I'm driving that night on the Interstate toward Atlanta. I sleep for a few hours at a friend's house in Atlanta and then get up early in the morning and drive straight through to the hospital.

Once I get there, I tell them again: "No morphine. I know she says she's in pain. But no morphine."

I tell the doctor about the last time she was in the hospital when they loaded her up on Sister M. and she got so loopy we thought she'd had a stroke. She couldn't complete a sentence. Thoughts were amorphous things floating like clouds far above her grasp. Sentences fell apart in her head. Words got stuck on repeat. It lasted for months.

The doctor promises he won't give her any morphine, but that night someone gives her morphine anyway.

The next day I am sitting in the green chair in my mother's hospital room and she's methodically examining her cover sheet, the effects of the earlier drugs have not worn off. She has a pen in one hand and a partially completed crossword but she is not doing the crossword puzzle. Instead she runs the edge of that sheet through her fingers. When I ask her what she is doing, she has no idea. Finally, she drifts off.

When I tell the doctor what happened, he writes that she is allergic to morphine in her chart. Maybe that will stop the dope pushers.

Later my mother is sitting staring blankly out at nothing, wearing a green hospital robe, a purple DNR wrist band and a heart monitor. She has expressly stated that no rescue attempts should be made in the event she gives out. But she's not really that sick. She's 91. She's in constant pain. She's often confused, but there is nothing drastically wrong with her, nothing a few months of blood thinner and ten or so other pills a day can't cure.

In addition to a blood clot, she has a tiny fracture in her ankle, and the orthopedic surgeon wants her to wear a big plastic boot when she leaves.

My friend Patti says, "So many of my women friends have been taking care of their mothers longer than their mothers took care of them."

Good God, I think. Decades.

■

Celina is entering another year of college. I hope she remembers the instructions I give her on my cell phone as I sit in the parking lot of the hospital: "Honey, if they want to give me blood thinner, antibiotics, anything, just say no to drugs. Let nature have its way. Do you hear me?"

She says that she does, but who knows what it will be like when we're there. Nightmare scenarios of nano-technology prolonging our lives for centuries haunt me.

My mother says to me in the hospital: "When my time comes, I don't want you to be sad. I want you to be happy for me. My life as me is effectively over."

"I will miss you terribly," I answer. "But I will be happy for you."

■

The third day: she's sleeping fitfully. You think of hospitals as busy places with doctors and nurses and med techs running around in the thrall of beeps and signals, doing important life-saving work, but really they are often more like holding pens for patients who are waiting for some number, some blood count, to rise or fall.

We've been here before. A 91-year-old body needs a lot of repair work. During those other excursions, I planted myself in the room like a lodger. And today as well. But this time I won't stay here all day and half the night. This time they're not giving her morphine, and she doesn't have an infection. We're gonna make it outta here okay.

When my mother wakes up, it's as if she's catching herself. She looks around confused. Then falls back to sleep. I wonder why I'm here, sitting in a little room with a sleeping woman.

A few days later my mother is sent back to rehab – another familiar place.

On Monday I leave work early to see about getting my mother re-certified for Medicaid. She's in the rehab center while her broken ankle heals. Medicare covers 20 days in rehab but she's in some insurance HMO plan that sucks out the Medicare money and doles it out the way they want to. For some things it's better than Medicare. But for others it's not. This, for instance. Instead of covering 20 days in rehab, it covers ten. She's on day seven. After that I have to start shelling out one hundred bucks a day to keep my mother there. That's why I'm driving to the Medicaid office instead of sitting in yet another meeting at my school.

During my lunch break I had called the SSI office. A message told me I was "caller number twenty in queue." I finally got to a human, but he managed to cut me off. So I dialed again and in only fifteen minutes I had another human.

"Please don't cut me off," I said to him. "It takes way too long to get to a human." He promised he wouldn't.

I told him my story: my mom had been on Medicaid 18 months ago, the last time she was in the rehab center. I explained that when she got better we put her in a private pay facility because there were no long-term Medicaid beds available. But now she was back in rehab and we needed the Medicaid again.

He transferred me to someone else and I got a voicemail. She didn't call me back. So a few hours later I leave work and call her again. Lo and behold, she answers. In my utter naivete I was sure that this was something that could be done by phone or online. Wrong. I am required to go to the office and fill out an application in person.

As I drive to the office, I wonder how this would get done if I were not here to do it – or if I had the kind of job where I couldn't leave to go take care of my mother's medical problems. Or what if I was sick myself, or disabled? This is how people's lives spiral out of control, how they go bankrupt, how they die forgotten and alone.

The Social Security Administration building in Charlotte is an imposing brick structure not far from uptown. As you approach the entrance, you join the huddled masses yearning for healthcare. Most of the people milling about are minorities. According to a Healthcare Forum I went to recently, 35 percent of African Americans are without health insurance. I don't know what the figures are for Hispanics. For whites, it's six percent. I've been part of that six percent. I know what it feels like to simply decide you can't get sick. Many of the people here are women. They have children or they are pregnant or both. I wonder why so many Americans are so poor.

I go inside and a woman at the information desk gives me some form to fill out. No pen, but I've got my own. I find a little desk and fill out the form, then I go stand in a line. When I get to the front of the line I have to sign a piece of paper. Then go sit in another area and wait. Okay, maybe this is what the crazy "keep your government hands off my healthcare" screamers are picturing. I know it doesn't have to be this way. Government manages to do a lot of things pretty damn well. Education, road building, libraries, policing, firefighting. But maybe this sucks because it's for poor people. Maybe if it was for everybody they'd get more efficient. (I'm still angry over a video I recently saw of a jet plane for insurance company executives with gold-plated dinner ware.)

This place has a kind of festive air about it. I watch a preteen girl herding her younger siblings; a dad and his severely disabled son; a lean, athletic young black man in a wheelchair with his hands in bandages. Everyone has a story. After an hour of sitting I'm still wondering why this process couldn't be done online or by phone. A couple of minutes before five, just before the place closes, a case worker leads me back into the warren of cubicles for an interview. The cubicles are small; the walls brown. I sit down in a plastic chair and stare at a line of screws sticking out of the wall.

The case worker, a strapping bald man, seems like a really nice guy but I'm remembering a guy I knew who worked for social security in another town and who had a predilection for smoking pot and exposing himself to teenage girls. Whatever this particular guy does in his spare time, he seems perfectly willing to approve my mother's application.

There's just one problem. I'd forgotten that when you get on Medicaid, they take your social security check and leave you thirty bucks a month for spending money.

"But . . .but . . .how will we pay for her room at the assisted living place?" I ask. "Her social security check pays for a good chunk of the rent. Then my brothers and I make up the difference."

"My hands are tied," he says with a shrug.

Tears start marching down my face. Words of doom and desperation swirl around my brain.

"But . . . but . . ." I begin again. "She's only supposed to need rehab for a couple of weeks and if she loses her place, then where will she go?"

"I understand," he says. "Some people have mortgages and they have to choose between their homes and their healthcare."

This makes me feel *so* much better.

"It's not going to work," I tell him, trying to keep the whine out of my voice. We continue with the application.

Like a rat backed into a corner, my brain begins scurrying around the problem as I wait for him to print out the forms. What can I do? Will I need to yank her out of rehab? Surely The Sanctuary won't take her back in this shape. She can't put any weight on her right foot. She needs help getting off and on the toilet, getting in and out of the bed. Will I need to go over to her place and move all her stuff out? Money for movers, money for storage. What will I do about that albatross of a bed she has? Is it time for her to move in with me? Will my new roommate be willing to help me out with her? If she moves in with me, will I ever get any work done again? Will I ever be able to travel? What about sleeping? And how can I get her in and out of my house without a ramp?

Finally, I stop. I realize I can't make any decisions without more information. I'll figure this out tomorrow.

■

Friday is the last day that my mother is eligible to stay at the rehab center before I have to start paying a hundred bucks a day. I've called The Sanctuary to try to get her back in on Friday, but the nurse won't be there on that day so it has to happen on

Thursday – if it can happen at all. So even though I'm supposed to be at work, I slip out right before lunch. I've got Mom on her way to the orthopedic doctor, who I'm hoping will say she can put some weight on that leg. In the meantime I'm calling back and forth to the rehab center to see if they'll release her, and The Sanctuary to see if they'll admit her. The hell with Medicaid.

Oh happy day when the social worker at the rehab manages to get the right signatures and finish all the forms and says yes, she can leave. After the doctor has put mom's leg in a cast that allows her to put a little weight on her foot, I drive to the rehab center, sweep through, gathering her things, signing papers, saying sayonara, even stopping to pat Miss Rebecca, who is terminally depressed but still ever so grateful for the flowers I brought her one night, on the back and say, "I hope you feel better."

She looks up at me, her gray hair stringy, her pants baggy and stained, her eyes like the eyes of the dog you left behind at the shelter, and says, "Pray for me."

SEVEN

FALL 2009

Ever since Mom got back to the Sanctuary, she's shakier than ever before. On Monday I go to visit her after my class. We sit outside to absorb some vitamin D, and then she says the inevitable: "I have to go to the bathroom."

I grumble a bit because she'd been upstairs only fifteen minutes earlier, but I push her up to her third floor room, then wheel her into the bathroom, lift her cast off the leg lift, and move both leg lifts out of the way.

"One, two, three," and I hoist her up. "This way, Mom. Pivot this way."

I lift her dress, move the wheelchair, support her body and guide her around, pulling down the pull-ups, trying to get them down before she collapses onto the elevated toilet seat. Lord have mercy.

After the bathroom ordeal, we go downstairs for a game. She's lost a lot of ground in the past few weeks. She has the Q, a blank for a U and an I. I show her where there is an available T, but she can't put those letters together. She cannot figure out the word, "quit." Until finally, exasperated, I just tell her what the word is and where to put it.

Then it's time for dinner. When I wheel her up to the table and give her a hug good-bye, she clasps my arm and begins to kiss it.

That night my old friend Joe from Tallahassee calls me. His mother is in the hospital. She's got a touch of pneumonia. She's only 84. That seems so young to me now! But she's lost the will to live. She tells Joe, "Just kill me, please."

I can tell that he feels like he's been run over by a truck. He's confounded by her hallucinations. "Those are common," I tell him. "It's called hospital dementia."

"There's a name for it?" he asks.

We engage in a dialogue I seem to have with all the friends and acquaintances in my age range: how are we going to avoid this? One of my friends plans to take a boat out into the ocean along with a bottle of vodka and sleeping pills. A nice couple I know has their suicide pact all figured out. Joe is hoping he'll get hit by a bus. My strategy is this: no doctors and no medications after the age of 84.

"You have to start indoctrinating your children. My mom thought it was good to say 'no extreme measures,' but what you have to say is 'no measures at all.' They can keep you alive forever. They just keep patching you up. You'll never die."

Joe's mother is on an IV for fluid, but if she doesn't want to live, should they take her off the IV and let nature do what it does? He doesn't know. Who wants to be responsible for letting a parent fade out, especially a good, beloved parent?

My mother, on the other hand, clings to life no matter how awful she feels. I think she's afraid of death. Hell, she's afraid of sleep. I told her once when she was really miserable and expressed a wish for her life to end that she could stop taking her medicines anytime she wanted. It was her choice. She answered, "I know, but when it gets close it doesn't look so attractive."

282

Meaning death. So perhaps I'll feel differently when I'm very old and maybe I'll want to suck every bit of juice out of my life, suck it till its dry as salt. But if I do, I'm going to do it without the help of their magic potions.

"You know, we're conditioned to believe that life must be preserved at all costs," Joe says. "If your mother is depressed and wants to die, well you give her antidepressants. Even though it's never going to get any better."

But where is that line? Where is the line at which you say, "You're right. Better to leave the party now before the police come and throw everyone in jail." This is what we need to figure out and we only have two or three decades to do it. Not much time. Not much time at all before you're there, before it's you.

■

The next morning I get an email from Joe. His mother passed away peacefully in the night. She was 84. She'd been sick for a couple of months and Joe and his brothers each had spent some time with her in recent weeks. Now she's gone.

■

Halloween day. I'm motivated to clear out some space in Hank's office for an extra bed so that Lorri can have a place to sleep when Celina comes home. In order to do that, I need to clear off a table covered with nails, levels, clamps, tools, and paint cans, move the table out of there, and put it in his room in the hopes that someday the half-demolished bathroom will be fixed – by somebody. As I stand in Hank's room, I am filled with an ineffable sense of sadness. I can't bring to mind all the things he said or did that hurt me so deeply this past year. I can only feel a deep regret for how unhappy he was. I have a sense that I didn't try hard enough, didn't care enough. I simply let him be. I had the life I wanted and that was all I cared about.

Of course, I couldn't force him to participate in life, in my life. I tried to get him to go on trips with us, but at some point I gave up. We ate dinner together, we shopped for groceries together. That seemed like enough.

Standing in this large room with the poplar tree all yellow outside his big bay window, I realize I will never again celebrate Halloween with my husband and child, watching our favorite movies, making caramel apples, trying to keep the dog from sneaking off with the candy. Those years are over. I run a finger through the dust on his armoire. Finally with my barge ship of a heart, with the beat of lost love still thrumming in my veins, I walk out of the room and close the door.

That night I go see a movie with a friend and leave Lorri to give out candy to the few little groups of children who brave the wet night in search of sweets.

EIGHT

THANKSGIVING, 2009

When I learned that my friend Michael Gearhart died of congenital heart failure in 1996, I felt as though I'd fallen through ice into freezing waters. My phone had rung at seven that morning as I was getting my young daughter ready for school. When I picked up the phone, my friend Mary Jane said in a soft voice, "Trish, have you heard? About Mike?"

"Heard what?" I asked. I remember feeling annoyed. That was my response to the creeping fear I felt.

"He's dead," she answered. "It's in the paper."

"No," I told her. "No, that's not true."

I hung up the phone and tried Mike's phone number. I got his answering machine and heard his voice. See, he can't be dead, I thought, there's his voice. And yet I knew that only meant that he wasn't there to pick up the phone. I put on my flannel bathrobe and went outside. The night before, my family and I had stood outside in the street with our neighbors looking through a telescope as the moon turned a deep ruddy color during a full lunar eclipse.

My newspaper lay folded up at the end of my driveway on that sparkling September morning. I sat down on the concrete drive and opened up the local section. I found the article that told of my friend's death. He'd been driving his antique Ford pick-up truck and had an accident two blocks away from my house at the same time I was gazing up at the eclipse of the moon. A witness said he had slumped against the wheel before hitting the other car. I looked up at the sky. A black balloon hovered over the pine trees in the yard across the street. I watched as the balloon floated away, and I understood that my friend was gone.

It had been a long time since I'd experienced the death of someone close to me. It seemed as if a giant hand had torn a hole in the universe. A grief the size of Nebraska engulfed me. My friends and I clung to each other for days in stunned disbelief. Mike was young, healthy, funny and handsome – admired by men and desired by women. Now he was gone. One day here. The next day deleted.

■

I think of the shock of that sudden death now, contrasting it to my mother's slow tortuous slide into the abyss.

Thanksgiving 2009. Hank and I have been separated for nearly a year, and Lorri has become a part of my new makeshift family. Celina is coming home from college for the break. Hank never enjoyed entertaining so I am looking forward to having Thanksgiving dinner with friends at my house for the first time ever. But I don't want to do all that work – roasting turkey, peeling potatoes, etc. Celina hates turkey anyway, and it has been at least a year since I've eaten meat. Not to mention, I'm not much of a cook.

So I order a big spinach lasagna from Pasta & Provisions, make a salad with Romaine, arugula, edamame beans, shrimp, avocado and candied pecans; steamed some asparagus and bake pecan pie bars for dessert. One of my former students, a fantastic chef, delivers the most incredible soup (see recipe below) and broccoli gratin the day before. My friend Darryl is bringing over a turtle cheesecake. Not a traditional Thanksgiving dinner but a feast nonetheless.

The guests include four friends of mine along with Lorri, Celina and my 91-year-old mother. That's the Olympic challenge – getting my mother out of her assisted living place and over to my house. She used to go a little crazy staying in one place, but now she doesn't like to leave. I know she is going to balk when it comes time to go, but I've already steeled myself for that. It's kind of like taking the cat to the vet except that once my mother gets to wherever I've made her go, she realizes she wanted to do this all along – as opposed to my cat who goes psycho and tries to eviscerate the doctor. Mom was so happy I'd dragged her out last year to vote, and was eventually delighted when I made her go to the mall with me and my brothers last summer to buy her a dress. She loved it when we went to the symphony in the park – after we got there. And I figure this will be no different. She'll make all kinds of noise about getting in and out of the car (not easy when your legs don't work), but once she's at the house she will be happy as a bluebird in a tree.

I arrive at the assisted living place at 2:30. My mom wears a pretty red dress and a coat – it is plenty cold outside. Although she looks spry, she has a vicious cough. She keeps hacking up phlegm and spitting into a napkin. As we approach the car, just as I expected, she panics.

"Oh, I don't know about this," she says in a weak, frightened voice.

"You don't have to go," I answer. You know how you can say something and mean just the opposite? She gets my drift. I angle her wheelchair inside the open car door, put on the brakes, tell her to grab the top of the car door and help her get up. Then I deftly unbrake the chair, pull it out of the way and help her pivot onto the car seat. I lift her legs (one of them is in an enormous black boot to protect the ankle which was fractured a couple of months earlier), tug the seat belt around her waist, shut the door, and proceed to load up the wheelchair in the back of my car.

I live about fifteen minutes away, and want to make sure I got there before guests arrive. I pull into the driveway, extricate the wheelchair, reverse the actions, and wheel her down the winding leaf-strewn walkway to the steps at the front of the house. Standing at the bottom of the three rickety wooden steps I realize I forgot that Hank had removed the handrails to the steps in a fit of "renovation." We are facing three steps and she has nothing to hold onto.

My mother wears the facial expression of someone hanging over a cliff.

Not too worry. My strong 19-year-old daughter is here, and Lorri is fairly strong as well in spite of a bum knee. Surely we can maneuver one little old lady up those steps and into the house. My mother clutches the wheelchair.

"What do I do?" she asks.

"Let go of the wheelchair first," I instruct.

We get her up, but she isn't supporting herself at all. She doesn't know how to. The mechanics of movement have become foreign to her.

"Come on, Mom," I say, helping her to lift one leg and then the other. Miraculously we get her onto the first step. But the next step is impossible. She can't or won't lift her legs on her own even with us supporting her. She gets heavier by the second. We're at an impasse. We have to retreat.

"Go back," I say. My mother's rear end begins to lower but her feet stay planted on the step. Disaster looms.

"No, no!" all three of us yell.

"I meant step back, Mom!" I say, trying to hold on to her and maneuver the chair under her descending body. Then to heap insult onto her injuries, I start to laugh. I can't help it. It's all so terrible, my mother is going backwards, and we can't stop her. Celina catches the giggles from me and Lorri follows suit. Which just enrages my mother who yells at Celina, "It's not funny!"

Celina glares at me at the same time that my mother lands half-assed onto the wheelchair. But by then I am laughing so hard I've peed on myself, which brings on the idea that maybe my mother isn't the only one who needs "extra protection." Fortunately, at that moment, Darryl and his very strong friend Eric arrive. They lift up my mother, wheelchair and all, and cart her up the steps onto the front porch. Eric, who took care of an elderly couple for several years when he first moved to the United States from Poland, pulls the wheelchair over the last step and across the threshold while I run upstairs to clean up and change clothes. All's well that ends well, right?

Maybe it's because she's sick with the cough, but my mother is listless and confused from our pre-dinner gathering in the living room for appetizers through dinner. Like all of us, she does make special mention of the splendid soup. While the rest of us talk about various topics (Eric from Poland fills the Americans in on Abe Lincoln's connection to Thanksgiving and how he established the holiday for morale), my mother's eyes droop. I worry about whether she needs to go to the bathroom and if that is possible in the tiny first-floor "powder room." A couple of times she tries to keep up with the conversation but her hearing has gone and not everyone knows to speak loudly to her. She does, however, notice the lace tablecloth and the place settings – remnants of her mostly vanished life.

After dessert, we waddle like hippos back into the living room, where Celina lights a fire in the fireplace and entertains us with stories of riding back to school recently on a train packed with drunken football fans. Darryl, Eric, and Steve wax philosophical. Lisa informs us of the real skinny on 2012. Lorri laughs at the jokes. I watch my mother.

Her head slowly lowers, eyes shut, and she peacefully dozes until suddenly – as if she were falling – she screams, "ooooh!" and her body jerks upright. The conversation skids to a halt every time it happens. I find myself wishing the festivities would just end so I can get her back to the assisted living place where she has an accessible bathroom and her adjustable bed. Finally, about 7:30 I tell my guests I have to take her back home. Steve and Eric carry the wheelchair to the sidewalk, and I wheel her back to my car.

Unlike my friend Mike, my mother's life has ended in degrees. Tonight, I realize, we've lost a few more of them. This will be the last time I'll bring her over to my house. I don't have the income to build a ramp and retrofit my bathroom. Besides, if it isn't enjoyable to her, what is the point? I decide I will not force her out again. The thing that worries me is the Requiem performance. The date is set for February 21. Everything is a go. But how will I ever get her there? I'm thinking we might have to do it without her. I shut this awful thought out of my mind.

Mom surprises me on the way home.

"What a lovely evening," she says.

"It was nice, but I'm so tired," I admit.

"Well, don't fall asleep before you get me home," she says. And I laugh. Though my mother's long slow decline saddens me more than I can say, I feel grateful that she still has that spark of humor, that I've gotten to have one more Thanksgiving with her in my house with the old lace tablecloth that belonged to her grandmother and the beautiful hand-painted plates that had belonged to my grandmother, and that back at my house, a large pot of leftover Thanksgiving soup will keep me warm for the coming days.

Here is Greg's recipe, with his permission:

Greg Guthrie's Absolutely Delicious Butternut Squash and Lentil Soup

VEGETABLE STOCK:

Mirepoix:
2 parts onion
1 part celery
1 part carrots
6 garlic cloves
Bouquet Garni:
1 bunch of thyme (handful)
1 bunch parsley stems (leaves make it bitter)
10 whole black peppercorns
3 bay leaves

Cover with water two inches above solids and simmer for at least an hour

SOUP:

Butternut Squash, cubed and roasted
Lentils, cooked separately with vegetable stock
Onions, brunoise
Carrots, brunoise
Celery ribs, brunoise
Garlic, minced
Ginger, minced
Cremini mushrooms, diced

Shitake mushrooms, diced
Fresh oregano
Fresh flat leaf parsley
Fresh cilantro
Curry powder
Shaved nutmeg, tiny bit

CILANTRO GARNISH:

Cilantro, chopped
Parsley, chopped
Garlic, minced
Lemon zest
Orange zest

MOP:

Sauté vegetables until tender adding each vegetable one at a time. Onions, celery, carrots, garlic, ginger. Deglaze with vegetable stock or dry white wine. Add vegetable stock and simmer for half hour. Add mushrooms, curry, cooked lentils and squash and cook for another half hour. Finish with fresh herbs and nutmeg. Salt and pepper to taste. Add garnish when serving. Can drizzle truffle oil or olive oil to taste.

NINE

I am traveling across North Carolina in an Amtrak train – warehouses of brick and corrugated steel, tanks, leafless trees and evergreens, brown or pale yellow lawns, small clapboard houses with metal carports attached to the sides, factories, anonymous brick buildings, trucks. We pass over highways and see people heading to work, cell phone towers, roofing businesses. I love the train, the easy forward momentum. These trains don't rock the way trains used to. They glide like steel serpents.

We pass small towns: a faded painted sign "Central Grocery" on old brick, enormous steel water towers like space ships gleaming in the blighted rural area, an old man in a Stetson hat creakily getting out of a truck, an electrical forest of towers and wires, backyards and apartment complexes, tiny houses with their Christmas decorations still up. The train blows its one chord, sometimes long, sometimes short – an indecipherable Morse code.

I'm on my way home to Charlotte after visiting Celina at college in Chapel Hill. As we walked across the campus, she told me about the phone call she recently had with Hank, how the conversation was unstrained and happy, how they laughed together. I'm grateful the two of them are finding their way back to each other.

The train continues west and the sun slides by in window-sized patches as we round bends. Outside I watch the scenery: farm land, wet lands, a tiny log cabin, a hawk scouring the land for breakfast, a landfill with a dump truck spilling black dirt, and a back hoe with its head on the ground as if it is sleeping.

I'm worried about the Requiem performance. Everyone is expecting Mom to be there. They have a different idea of who she is. They think she will be happy and honored. I think so too, but I think it will be her ghost who is happy and honored. I

293

believe that her former self still lingers near her body. I believe that even though she may fall asleep during the performance, some part of her consciousness will register this homage to her work.

I haven't been able to do much to make sure the performance goes the way it should. My brother Jo has taken the reins, but he is making all the arrangements by long distance. There's a committee of Mother's old friends, working to make it happen, and apparently there have been unspecified problems. Have we imposed too much, I wonder. We don't have any money to pay for anything. The most important thing to me is getting a good recording of it, but so far I haven't had much luck finding someone who can do it. I have to trust that Jo will make it happen. He seems pretty confident.

We're pulling into Greensboro – a small, pretty city with a few mid-sized buildings.

At least Mom has been better mentally, more alert, more like her old self since she got over her cold. And I know I have no choice now. She has to go to Jacksonville where the Requiem will be performed. The only hitch in the plans is that Celina can't come with us so I'll have to get my brother David and his son to help me transport her. She's so afraid of travel now, of leaving the confines of The Sanctuary. I'll have to find some way to convince her.

"Mom, you know how much you love me?" I will ask. "I need you to do this for me. I need you to not be afraid, to be strong and to be happy. Please do this for me." If I can just frame it that way and tap into that old drive of hers, then she'll do it. She'll go to the ends of the earth. All my life I have known this, that if I really needed my mother to do something for me, she would battle dragons. I once used this power to persuade her to get drugs for me from her friend the dentist. I still feel bad about that.

It's not just for me. This is a chance for others who have loved her and learned from her to express their feelings. It's a chance for people who never heard the Requiem to hear it. And it's one more chance for her to realize the impact she has had. And no, it won't just be her ghost that will get it. She'll thrive in all that attention. I only have to get her there.

The mystics say that old age is a time of return to the essential self. What looks like the worst thing imaginable to us is actually a spiritual process at once beautiful and liberating. I have judged my mother's aging time and again, but I also know that there is something holy and ineffable about the slow erasure of her worldly persona. And the Requiem feels like a way to honor not just her, but the transformation that is taking place.

The train is moving again. We slowly move through a tangle of wood, some trash on the ground, big muddy puddles, bare trees with brown desiccated leaves. The ground is covered with leaves and sticks. A few pines lift their green branches like chalices; they toast their imperviousness to the weather.

Soon I will be back in Charlotte. I will drive to work. I will teach my classes as always, collecting papers, listening to presentations. My students will suck me into their world as they always do. And suddenly I'll start caring. *Yes, you can turn that paper in next week. Sure, I'll look at what you've written. Now, what are you really trying to say right here in this opening paragraph?*

And then I'll drive to my mother's.

■

After days of feeling like a petri dish swirling with cold germs, I wake up Saturday – departure day – feeling like the universe is on my side no matter what. The cold germs have vacated the premises.

My brother David and his son Edward are still sleeping in Celina's room when I pop out of bed (something I haven't done in weeks) and take a shower. I've been dreading this day in a way. Feeling like it was more of a chore than an exciting event. But this morning feels like a rose in full petal. I make oatmeal with blueberries and walnuts and raw honey and manage to impress my brother – which is something that, after all these years, I'm still trying to do.

While David showers and Edward goes off with Lorri to take our broken TV to the dump, I decide to squeeze in a short walk. The cold morning air nips at my cheeks, but the sun shines like a Happy New Year hat. It's February 20, the day before the day.

I shiver in my fleece jacket and puff up the hill. At the top of the hill, I emerge from under the trees, and cross the street into the next neighborhood. As I walk along the sidewalk past the brick houses, I notice two trees with branches bare of leaves but filled with birds. Red-breasted robins. Spring is sneaking up on us. The sun hovers over the horizon, and its beams slide across the planet to illuminate the breasts of the robins so it looks like the trees are full of gold coins. I am paralyzed with delight and wonder. Suddenly the birds all take wing. I stand on the sidewalk, head tilted up, watching them whirl around like a tornado of feathers above my head. Then I see the cause of the disturbance coasting slowly over the houses at the end of the street. Two hawks with nowhere to go and nothing in particular to do. The robins are spinning *en masse* – little missiles. As the hawks pass them by, they settle back down. The marvelous little show is a good omen for the weekend.

We go to pick up my mother at The Sanctuary. Edward is 22 now, a college graduate getting ready to enter the Navy. My mother looks up at him in wonder. Of all the grandchildren Edward is the one who makes a point of being her grandchild. He's always had this in-born loyalty to the concept of family. He's the only grandchild who came to our father's memorial service. He tried to understand why our father didn't relish the company of his three children, but our bitter answers left him only more baffled.

"So you're my grandson?" Mom asks. She has not seen him in several years though he has sent cards and letters, including the speech he gave at his college graduation.

"This is David's son," I tell her.

"David, my brother?"

"No, David your son. He's here, too, in the cafe washing some fruit for the trip."

"What trip?"

"We're going to Jacksonville today," I tell her.

"Really? Today?" she asks.

"Yes." I begin pushing her wheelchair down the hall.

"I thought you meant next week."

"Remember you agreed to do this. For your daughter who has done so much for you." I nuzzle my cheek next to hers.

"I don't think you've proven yourself yet," she says.

But she comes along easier than I dared to hope. She knows resistance is futile. I've made that much clear.

■

The drive down is easy as well. We stop periodically at rest areas. We have a drill. Edward gets the wheelchair out of the back. David maneuvers Mom in the wheelchair and I bring her into the bathroom, take the leg rests off and get her onto the toilet. I've developed my own little patter: "Okay, plant your feet, Mom. Plant them under your knees. Are your feet planted? Now I want you to grab the bar here and stand. Stand all the way up. One two three. Good. Okay. Now pivot, move your foot, pivot, pivot, and go ahead and sit down, Mom. Good."

I schedule eight hours for the trip but it takes less than seven. Then we are in the hotel. My brother Jo and his girlfriend Connie are already there with Sharen, my niece, who is going to sing the soprano solo in the performance on Sunday.

We gather in the sitting area of David's hotel room and Jo pulls out the newspaper. The front page of the Florida Times-Union on Saturday Feb. 21 shows a contrite Tiger Woods and the words "I am so sorry" emblazoned above his face. But we are not interested in section A. We are interested in the state and local news. And on the front page of section B – above the fold even – is this headline: "City's Music Master Returns." The story takes up a solid column at the bottom of which is a picture of my mother from 1967. She looks like a movie star, like Joan Crawford or Jane Russell.

The story continues inside and includes quotes from yours truly and mistakenly refers to my brother David as "Mark MacEnulty." We get a laugh out of this, but none of us is too worried about the name mix-up because the writer has the essence of the story – the grand dame is back for a special appearance at her old home, the Church of the Good Shepherd.

Jo and I later congratulate ourselves.

"We did it!" Jo says.

"You're the wide receiver, man," I tell him. "All I did was throw the ball. You're the one who caught it and made a touchdown."

It's true. He spent countless hours making scores for the chorus and orchestra and organist. He raised money. All his talents and skills from his former stint as conductor and managing director for an orchestra in Illinois have paid off. I had planned to pay for any expenses myself. But it turns out all I'm paying for is gas, some food and a hotel room.

Our family friend Karen managed to find the chorus and conductor for us, generate publicity, and get us a deal on the hotel rooms. And now she's invited our family over for dinner at her house. But when Jo and David are together, conversation and reminiscence take precedence. I actually do have a duty – herding this family of cats outside and into our respective vehicles.

The dinner is wonderful. Even though not everyone is here, there are more of our family members in one spot than have been together since Sharen's wedding ten years earlier. They start telling Roz stories at the table. Karen tells us about a man who, for some reason, stopped Mother on one of her walks and began to tell her his woes. He lost his wife and now his dog. He told my mother he couldn't see any reason to keep living. And apparently she agreed with him. I'm thinking that's not the sweetest story in the world. I'm thinking she was a more sympathetic person than that. But perhaps her methodology in this case was to shed light on his self-pitying.

My favorite story is the one where a young couple interrupted a choir rehearsal asking for money. They said they were hungry so Mom gave them five dollars. The choir members chided her for believing their story but after choir when they all went to the Derby House for their usual repast, and there was the young couple eating hamburgers. Mom's faith in humanity was vindicated.

Even though earlier in the car she asked if the four of us were all somehow related, Mom holds her own in the table conversation. If she's not fully cognizant, she's got a hell of a good act.

This day has gone so well that it's inevitable that I screw up. I do this by taking "just one bite" of the delicious chocolate cake that Karen made. Oh hell. You might as well tell a crackhead "just one hit." I scarf down my piece and half of my mom's. While this may not seem a terrible sin, you have to know that chocolate has caffeine and my body is akin to a finely tuned scientific instrument geared to detect the most minute portions of caffeine in any substance. I am not going to go to sleep for hours.

■

We come back to the hotel. The bed is too high for Mom, so I put her in the fold out bed in the "suite" area. There's a wall between us but it only goes halfway into the room. The time we spent together today was fun, and we're both feeling rather sisterly. I lift her from the wheelchair and she drops onto the bed. Then I stand on the bed and pull her into a prone position. I place pillows under her head and feet and cover her with a blanket, leaving her feet uncovered per her instructions. At 10:30 I actually lie down in the king-size bed as if I'm heading directly to that adored world, that realm of happiness: sleep. But it is not to be. The chocolate cake has sent its caffeine brigands to hijack my brain. They are celebrating Carnivale with lights, music and dancing.

Eventually, however, the relaxation herb I take kicks in and I can just begin to taste the elixir of sleep. About midnight as I'm finally thinking I might go down the tunnel, the horror show begins. The whimpering, the groaning, the moaning, the tiny grunts.

"What is it, Mom?"

"I hurt."

I get up and give her some pain pills and crawl back into bed. Oh rapturous sleep. The thoughts in my head are deliciously nonsensical, a sure sign that I'm entering the sacred realm.

Then my mother whines and I am yanked out of paradise.

"Stop it!" I growl.

For maybe five minutes there is silence. Then it comes back.

I beg, I plead, I cajole, I threaten, but mother cannot be quiet. Every time I start to drift off, it's like she cuts off my oxygen supply. The CIA should employ my mother to torture terrorists. About five in the morning out of helpless desperation, I take the comforter and a pillow into the bathroom where I shut the door and lie on the floor. I quickly drop down into oblivion and for maybe 45 minutes it works. I cannot hear my mother.

So she ups the ante. She no longer whimpers. Now she yells out: "Help! Help!"

I stagger out of the bathroom.

"What is it, Mom? What's wrong?"

She looks up at me helplessly and says, "I need some water." She's already had a glass of water.

In a dry voice, I tell her, "If I had a gun right now, you'd be dead."

"Why? What have I done?" she asks. Then she turns her face from me and says, "No one has ever treated me with such hatred, and it saddens me."

"I'm just trying to sleep. Can you please please please just give me that?"

But she can't. And I can't help myself either. We're playing our roles – the victim and the martyr. Later I will realize she does not know what she's doing, but right now I'm cranky as hell and desperate for sleep. Later when I'm complaining to all and sundry about my sleep deprivation Sharen will mention that her other grandmother was the same way. The call it "sundowners." The sun goes down and some old people lose their minds. Her other grandmother thought people were trying to kill her at night.

"I'll just leave," my mother says. "I'll go back where we came from."

"You can't do that," I say.

At 6:30 a.m. I call Jo.

"She's killing me," I tell him. He shows up at my door a few minutes later. We get her out of bed. I take her into the bathroom and clean her up and get a pretty dress on her. Jo takes her downstairs for breakfast. I try to get some sleep. But it's hopeless. I cannot sleep now. I get up in frustration and head downstairs, too.

■

That day I am a zombie. The performance is at 6 p.m., and I can't begin to imagine going there and smiling at people and trying to traverse the pathways of common conversation. People I haven't seen in forty years will be there. And I'm going to look like someone who just escaped from a mental institution. I look in the mirror and am frightened.

While Jo and Connie go to my father's old Unitarian church where Jo is giving a flute concert, the rest of us wind up having lunch at some bizarre place on the river decorated with stuffed wild animals.

We order gator tail for an appetizer. I don't eat mammals and have even stopped eating fowl, but a gator is a different story. I eat gator in the hopes that someday I'll stop having nightmares about the scary bastards. I order for Mother, just like I used to do for Celina. We gorge on fried shrimp and fabulous creamy key lime pie – *de rigueur* Florida fare. Then we zoom over to the church so Sharen can vocalize before the rehearsal. David wants to take pictures. Mom wants to stay in the car. I wander around with Edward, first showing him where the choir kids all scrawled their names on the wall.

"There's my name," I say and point it out, remembering the hours I spent in this room turning pages for my mother as she played the piano.

■

As we leave the church parking lot and head back to the hotel, my mother asks where we just were.

"At the church," I tell her.

"What church?"

"The Good Shepherd. The church where you worked for thirty-something years."

"Oh, that church," she says.

The day is bright with a yellow sun in a merciful sky. But I'm totally off my game. My brain is filled with awful buzzing. Pam, Gary, and Joe arrive from Tallahassee and call me on the cell phone, but I can't go hang with them. I send them off to eat. The big night is finally here and I'm in misery.

■

When we get back to the hotel, I leave Mom with David and Edward. For an hour I sleep! Sleep, glorious sleep. When I wake the world has been magically restored. Everything that was fractured is now whole. The night is almost here, so I slip into pantyhose and a shimmery dress and high heels. I brush my hair and put on makeup and damn – I can actually pass for a member of the human species.

Joe, Pam and Gary come over to the hotel. They come upstairs with me and my mom and wait in the sitting area while I get Mom ready for the performance. They can overhear me in the bathroom.

"I'm going to get you your pain pills," I tell my mother in a loud voice because her hearing is "not what it used to be" as she says.

"What?"

"Pain pills."

"What? Petticoats?"

"Pain pills, Mom. Pain pills," I shout.

I go back to the sitting area where Mom's bag of medicine is and pull out the sheet of Tramadols.

"Do you have enough for all of us?" Gary asks. Within seconds Pam and I are staggering with laughter.

I return to the bathroom with my mother's pills. Although the night before was one of my worst nights ever with my mother, today is filled with tenderness and connection. I stand behind her in the bathroom, facing the mirror, gently massaging her face with oil and then lightly rubbing in foundation.

"You do know I love you," I say, and she knows I am asking for forgiveness.

"Yes," she says. "I know."

We have been as close on this trip as we have ever been. My disappointment that Celina's school work prevents her from being with us sits like a stone in my gut, but I realize that this time is for me and my mom. If Celina were here, it would not be the same. I would be focused on my daughter and not on my mother.

A few minutes later Mom is dressed in her purple velvet dress with tiny pearl beads sewn into the collar. Her silver mane is brushed and I've put make up on her. She converses with my friends while I finish getting ready.

"Your mother is so eloquent," Pam tells me as we head outside. "Her language is sophisticated and playful for someone her age and in her situation. It's such a contrast—there she is in a wheelchair, with her memory going, but her mind is still journeying all over the place."

My mother's wit refuses to die.

■

We arrive at the church; nothing is as I imagined it would be. The church is not too cold as we feared it might be. A half hour before the concert and already the place is getting filled. Edward takes charge of pushing Mother's wheelchair. And the homage begins. Friends from thirty, forty, fifty years ago file in. They all want to see her. I watch her face as it lights up in recognition over and over again. She yelps in delight when her old friend Henson shows up. Another woman introduces herself to me, and my mother wheels around. "Did I hear you say Kaye? Kaye Bullock??" She knows everyone. She laughs joyfully. And they are so pleased to see her, to hold her hand, to tell her she hasn't changed.

"Oh yes, I have," she says with a laugh.

We are surrounded. Not just with her friends but with some of mine, too. Walking in the door is Katie and Nella. Katie was my best friend from the age of five to about ten. And her mother Nella was my second mother.

"I always said, we moved in and you moved over," Nella tells me. Nella is the one who opened the door for me on the terrible night. And I still feel a bond with her all these years later.

By six o'clock, the church pews are filled. We have seats in the middle. I have Mother's wheelchair right next to me. Joe, Pam and Gary are on my other side. Jo, Connie and Edward are in the row behind us. David is in the balcony with his camera. The new organist – a young man – plays a couple of pieces as an opening act, to let my mother hear the organ she played for thirty-two years. She was a ship captain and the organ was her vessel.

Then the priest comes out to give an introduction to the Requiem. He starts by telling the audience about her past service to the church and to the community. Most of us know all this, but everyone wants to hear him say it anyway. He's a good speaker, and at the end of the introduction he looks down the aisle and says to my mother, "Welcome home."

Then everyone (somewhere between 300 and 400 people) stands and turns to face my mother, clapping and clapping. Holy shit, I'm thinking. I wasn't expecting this. Tears roll out of my eyes in hot beads. Mom is confused at first, but then I tell her they are clapping for her. And she gets it. Tonight is about her. And her Requiem.

Finally, the clapping ceases and the performance begins.

The concert is heartbreakingly beautiful. When my niece Sharen stands up and sings the soprano solo, her necklace glitters in the light from the hanging lanterns, and her voice soars into the nave. I have loved her madly ever since she was five and I was fifteen and we lived together one year in my brother's house in Webster Groves. We pretended we were sisters. When I was in prison in Florida, she came to visit me once. She was a teenager, and I remember running down the sidewalk to the visiting park, my hands waving in nervous excitement. Years later I saw her as Maria in West Side Story at the Fox Theater in Atlanta and wept the whole time. She has that kind of effect on me. So now when her voice arches its back and fills the room, my chest tightens and for one holy moment I am fully present – right there in the now with my fingers wrapped around my mother's hand.

Daylight leaves and the stained glass windows grow dark. The musical complexity of the piece is evident to my ears now. Layer upon layer of voices and orchestra. A beautiful young African-American man sings the tenor part. (One of Mom's friends recently told me that in the very first production Mom's choice of soprano was a young African-American woman. It was 1982, for heaven's sake, but there was still a furor. Didn't matter. Mother insisted and the young woman was her soloist.) Now, this young man's mother sits a few rows in front of us. Even from behind I can tell she is beaming. Sharen told us earlier that he was originally a gospel singer and that he enjoyed the challenge of this classical piece. Tonight he is meeting that challenge in full metal jacket.

Not only is my blood family here, but my church family is here, too – all those gentle people who hovered in the background of my childhood. Not one of them ever judged me when I went off the rails – or if they did, they've let it go by now. And I am happy because my friends are here, too, and they had no idea that my mother is this woman–this woman who composed such a work of art. Maybe the rest of the world doesn't know about her. But everyone in this room does. We know we are privileged tonight.

I clutch my mother's hand throughout the performance, watchful to make sure she doesn't drift off. But my fears abate. She's thoroughly engrossed as if hearing it for the first time. And in a way she is because in the past she was always behind the organ. This is the first time she's gotten to hear her music the way her audience has heard it.

At the end of the concert, Edward runs to the back of the church and comes back with flowers for my mother and once again it happens. Again the people stand and turn to face her and they clap for all they are worth. Somewhat abashed she raises a regal hand and waves, saying graciously "Thank you. Thank you."

■

I thought I would feel relief that the whole thing was over. I thought that I would be happy once it was successfully completed. But instead what I feel is a rare elation. I want this moment to last forever. My brothers and I exchange hugs and high fives. My godfather hugs me. My former flute teacher shows up to warmly shake my hand. And her husband, Bill, who owned the music store where Mother shopped for sheet music and manuscript paper is there, too. His child was one of the sons who died, one of those who inspired the original Requiem. Bill is ninety years old now. I can still remember the sweet musty smell of his music store and following my mother around as she perused the sheets of anthems.

People line up to pay their respects to my mother and I leave her in Edward's capable hands. I stop the young tenor to congratulate him.

"Oh, I just love her," he gushes. "As soon as I saw this piece, I loved her. It's such a powerful piece of music. And such a challenge. I learned so much."

We look into each other's eyes. He is someone who will never have to read a self-help book, I'm thinking. I'm also thinking that she's gone and done it again. Touched another generation.

In the reception hall, my friend Mike with his thick hair in a ponytail and an arm draped over his wife Katherine comes over. They drove over from the beach to be here. I feel like a birthday girl.

When Mike was a teenager he played drums in a band that would later become Lynyrd Skynyrd without Mike, who ultimately chose surfing over drumming. The earlier version of the band played many a Friday night in the church hall across the courtyard from the sanctuary.

A few days earlier Mike and I were talking on the phone. His father had recently died, and Mike had warned me to make sure that all my mother's assets were in order. He was having to pay an attorney to straighten out his deceased father's financial affairs.

"It's not a lot," he said. "Maybe a hundred grand, but still."

A hundred grand? I swallowed. "I don't think that will be a problem for us. Mom is basically living on social security and our monthly contributions." If you're middle class you're supposed to have parents with "assets." We feel we're entitled to some kind of inheritance. My brothers and I had thought that surely our father would have left us *something*. He didn't. But standing here tonight, I don't care about that. I've gotten all the legacy from my mother I'll ever need.

Just then Edward proudly wheels his grandmother into the reception. A group of young female singers in their long black dresses look at her, awestruck. My mother smiles happily. Her eyes glow.

Joe, who has become an increasingly important presence in my life, comes up and places an arm around my shoulders.

"Good job," he says.

Yes, I think, I was the catalyst for this event. But she's the one who tore out her heart and put it on a stave for all the world to hear.

Ten

I pull out of the parking garage at the Charlotte Airport and into the bright morning light. I have just watched Celina walk through the line to the security check point. She glanced back at me with a nervous smile. We waved good-bye. She is on her way to see her father for the first time in two and a half years.

As I drive along the Interstate, I am not sure how I feel. I try to imagine their reunion. Will she burst into tears? Will he? Or will they simply hug and be done with it?

So often in the past when Celina has gone away, I've felt as hollow as a bell. Today I search for signs of impending sorrow that she will not be with me for Christmas. Traffic on the road is light, and the sky is laced with wispy clouds. I notice a swelling in my chest – not of unhappiness, but of something like joy. This is the right ending to this story, I realize. Because every ending should also be a beginning. And I am pretty sure this is a new beginning for Hank and his daughter.

As for me, I've got to get back home and start cleaning for the party Lorri and I will have for my circle of friends on Christmas Eve. Joe will come to visit and we'll have Christmas dinner with my mother at the assisted living place before driving down to Florida for a few days.

I eject the Bright Eyes CD that Celina and I were listening to on the way to the airport – Celina's comfort music. And I randomly select a different CD and slide it into the player. It's the Birthday Mix – old show tunes and popular standards Joe made for me. For some reason I've fallen in love with the songs that my mother's various community choral groups sang over the years: "More," "The Look of Love," "Autumn Leaves," "Moon River," "Summertime," and "My Funny Valentine." I thought the music was schmaltzy when I was a kid, but a few weeks ago listening to my mother play one of the them on the piano, I yearned to hear them all again. Now the music I once disdained sounds both hip and glamorous. I smile when I hear the first track: Frank Sinatra singing "Let's take it nice and easy. . ."

I pull off the highway onto the road that leads home. The trees are bare, their spindly branches reaching toward the pale blue sky. I look up at a tiny point that I know is a jet cutting a straight white line like an arrow. The road rolls underneath me as I drive toward the rising sun, listening to Frank. It's Sunday morning, and I am fine.

Afterword

This book was originally published by The Feminist Press, CUNY, under the title *Wait Until Tomorrow: A Daughter's Memoir.* It came out in May, 2011. I brought a copy to my mother, which she proudly showed to any and every one at her assisted living facility. She couldn't read it. Her mind was no longer capable of that, but she knew it was about her and that I wrote it.

My friend Lisa and I went on a mini-book tour in June and right after I finished giving a reading at a bookstore in Elizabeth City, NC, I received a phone call from the facility. Mother had taken a bad turn.

Lisa and I sped back home — a five-hour drive.

When I got to the facility, my mother was planted in the back hallway in her wheelchair, calling for help — in her sleep! Her caregiver told me she wouldn't let him put her to bed. She'd been calling for help for two days, apparently, but no one knew what to do about it. I tried to rouse her, but her eyes would only flutter open briefly and then close. I wheeled her to her room and got her into bed.

We called hospice.

Dying is hard business, and the life force inside my mother was like the water in a fire hose. She was not going gently into that good night, and why should she? My job was to stand on the sidelines like an angry cheerleader, who knows her team is not going to win, and tell my mother she's doing a helluva job.

My oldest brother, Jo, arrived with Connie. Then David came. We took shifts sitting with her. Jo and Connie, then me and David.

On June 18, she died early in the morning while we were all my house catching up on our sleep. It was as if she knew: David had to get back to New York, I had more readings scheduled in Florida. It was just like her. She always put her children first.

We had a small service for her at the facility, and then in November — on my birthday — we had another service for her friends in Edenton at St. Paul's, where the choir sang one of the songs from her Requiem. Her ashes were poured into a hole in the ground beside a wall with a plaque.

Hank and I got officially divorced in 2012, and in October of 2020, Joe Straub and I were married. Joe's son, Jack, has helped me to digitize some of my mother's compositions, including the Requiem. You can find them at the website: *RosalindMacEnulty.com.*

If you want to know the other part of the story — the one where she saved me from myself (over and over again), you can find it in my other memoir: The Hummingbird Kiss: My Life as an Addict in the 1970s.

By the way, both of my brothers have written books about their own lives. Jo's book is called *This is My Story and I'm Sticking to It* and covers growing up in the 1950s, playing for the St. Louis symphony, conducting for another symphony, his spiritual journey, and more. David's book, *Sunrise in the Bronx*, details his extraordinary and inspiring journey as a chess coach.

Another Perspective

I was looking through a copy of my brother's book of poetry
Amazing is Quite Often and came upon his own remembrance
of our mother and the performance of the Requiem. As a musician he has a slightly different perspective, so here is a different
(and much shorter!) version of some of the events described in
the book:

Mom's Story
I was driving my mother through Edenton, North Caro-
   lina.
There was road construction everywhere.
We had to stop constantly.
It was all over the town.
Finally, as we were waiting for a flag man
to wave us ahead
she looked at me and said,
"You'd think that after two hundred years
They'd have this country finished."

She is known for her constant unpredictable responses
Her friends say,
"Let's hear what Ros has to say about this"
and they'll ask her a question like,
"Ros, what do you think of the ladies of Edenton?"

Her response, "I think they're the sweetest
uneducated women I've ever met."

So she's a character, a genuine character.
But she's more than a character.
She's a graduate of the Yale University School of Music.
She was there back in the thirties
and studied composition with Hindemith.
She was a brilliant pianist and composer
and she was a church organist
for nearly eighty years.
Every place she has been
she has developed a following, a fan club,
admirers who have learned to sing under her
and who have been wildly entertained in the process.

"Ros, what do you think of God?"
"Well, He really shouldn't have rested on the seventh day.
There was so much more He should have done.
I think that was a big mistake."

Or, "Ros, why is there so much pain in the world?"
"What do you expect on a planet where we evolved
by eating each other?"

So here it is two thousand and ten
and Mama's living in Charlotte
in an assisted living place.
She's ninety-one and in constant pain.

See, when she was eighty-four she was music director
of an outdoor theater production,

The Lost Colony, a dramatization
of the story of Sir Walter Raliegh's Lost Colony.
She was going to New York every winter
to audition singers for the show,
which attracted several hundred thousand people
every summer,
and she had a problem with her lower back
and the surgeon screwed up big time.
He nicked the nerve that controls her right leg.
Paralyzed her instantly.
She'd probably still be doing the Lost Colony
if he hadn't paralyzed her leg
and given her a chronic pain problem
from the damaged nerve in her right leg.
She'd probably still be training young singers
in Elizabethan style singing
and doing concerts with the young, aspiring professionals.
She had them doing special performances
for their own musical growth and enjoyment.
Like the Mozart Requiem,
and various oratorios and musicals.

She had them perform her masterwork,
An American Requiem,
had me conduct it,
(part of her plan for me to be a conductor)
and we took it up to Chapel Hill
and video taped it for broadcast on PBS.
Everybody loved what she did.

After her leg was paralyzed
I took her back to see the show.

It rained cats and dogs and just quit
the moment I drove her into Manteo
to see the performance.
As I wheeled her up the sidewalk
we encountered a group of madrigal singers
in full Elizabethan regalia.
When they saw her they were in the middle of a song.
They began dancing toward her
and surrounded her, singing and hugging and kissing her.
They asked her what she'd like to hear
and they sang requests for her,
Elizabethan madrigal requests,
until it was time to get her in for the performance.

It rained cats and dogs all over again
and I had to wheel her to shelter.
We were headed for the light shack,
her old hangout during the shows.
There was a set of about ten stairs
leading up to the light shack.
As I was pondering how to get her up the stairs
a gaggle of about six of the very gay dancers
lifted her wheel chair
and danced her smoothly up the stairs
and into the light house
which was filled with ten or fifteen performers.

Word trickled out that Ros was in the light shack.
So while the rain fell outside
the light shack began to be filled with performers.
They formed a circle
and began to sing broadway songs and madrigals.

There were finally over thirty people in costume
singing like an old Bing Crosby movie with the chorus ri-
    diculously, spontaneously singing beautifully, perfectly.

Well, it actually happened, the movie thing in real life.
They gave a spontaneously improvised concert
that went on for a good forty-five minutes
while it rained cats and dogs outside.
My eyes slowly flooded
and I just stood there watching the love pour out to her.
"Ros, what should we sing now?"
and she'd say, "The Sound of Music"
and someone would start singing
and suddenly there was a polished performance
emerging from the group.
And there was laughter and hugging
in a scene that I thought would never be surpassed
in my lifetime
as it just went on and on,
love, love, love flowing like a big choral river in the sky.

It would never be surpassed until....

The church was filled with people,
around three hundred of them.
A performance of An American Requiem
was about to begin.
There had been an article
in the Florida Times Union,
headline: "City's Musical Master Returns."
We showed it to her,
read it to her.

She was confused, didn't get it.
"That's about you, Mom."
"Me?"
a huge grin crossing her face,
a deep self conscious happiness.
She's never been able to love herself,
always thought she could have done so much more.
I've tried and tried to convince her
that she was a wonderful, extraordinary person,
had brought so much into so many people's lives.
But her comparison was Mozart and Bach and Beethoven.
She just hadn't made her mark.

She had the kind of musical skills
that you only read about:
perfect pitch, the ability to write out anything she heard
    from memory.
She composed choral works and wrote out the parts
without bothering to write a score.
She could improvise a fugue
from a telephone number handed to her.
She was a bonafide musical genius
and people loved her and her music.
They gathered around her wherever she went
and she just kept organizing things,
training singers, starting choruses.
It was just her way of being.
In the retirement home
she started a chorus of seventy year olds.

And here she was, sitting in her old church,
the Church of the Good Shepherd

with its magnificent old Aeolian-Skinner organ,
a famous organ, known by organists
as an organ they'd kill to play on,
and the priest got up and gave a little pre-concert talk.
He talked about her contribution to music in Jacksonville
and to the Church of the Good Shepherd
and how the church was filled with those
whose lives she had touched
and how deeply we all felt that special gratitude
to Ros for all she had done
and he just wanted to say one thing,
"Welcome home."

Everything went into another zone when he said that.
Time stopped, shifted.
My eyes flooded again
as I watched three hundred people silently rise together
as if it had been rehearsed.
And the applause began to rise like an ocean around us.

Again, she was confused.
My sister leaned over to her as she sat in her wheel chair
in the aisle beside the pews.
She whispered in her ear,
"They're clapping for you, Mom."
She looked surprised
and the applause continued,
a standing ovation to her life.
She began to get it
and the roar deepened
as she finally raised her hand awkwardly
to wave and acknowledge the applause.

She couldn't stand and bow
but she waved and smiled.
And the applause went on,
everyone sensing something special, something historic
for this Jacksonville musical community
who were experiencing their beloved friend,
teacher, choirmaster, organist.
It was all packed into that standing ovation
and my brother and sister and I
stood in the rushing flood,
recognition and honoring, a rising tide.

The priest came and hugged her
and it was time for the Requiem.
The choir began softly and the sound rose
in the reverberant stone walled church.
It was magnificent.
The music was beautiful.
Her piece was speaking to everyone.
No one was surprised.
They expected that from Ros.
The music was beautiful.
The performance was beautiful.

Her Granddaughter, Sharen, now grown up into an
accomplished, professional coloratura soprano,
brought her beautiful voice to the soprano solos so carefully
    crafted in the Requiem.
The chorus of young college students had gotten
what it was all about.
They got the reverence of the whole thing
and the music wasn't easy.

It was a major challenge, this modern work
that switched from 7/8 to 9/8,
to 4/4 to 3/8 in the Sanctus
and had them singing an e-flat
against an e-natural in the organ pedal.
But it flowed, changed color and pace, mood.
And when it was done forty-five minutes later
there was another standing ovation
and flowers brought to her.
We were supposed to take her to the reception
after the concert
but there were people gathered around her
and there was another half hour, maybe an hour,
who knows in this timeless universe,
while everyone said hello, told her they loved her,
that she had changed their lives forty years ago,
that they were so glad to see her again.
It seemed that every one
of the three hundred people there
had actually known her,
remembered her, personally.

We stood there waiting
for the handshaking and hugging
and the occasional tears to subside.
Then off to the reception
where the same thing happened.
Man, was she up to it.
It fed her more than anything we had ever seen.
She had been unfeedable for so many years.
The only thing that helped her
was playing Scrabble with my sister

or a visit from my brother and me
and we had to resort to Scrabble after the first day

The evening ended with going to a fine seafood place
and she was up for that too.
She was on a roll.
In Charlotte she would have been done pretty quickly,
would have needed some pain medication, fallen asleep.
Now she was awake, alive, herself again
that wonderful self we have loved so much
and for so long.

There's no ending to this story.
Just a lifetime marking weekend for Rosalind MacEnulty,
returning master musician of the City of Jacksonville,
coming home
to discover she was still loved, remembered.
She had completely forgotten what she had done.
It took all this to remind her.

ACKNOWLEDGEMENTS

My dear friends Pamela Ball and Patti Wood read this book in its patchwork quilt form and gave invaluable support and advice. My Charlotte writing group read and gave great suggestions for many little sections. Joe Straub provided the final proofing. Thanks and love to all of the above.

Much gratitude to Sy Safransky and the editors at *The Sun Magazine* for publishing "At Her Feet" – the essay that was the seed for this book. Much gratitude to Amy Scholder, editor for my first four books and now this, for her support and encouragement as well as her discerning eye.

Without my brothers and my daughter, I couldn't have survived this era of my life much less written about it.

Much thanks to my brother Jo for all the work he did to make sure the "American Requiem" performance happened; to Sharen Camille Becker for contributing her amazing vocal talents; to David and Edward for helping me transport my mother and keeping me sane; to the "Requiem Production Team" especially my godfather Jim Taylor for logistical support; to R. Wayne Bailey and the Chorale of Florida State College at Jacksonville (including soloists Ebony Johnson, Andre Troutman and Mark Mansilungan) as well as the orchestra performers and organist Shannon Gallier – an extraordinary group of talented people; to the many friends and admirers of my mother who contributed money and time and energy to make the performance happen. Thanks to Reverend Douglas G. Hodsdon and all those at the Church of the Good Shepherd for welcoming us home.

And of course undying gratitude to my mother, Rosalind MacEnulty, for her endless patience, love, and forgiveness and for giving me her blessing to write this book.

ABOUT THE AUTHOR

Trish MacEnulty is the author of the historical fiction series, Delafield & Malloy Investigations. She has written four other novels, two memoirs, a short story collection, and children's plays (some of these under the name Pat MacEnulty). She currently lives in Florida with her husband, dog, and cat. She teaches journalism classes at Florida A&M University and writes reviews and features for the Historical Novel Society.

For more information about my books, visit my website, trishmacenulty.com.